COUNTRY WALKS and BIKEWAYS

IN THE PHILADELPHIA REGION

by Alan Fisher

RAMBLER BOOKS

Baltimore

COUNTRY WALKS AND BIKEWAYS in the Philadelphia Region

by Alan Fisher
Maps and photographs by the author

Rambler Books
1430 Park Avenue
Baltimore, MD 21217

If you notice errors in the text or maps, please point them out in a letter to the publisher.

Printed in the United States of America

FIRST EDITION 1 2 3 4 5

Some material from this book appeared previously in *Country Walks Near Philadelphia.*

ISBN 0-9614963-4-7

CONTENTS

	Preface	9
	Comfort and Safety	10
	Ticks and Lyme Disease	12
1	Delaware Canal State Park Hugh Moore Historical Park and Canal Museum at the Lehigh Canal Delaware & Raritan Canal State Park	15
2	Hopewell Furnace National Historical Site French Creek State Park	35
3	Valley Forge National Historical Park	49
4	The Schuylkill Trail: Philadelphia-Valley Forge Bikeway	63
5	Mill Grove: Audubon Wildlife Sanctuary	75
6	Evansburg State Park	85
7	Peace Valley Park Peace Valley Nature Center	97
8	Tyler State Park	109
9	Washington Crossing Historic Park Washington Crossing State Park	119
10	Morris Arboretum of the University of Pennsylvania	133
11	Wissahickon Valley	145
12	The Schuylkill Center for Environmental Education	163

13	**Pennypack Park** **Lorimer Park**	169
14	**Fairmount Park** **Riverside paths** **Belmont circuit** **Tour de Fairmount**	179
15	**Ridley Creek State Park**	197
16	**Tyler Arboretum**	213
17	**John Heinz National Wildlife Refuge at Tinicum**	223
18	**Brandywine Creek State Park**	233

MAP 1 — Orientation

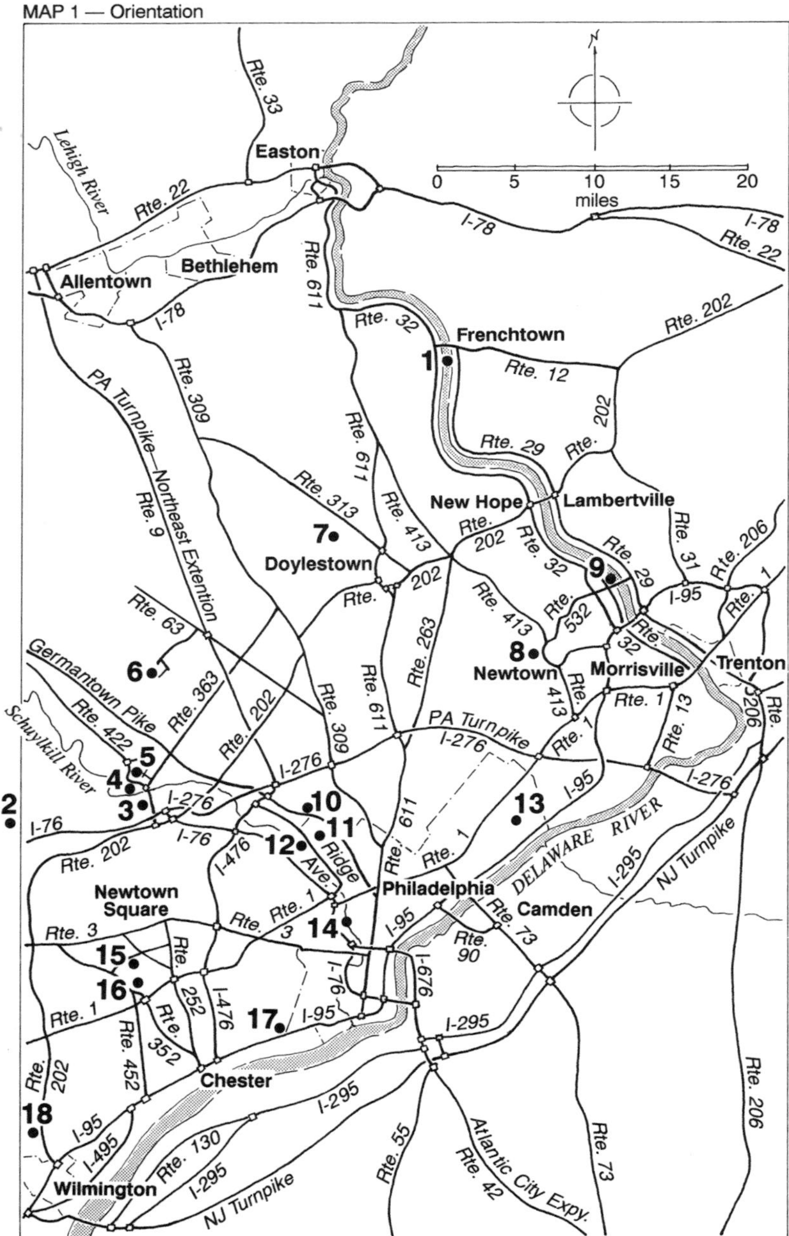

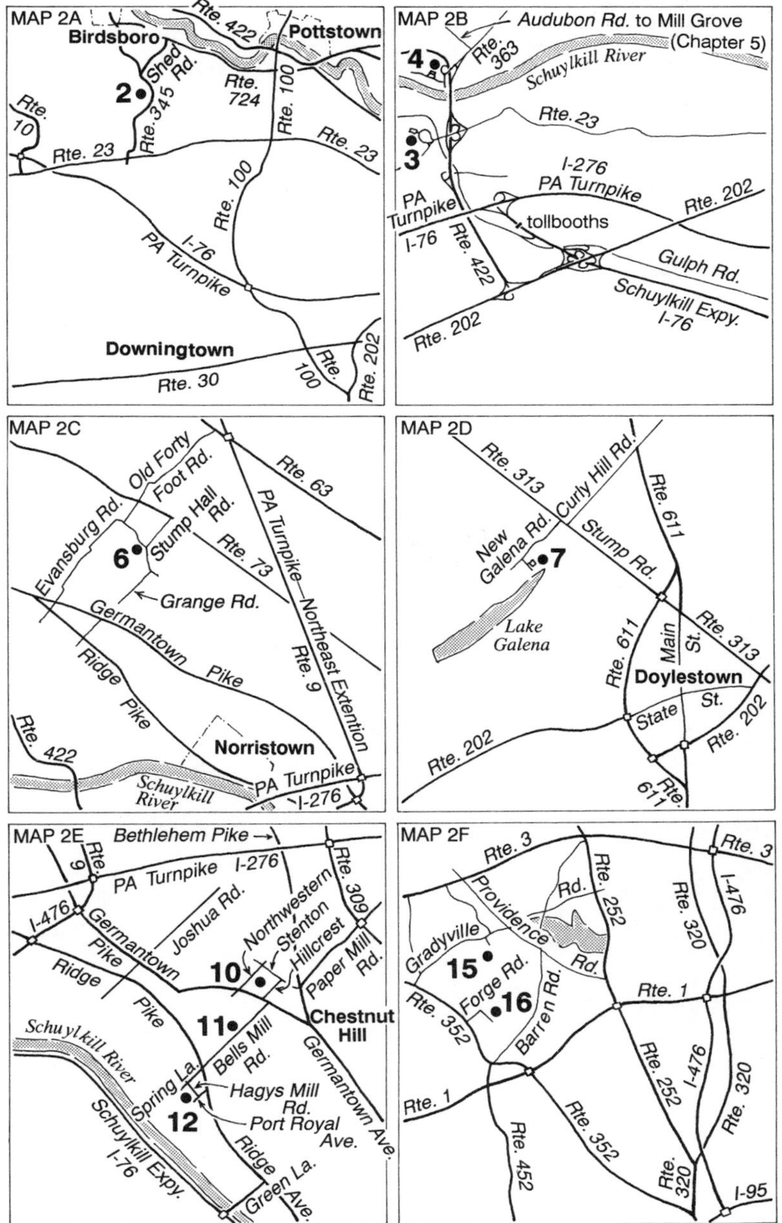
MAP 2A
Birdsboro
Pottstown
Rte. 422
Shed Rd.
Rte. 345
Rte. 724
Rte. 100
Rte. 10
Rte. 23
I-76
PA Turnpike
Downingtown
Rte. 30
Rte. 202
MAP 2B
Audubon Rd. to Mill Grove (Chapter 5)
Rte. 363
Schuylkill River
Rte. 23
I-276
PA Turnpike
Rte. 202
tollbooths
I-76
Rte. 422
Gulph Rd.
Schuylkill Expy.
MAP 2C
Old Forty Foot Rd.
Stump Hall Rd.
Rte. 63
Evansburg Rd.
Rte. 73
Grange Rd.
Germantown Pike
Ridge Pike
PA Turnpike—Northeast Extention
Rte. 9
Rte. 422
Norristown
Schuylkill River
PA Turnpike
I-276
MAP 2D
Rte. 313
Curly Hill Rd.
Rte. 611
New Galena Rd.
Stump Rd.
Lake Galena
Main St.
Doylestown
State St.
Rte. 202
MAP 2E
Bethlehem Pike
Rte. 9
PA Turnpike
I-276
Rte. 309
I-476
Germantown Pike
Joshua Rd.
Northwestern
Stenton
Hillcrest
Paper Mill Rd.
Ridge Pike
Chestnut Hill
Schuylkill River
Bells Mill Rd.
Germantown Ave.
Spring La.
Hagys Mill Rd.
Port Royal Ave.
Schuylkill Expy.
I-76
Ridge Ave.
Green La.
MAP 2F
Rte. 3
Providence Rd.
Rte. 252
Rte. 320
I-476
Gradyville
Forge Rd.
Barren Rd.
Rte. 1
Rte. 352
Rte. 452
I-95

PREFACE

THIS BOOK IS FOR PEOPLE who want an outing in a country setting without wasting half the day getting there and back. If you live in the Greater Philadelphia region, the excursions described here are close at hand. The walks and bicycle rides show the best parts of the Delaware Valley's large parks, wildlife refuges, arboretums, and extensive trail networks.

I have tried to provide variety: short walks and marathon hikes; cycling circuits and linear bikeways ranging from a half-dozen miles to 50 miles; and excursions rich in scenery, history, and wildlife, especially birds. The routes cover the gamut of the region's Piedmont landscapes: steep-sided river valleys, rolling hills, flood plains, woods, farmland, meadow, and marsh, as well as historic villages, houses, mill sites, and ruins along the way. Successive visits during different seasons—to see the changing foliage, views, flowers, and birds—provide an added dimension of enjoyment.

Each chapter of this book includes a brief introduction, a discussion of the area's natural or social history, detailed directions, and one or more maps. Because it is anticipated that readers will be driving from different places to reach the sites described here, the automobile directions outline different avenues of approach. Necessarily, there is much repetition, so focus on the set of directions that applies to you and skip the others.

Most of the places described here can be reached by SEPTA bus, trolley, or train. The SEPTA directions in the various chapters merely note the route number and stop for the destination. Telephone (215) 580-7800 for current information on schedules, routes, and connections from your starting point. To obtain a SEPTA "Bike-on-Rail" permit, call the Customer Service Office at (215) 580-7852.

The following people helped me with this book by reviewing the text for different chapters and making suggestions: John Auciello, Lee Boyle, Rick Colbert, Kelly Connor, Jonathan Edwards, Jr., Jack Graham, Agatha Hughes, Steven Humphrey, Richard L. James, Carolyn Jarin, Sandra J. Kadis, Catherine Larkin, Matt Marcinek, John McIlhenny, Walter W. Robson, III, Mike Seasholtz, and H. Kels Swan. Many, many thanks.

Alan Fisher

COMFORT AND SAFETY

PLEASE READ THIS. It is customary, in guidebooks such as this, to include a catalog of cautions about possible nuisances and hazards. Such matters do not make for scintillating reading, but really, I think that you will be glad to have read here about a few potential problems—so that you can avoid them—rather than learn about them through uncomfortable (or even dangerous) experience.

For walkers, wear sturdy shoes that you do not mind getting muddy or wet. In winter wear hiking boots that will keep your feet dry and that will provide traction in snow. I usually carry a small knapsack containing a snack, a water bottle or juice carton, insect repellent, and an extra layer of clothing, such as a sweater or rain parka.

Bicyclists should wear helmets, yield to pedestrians and horseback riders, pass with care, and keep their speed to a moderate, safe pace. Some of the bikeways occasionally make use of local roads (the Tour de Fairmount is nearly *all* on roads), and these excursions are clearly unsuitable for children or even adults who lack experience in traffic. Even on bikeways from which cars are excluded, your children must have the skill to steer steadily and the discipline to ride single file, to stay to the right where necessary, and to cope with cars at crossings and parking lots. Some of the parks described here present good opportunities for mountain biking, provided that you are prepared to dismount occasionally because of steep slopes, rocks, and other hazards. Also, do not go mountain biking alone; always have a companion in case you fall and suffer a sprain or fracture. Finally, as a courtesy to hikers and horseback riders, mountain bikers should dismount when passing on narrow trails.

Hunting is allowed at some of the state parks and other areas described in this book. Where appropriate, I try to alert you to the possible risk from hunting, but for precise information on hunting schedules, call the telephone numbers provided in the introduction to each chapter, or call the Pennsylvania Game Commission at (610) 926-3136. If you go walking or off-road cycling in areas where hunting is underway, wear a bright orange jacket or vest. Generally speaking, most hunting is restricted to the period October through February, but some animals may be hunted year-round, even on Sundays.

Some of the trails described in this book traverse steep slopes. Bear in mind that terrain presenting only moderate difficulty when dry can be treacherous when wet, snowy, or icy. Turn back before you find yourself sliding down the hillside. And unlike some people I have encountered, don't undertake impromptu rock climbing, only to find yourself perched on a ledge and unable to extricate yourself.

During winter, all to often drownings occur when people fall through the ice after venturing out onto frozen ponds and rivers. I am sure that you have heard this before; everyone has. And yet each winter a few more people die in this manner. So stay off the ice. And tell your kids.

Other sound advice that is ignored with puzzling regularity concerns lightning. If you are in an exposed or elevated area and a storm approaches, return to your car immediately. That is the safest place to be. And if a storm arrives before you get back to your car, hunker down in a low spot. Don't worry about getting wet or feeling stupid as you kneel there with the rain pouring down. Clearly it is better to get wet and yet be safe than to try to stay dry by huddling under an isolated tree or pavilion or some other target for lightning.

Every year the newspapers carry stories about people who pick up a squirrel, a raccoon, or some other animal and get bitten. They then have to undergo a series of painful anti-rabies shots. Don't be one of these people; don't handle *any* wild animals. In somewhat the same vein, remember that poisonous copperhead snakes occur in the Delaware Valley region. Be careful where you place your feet and hands, particularly in rocky areas.

Where the trails described here follow roads briefly, walk well off the road on the shoulder to minimize the risk of being hit by a car, and use caution, especially at dusk or after dark, where the routes cross roads. Studies show that in poor light conditions, motorists typically cannot even see pedestrians in time to stop, so your safety depends entirely on you. And if you are bicycling, get off the road or trail before dusk.

Finally, one of the pitfalls of writing guidebooks is that conditions change. Just because I say to do something does not mean that you should forge ahead in the face of obvious difficulties, hazards, or prohibitions.

In sum, use good judgment and common sense to evaluate the particular circumstances that you find. Heed local regulations and signs, and do not undertake any unusual risks.

TICKS AND LYME DISEASE

I WANT TO DRAW particular attention to the problem presented by ticks, which unlike the hazards discussed in the preceding section, are not so obviously a matter of common sense. Some kinds of ticks (chiefly deer ticks, which actually feed on a wide variety of animals) may carry Lyme disease. If not diagnosed and treated, Lyme disease can cause long-term arthritis and neurological and cardiac disorders. Standard advice about ticks includes how to avoid being bitten, what to do if you are bitten, and what you should know about the symptoms of Lyme disease.

Ticks can be a problem from spring through fall, and especially from May through September, when nymphal deer ticks are so tiny (smaller than the head of a pin) that they are not easily noticed. Although adult ticks are active late into the fall, early in spring, and even during mild weather in winter, they are bigger and so are more easily seen and removed before they bite. It is also thought that adult deer ticks are more discriminating than nymphs and are less likely to bite humans.

The main way to pick up ticks is by walking or mountain biking through tall grass and weeds or along narrow paths where you brush against foliage as you pass. One simple precaution is to walk in the middle of paths or even, from late spring through early autumn, to confine your walking and riding to wide mown or paved paths and dirt roads, such as are discussed in most chapters of this book. Other standard precautions, especially if bushwhacking or using narrow, overgrown paths, is to wear long pants and a long-sleeved shirt and to tuck your pant legs into your socks and your shirt into your pants in order to keep the ticks on the outside, where you can pick them off. And wear a hat to keep ticks out of your hair. Spray your clothes—especially your shoes, socks, and pant legs—with insect repellent containing DEET (N-diethylmetatoluamide) applied according to the directions on the label. If your clothes are light colored, it will be easier to spot any ticks that may get on you. Inspect yourself from time to time during your outing (have a friend examine your back) and when you get back to your car. And when you get home, wash your clothes, take a shower, and examine your body closely. Pay particular attention to your lower legs, the backs of your knees, your groin, back, neck, and armpits, which are all places where ticks are known to bite.

If you are bitten by a tick, remove it immediately. Grasp the tick with sharp-pointed tweezers, as near to your skin as possible, and gently but firmly pull straight out until the tick comes off, then blot the bite with alcohol. Make a note of when and where you were bitten. Some authorities recommend saving the tick in a small jar of alcohol for later identification. If the tick's mouthparts break off and remain in your skin, see your doctor immediately so that he or she can remove them.

The main early symptom of Lyme disease is a circular, slowly expanding red rash, often with a clear center, that may appear a few days or as long as two months after being bitten by an infected tick. Not all patients, however, will have this rash. Flu-like symptoms are also common, perhaps accompanied by headache, swollen glands, a stiff neck, fever, muscle aches, nausea, and possibly general malaise.

If you develop any of these symptoms after being bitten by a tick, or after visiting an area where you may have been bitten, see your doctor promptly and mention the possibility of Lyme disease so that one of a variety of blood tests can be conducted. Don't put it off, because Lyme disease in its early stages is easily treated with some antibiotics. The tests are not altogether reliable, so some doctors and researchers say that if signs and symptoms consistent with early Lyme disease are present, treatment should not be withheld while waiting for the results of a blood test or because the test results were negative. If allowed to progress untreated, the early symptoms of Lyme disease usually disappear but may eventually be followed by such disorders as swelling in the knees, hips, and ankles, arthritis, severe headaches, numbness, tingling in the extremities, palsy on one side of the face, loss of concentration, heart palpitations, heart block, and other problems that are so varied that diagnosis can be difficult.

In short, although the risk of getting Lyme disease is small, there is no good reason not to take simple precautions that will help you to avoid tick bites in the first place or—if you are bitten by an infected tick—that will help you to minimize the consequences.

1

DELAWARE CANAL STATE PARK
HUGH MOORE HISTORICAL PARK and CANAL MUSEUM at the LEHIGH CANAL
DELAWARE & RARITAN CANAL STATE PARK

Walking, jogging, ski touring, and bicycling. The bold lines on Map 3 on page 27 outline a system of paths along both banks of the Delaware River above Morrisville and Trenton and along the Lehigh River upstream from Easton. For the most part, the paths follow old canals. Locks, locktenders' houses, spillways, waste weirs, aqueducts, and other fascinating engineering works punctuate progress along the waterways, which pass through a series of villages and historic towns, including Yardley, Washington Crossing, New Hope, Lambertville, Centre Bridge, Stockton, Lumberville, Frenchtown, and Riegelsville, where there are outstanding inns and restaurants and where bridges provide the opportunity to cross between the towpath of the Delaware Canal in Pennsylvania and the Delaware & Raritan Canal in New Jersey. For long stretches the paths border the Delaware River, where the views are sometimes spectacular. Although roads often border the canals, they are usually on the waterways' inland side, at a distance from the towpaths.

Maps 5 though 7 on pages 31 through 33 give details—section by section—on the canal system from Easton southeast to Trenton and Morrisville. Parking areas are shown on the maps. If you have never been to the canals, a good place to start is Bulls Island in New Jersey, to which automobile directions are provided on page 26. Two introductory circuits from Bulls Island along both banks of the Delaware—one circuit 18 miles for cyclists and the other circuit 7 miles for walkers—are discussed starting on page 28. Also, Interstate 95 provides quick access to both the Delaware Canal in Pennsylvania and the Delaware & Raritan Canal in New Jersey, as illustrated by Map 4 on page 29. (Automobile directions are included on the map.)

The Delaware Canal in Pennsylvania stretches 60 miles between Easton and Bristol, but the 10-mile section below

Morrisville is in poor condition and is not featured here. Short detours out to nearby roads and back may sometimes be necessary to bypass aqueducts or locks undergoing repair. To navigate through New Hope, you may have to consult the insert in the upper-right corner of Map 7, but the rest of the way is clear. The towpath is a grass and dirt track, excellent for walking and also easily passable by fat-tired and hybrid bicycles. For cyclists, however, the bumpy surface (from which rocks and roots sometimes protrude) dictates a fairly slow pace—about 8 miles per hour maximum. One more caveat is that after heavy rains, the towpath is sometimes flooded where it dips across spillways, which should not be crossed if the water is more than 2 or 3 inches deep. Route 32 and—at the northern end of the canal—Route 611 provide access to the canal at intervals. The Delaware Canal is managed by the Pennsylvania Bureau of State Parks; telephone (610) 982-5560 for the park office, which is open weekdays only, and (215) 297-5090 for a ranger station that is staffed on weekends and holidays. Dogs must be leashed on the Delaware Canal towpath and other towpaths also.

At its northern end in Easton, the Delaware Canal joins the Lehigh Canal, where an intertwined system of paved and grassy paths extend upriver 3.5 miles. Next to Route 611 at the juncture of the Delaware and Lehigh canals is the small but excellent Canal Museum, which is open Monday through Saturday from 10 to 4 and on Sunday from 1 to 5. An admission fee is charged. For information telephone the Hugh Moore Historical Park & Museum at (610) 250-6700. Eventually, a new and much larger National Canal Museum will be built in central Easton, which is easily reached by crossing the Lehigh River on the first bridge.

The path along the New Jersey side of the Delaware River extends 31 miles between Frenchtown and Trenton. For most of this distance, the path occupies an old railroad bed that in turn follows the Delaware & Raritan Feeder Canal south from the intake at Bulls Island. As shown on the cover of this book, the path is paved with rock grit that provides a smooth, hard surface suitable for walking and bicycling, although there are occasionally bumpy, gravelly sections. Route 29 provides access to the path at intervals. From Trenton the Delaware & Raritan Main Canal extends northeast 35 miles to New Brunswick in central New Jersey, but this section of the canal is not discussed here. The D&R Canal is managed by the New Jersey Division of Parks and Forestry; telephone (609) 397-2949 or (908) 873-3050.

A few more notes on bicycling may be in order. If you plan to bring your children, they should be old enough to steer steadily; if they can't and they veer off the path, they could plunge into a canal or down the steep embankment into the Delaware River. Use caution at road crossings and parking areas where cars are present. Also, cyclists must ride single file, yield to other trail users, keep their speed to a moderate, safe pace, and walk their bicycles across the Delaware bridges.

DURING THE PERIOD of its commercial operation, the Delaware Canal was called the Delaware Division of the Pennsylvania Canal. The Pennsylvania Canal was a system of interconnected, state-financed waterways linked with other canals built as private ventures. The state canals were managed by the Pennsylvania Canal Commission, which had been formed in 1822 to develop a network of inland waterways to transport the state's growing output of agricultural, mineral, and industrial products. Because of rapids, spring floods, low water in summer, and a strong downstream current against which river craft had to be poled laboriously upstream, even major rivers such as the Delaware were unsuitable for navigation above tidewater. Steam railways, of course, were still unknown—although their advent was only a decade away. Instead, canals such as those that had long been successful in Europe appeared to be the best means to improve trade and travel between the Eastern seaboard and the interior of the country.

The Pennsylvania Canal Commission was particularly anxious to compete with the Erie Canal, then under construction and designed to join the Great Lakes and the Hudson River. Pennsylvanians justifiably feared that the Erie project, which even before it was entirely finished was proving to be a huge success, would divert commerce from Philadelphia, at that time the nation's financial center. After the Erie Canal was completed in 1825, a wave of frenzied canal building swept the Eastern states. Within two decades approximately 4,000 miles of canals were built. By the mid-1830s, Pennsylvania's canal projects entailed state obligations exceeding three times the commonwealth's annual revenue. Pennsylvania alone built more than 1,200 miles of canals, of which the 60 miles of the Delaware Division were just a small part. Even after powerful steam locomotives and extensive rail networks were developed in the second half of the nineteenth-century, many canals continued in use to move extremely heavy bulk cargoes.

The main purpose of the Delaware Canal was to transport coal. In 1791 anthracite was found near the town of Mauch Chunk (Jim Thorpe) in the Lehigh Valley. At first, little came of this discovery. Transporting coal in wagons down from the mountains to the Lehigh River was difficult and costly, and the river was too rocky and shallow to ensure safe shipment of coal to market. For that matter, there was no market. Heating stoves of the day were designed to burn wood. The iron industry still used charcoal for smelting ore. Mills were driven by the region's abundant water power.

Gradually, however, a demand for coal was created. Josiah White, who with his associates leased the Mauch Chunk coal fields in 1818, promoted the development of new coal-burning stoves. The first models appeared in 1820 and caught on quickly. In 1822 the Lehigh Coal and Navigation Company was chartered, with White at the helm. Under his direction the coal company constructed the first coal railroad in the country. Powered by gravity, the loaded cars rolled downhill for 9 miles from the mines to the Lehigh River; mules pulled the empty cars back uphill. The coal company also made the Lehigh River navigable, after a fashion. Boulders were cleared from the channel. Dams with openings at their centers turned the river into a series of long pools and short chutes through which so-called arks were floated downstream. By 1823 arks loaded with coal were sent regularly from Mauch Chunk to Philadelphia.

The arks were made of dressed timbers strapped together with iron bands. These clumsy craft were strung together in tandem, sometimes reaching an overall length of 180 feet. Propelled by the current and guided by long oars, they were floated down the Lehigh River to its confluence with the Delaware River at Easton, and then on to Philadelphia. The arks were so cumbersome that they could not be brought back upstream, so after the coal was unloaded, they were dismantled and sold for timber. There were other disadvantages as well. Coal bound for other cities, principally New York, had to be transferred to coastal vessels for the second half of the journey. Also, navigation through the dam openings was hazardous. On June 8, 1830, *The Whig* of Easton reported:

> An ark belonging to the Lehigh Coal and Navigation Company sunk on the 6th instant, in passing the sluice of the dam in this place. The men hung onto the oars, and were taken off by a skiff sent from shore to their rescue. The coal (about 140 tons) was lost.

As the commerce in coal increased, so did the demand for dependable, inexpensive water transportation. With the newly opened Erie Canal as an example (it reduced freight costs by half), surveying began for the privately financed Delaware & Hudson Canal in 1825. This waterway was designed to carry coal from northeastern Pennsylvania to the Hudson River and New York. Also in 1825 the Morris Canal was started from the Delaware River opposite Easton to Jersey City and New York. It too was intended primarily to transport coal and was a private venture. The Morris Canal featured inclined railways to carry the canal boats between different sections of the waterway that occupied different elevations. Photographs of such railways can be seen at the Canal Museum in Easton.

In 1827 the Lehigh Coal and Navigation Company began construction of the **Lehigh Canal**, which turned the Lehigh River into a navigable waterway. A series of short canals, each with two or more lift locks, was built around the dams on the Lehigh River, as can be seen today at the Hugh Moore Historical Park in Easton. That same year the Commonwealth of Pennsylvania undertook construction of the **Delaware Canal**. It was linked with the Lehigh Canal at Easton and extended south to tidewater at Bristol, where boats could continue to Philadelphia under tow by sidewheel steamers on the Delaware River. Finally, in 1830 the privately financed **Delaware & Raritan Canal** was started. It connected Bordentown below Trenton on the Delaware River with the Raritan River at New Brunswick. From there the Raritan River was navigable to Raritan Bay just below Staten Island and New York City. A feeder canal was built to carry water from the Delaware River at Bulls Island above Stockton to the highest elevation of the main canal at Trenton. Later, outlet locks were added on both sides of the Delaware River at New Hope. Canal boats were transferred from the Delaware Canal, across the river in the deep water above the wing dam, to the Delaware & Raritan system. This crossing became one of the main routes for transporting Lehigh coal to New York.

The Lehigh Canal was completed in 1829. Construction of the Delaware Canal, however, fell behind schedule. The canal leaked because its raised banks, which are essentially dikes, were made of sandy soil. When the canal opened in 1832, the boats could be only partially loaded because the water level was insufficient. Large sections of the canal were reworked under the direction of Josiah White, and a water wheel was constructed at New Hope to pump additional water into the canal from the Delaware River. By 1834, when the Delaware Canal was declared satisfactory for boats loaded up to 70 tons, the cost of the project had exceeded twice the original estimate. That same year the Delaware & Raritan Canal—like the others dug mostly by Irish immigrants working by hand—was completed at a cost approaching $3 million.

A report of the Pennsylvania Canal Commissioners in 1830 summarizes the main features of the Delaware Canal:

> On this division the width of the canal at bottom is 25 feet, at top water line 40 feet, and its depth of water, five feet. In its course there are 23 lift locks, ranging from 6 to 10 feet lift, also 2 outlet and 2 guard locks. The canal and locks are arranged for boats of 67 tons burden. Eighteen lock keepers are necessary in this division.

On the Delaware & Raritan Canal, the dimensions of the feeder canal are slightly greater (50 feet wide and 6 feet deep) and the main canal is substantially bigger (75 feet wide and 7 feet deep). Boats on the Delaware Canal were pulled by mules—even into the twentieth century—but steam-powered tugs were introduced onto the Delaware & Raritan system by 1843 and gradually replaced mule teams. Also, in New Jersey the canal company merged in 1831 with a railroad company, and by 1855 the Belvidere-Delaware Railroad was completed alongside the feeder canal. It is this railbed that most of the path follows today. Even after construction of the railroad, the waterway continued in use, although, of course, it had to close during winter.

The Delaware & Raritan Feeder Canal was built at one level, without locks, and even the entrance lock added later across from New Hope no longer exists. On the Delaware Canal, however, lift locks are located every few miles. Eleven feet wide and 95 feet long, and with mitered gates at each end, they compensated for an overall drop in the Delaware River of 165 feet between Easton and Bristol. At any given time, one pair of gates for each lock was shut. Boats that were headed south toward Bristol entered the locks when the downstream gates were closed and the upstream gates open. The upstream gates were then closed behind the boat. Wickets in the downstream gates were opened to drain the water in the lock to the level of the canal below. Then the downstream gates were opened and the boat was towed out.

For boats headed upstream the procedure was reversed. After a boat had entered the lock and the downstream gates had been closed behind it, water was let into the lock by opening the wickets in the upstream gates. When the water in the lock had risen to the same level as above the lock, the upstream gates were opened and the boat towed out. The boat crews usually helped the lock keepers with the tasks of opening and closing the gates and wickets in order to pass though the lock as quickly as possible. In some places, such as New Hope, several locks in succession were managed by a single keeper.

In addition to the locks there were stop gates, waste weirs, and overflow sluices at various points along the Delaware Canal. The stop gates could be closed to seal off sections of the canal in case of flood or breaches in the canal bank. Waste weirs allowed the canal to be drained, and overflow sluices diverted excess water into the Delaware River. Many of these features still survive and are still used.

One of the great advantages of the canal system was that it allowed coal to be shipped from the mine docks to market without repeated unloading and reloading. Because the canal boats had to be able to fit though all segments of the canal network, a standard canal boat—called the *hinge boat*—evolved.

The standard hinge boat was 10.5 feet wide to fit the narrow locks of the Delaware Canal. It was 87.5 feet long, but the bow and stern halves—each of which floated independently of the other—could be separated. The two sections were held together by metal fittings and pins when the boat was under tow. On the inclined railway of the Morris Canal, the separate sections of the hinge boat could be handled more easily than could stiff (i.e., conventional) boats. When coal was loaded and unloaded, the hinge boats could adjust better to the unequal weight in the forward and aft sections. Also, by unfastening and turning each half separately, a hinge boat could be turned around more easily than a stiff boat.

The sides of a hinge boat were straight and the bottom flat to maximize capacity in the shallow canals and to rest easily on the flatbed cradles of the Morris Canal railway. The deck also was nearly flat and without superstructure so that the boat could fit under bridges, even when the hold was empty and the boat was floating high. The sides tapered abruptly in front to form a V-shaped prow with a vertical profile. A small cabin in the squared-off stern provided living and sleeping quarters for the crew, which consisted of a captain or helmsman, a bow man, and a mule driver to lead the team along the towpath. As a economy measure toward the end of the canal era, boats were operated without bow men, whose principal function was to help boats through locks.

Most of the boats that plied the Delaware Canal were owned by the Lehigh Coal and Navigation Company. The captains were paid for each trip completed from the coal mines to market and back. Some captains owned their own boats or worked for independent freight companies. The captains hired their crews—often members of their families—and supplied their own mule teams.

The Delaware Canal operated for eight or nine months each year from March or April through November or December. In winter, when the waterway was closed because of ice, the canal was drained so that repairs could be made to the embankment and to the locks, aqueducts, and other equipment. Before dredges came into use, accumulations of silt (particularly where streams flow into the canal) were removed during winter with shovels and wheelbarrows. Up and down the waterway empty boats were allowed to sit on the bottom of the canal near the homes of the boat captains. Occasionally during hard times a

boatman and his family might spend the winter in one of the coal company's boats, using not only the cabin in the stern but also the hold for living quarters.

As spring approached, the Delaware Canal boatmen refurbished their equipment. The mules were reshod, the harnesses repaired and rubbed with oil, and the cabins cleaned and repainted. If the captain owned his boat, he might repaint the entire hull. New tow lines and snubbing ropes were purchased. After a warning from the section superintendent, water was let back into the canal by closing the waste weirs and opening all the locks, including the guard lock at the juncture with the Lehigh River.

Once the boats started moving in the spring, they hardly stopped until late fall. On the Delaware Canal, the locks were operated between 4:00 A.M. and 10:00 P.M. In the dark the boats were guided by "night hawkers," which were oil lamps with large reflectors. Men and mules ate on the move. Quick round trips were achieved primarily by working long hours rather than by moving faster. A team of two mules could haul a loaded boat at a steady pace of about 2 miles per hour, day after day, wearing out six pairs of shoes per season. Horses, which quickly broke down, were no good.

The locks were major bottlenecks, and sometimes the boats backed up. On the Delaware Canal, markers were set an equal distance above and below each lock. When two boats approached a lock from the same or opposite directions, the one that passed the marker first was supposed to be given priority through the lock. At night the boats tied up along the bank and the mules were put into one of many stables that catered to canal traffic. Often the boats started before 4:00 A.M. in order to arrive at the next lock by the time it opened.

During the middle decades of the nineteenth century, coal traffic on the Delaware Canal steadily increased. In 1833 about 92,000 tons were hauled. By 1840 the annual total was 171,000 tons, and by mid-century 581,000 tons. The peak year was 1866, when 792,397 tons of coal were transported down the canal. Over a thousand coal boats may have been in use on the Delaware Canal that year, each making an average of twenty-three trips of seven to eight days' duration from Mauch Chunk to Bristol and back.

The Delaware Canal was used to transport other commodities as well, including limestone, iron and iron ore, cement, plaster, grain, flour, hay, and whiskey. In 1867 a total of 901,000 tons was carried on the Delaware Canal, of which 137,000 tons were not coal. Given the dominance of the coal traffic, it is not surprising that about 95 percent of the load carried by the canal was descending traffic. Most of the boats came back empty, although large quantities of guano, bricks, milled lumber, salt, and general merchandise were brought up the canal.

During its peak years the Delaware Canal was managed not by the Commonwealth of Pennsylvania but by the Lehigh Coal and Navigation Company. Anticipating a decline in traffic because of the advent of railroads, the state sold the canal in 1858 to the Sunbury & Erie Railroad Company, from which the waterway was purchased immediately by a newly-organized subsidiary of the coal company. During the period of its control, the coal company maintained the canal in excellent condition and even made many improvements, despite the decline in traffic that set in after the Civil War. By 1880 the canal was carrying less than half the coal it had transported fifteen years earlier. In 1904, after a year of destructive floods, only 75,000 tons of coal were shipped via the canal. Repairs were made and in 1911 the waterway transported 321,000 tons, still hauled by mule-drawn canal boats. During the next two decades, the annual traffic gradually declined as the coal company moved more and more of its output by railroad. On the last day of 1917 the canal superintendent, I. M. Church, wrote in his diary:

> This was one hell of a year—labor scarce, high water, no boatmen, food high, cost sheet going wrong way and everybody with chips on their shoulders. Nothing but fight, fight. Hell has no terror—can't be anything worse than trying to run a damn old ditch like this.

In 1931, with only twenty boats left in operation, the Lehigh Coal and Navigation Company declared the canal closed and gave most of the waterway to the Commonwealth of Pennsylvania. However, operations continued into 1932 until factories along the canal could arrange for the delivery of coal by truck. For a period the waterway reverted to the coal company when the gift was declared invalid due to legal irregularities, but in 1940, pursuant to a special act authorizing the state to acquire the canal by donation, ownership of the entire waterway was transferred to the commonwealth. Since then most of the canal has been maintained in good condition for recreation, although funds are chronically in short supply.

The decline of the Delaware & Raritan Canal as a freight waterway parallels that of the Delaware Canal. The peak years of the D&R were the 1860s and '70s, when 80 percent of the cargo was Pennsylvania coal bound for New York. As railroads took over most of this traffic, the canal gradually became a drain on, rather than a contributor to, its operator's profits. At the end of the 1932 shipping season, the canal closed. The State of New Jersey then took over the waterway and refurbished it to serve as a water supply system that today provides about 75 million gallons per day to farms, industries, and homes. The canal's water supply function in turn generates income for maintenance and improvement of the canal park, which was established in 1974.

The Delaware Canal, Lehigh Canal, and Delaware & Raritan Canal have all been listed on the National Register of Historic Places and are part of a system of national historic and recreation trails. A tourist canal boat operates on the Delaware Canal out of New Hope April through mid-November; telephone (215) 862-2842 for information. A canal boat also runs on the Lehigh Canal Wednesday through Sunday from Memorial Day weekend through Labor Day and on weekends in May and September; telephone (610) 250-6700.

≈ ≈ ≈ ≈

In addition to the vanished canal traffic, another colorful spectacle that is gone from the Delaware Valley is the running of logs. As early as 1750 huge rafts of logs from New York State and northeastern Pennsylvania were floated to market in Philadelphia. By 1828 an observer on the riverbank reported that fifteen or twenty rafts, some 200 feet long by 60 feet wide, could be seen at one time. Sawmills sprang up at Trenton, Morrisville, Yardley, Taylorsville (or Washington Crossing), Hendricks and Eagle islands, Lumberton, Lumberville, and other towns along the river. Spring flood was the chief rafting season. In early May of 1875 one raftsman was told by the record keeper at the Lackawaxen Dam on the upper Delaware that 3,140 rafts had been counted so far that year. Then as now, the wing dams along the river had gaps at the center through which the rafts could pass downstream. Most raft traffic on the lower Delaware ceased by the end of the nineteenth century. In 1911 a sawmill operator at Lumberton recalled:

> There were lively times during spring rafting freshets. I can see one float after another going down the river, the men looking like dressed-up ghosts as they silently swung their Brobdingnagian oars, as if going to some mysterious country from which there was no returning.

≈ ≈ ≈ ≈

SEPTA: The R3 Regional Rail Line from Philadelphia runs to Yardley, where you can join the towpath of the Delaware Canal. From the train station in Yardley, descend to Main Street visible in the distance diagonally across the station parking lot. Turn left onto South Main Street and follow it 0.4 mile to an intersection with College Avenue. Turn right and follow East College Avenue a hundred yards. After crossing the canal, double back to the right next to the bridge in order to reach the towpath.

The next (and last) stop east of Yardley on the R3 Regional Rail Line is West Trenton. Although the station is located a mile from the Delaware & Raritan Canal path, bicyclists may want to get off the train here. (See **Map 7** on page 33.) Descend the stairs at the end of the platform next to the bridge. Turn left and follow the sidewalk along Sullivan Way 0.6 mile to a crossroads with Lower Ferry Road. Turn right and follow Lower Ferry Road 0.4 mile across the canal to the path.

Telephone (215) 580-7800 for current information on schedules, routes, and connections from your starting point. And telephone (215) 580-7852 for information about taking your bicycle on the train.

AUTOMOBILE DIRECTIONS TO BULLS ISLAND: As shown on **Map 3** opposite, the canals follow the Delaware River above Morrisville and Trenton and the Lehigh River above Easton. Obviously, you cannot become acquainted with the entire canal system through just one visit, but a good place to start is Bulls Island, where there is a pedestrian bridge across the Delaware River, thus providing the opportunity to walk or bicycle up and down both sides of the river to other bridges, as discussed starting on page 28. Bulls Island is also the place where the Delaware & Raritan Feeder Canal starts, and the island happens to be located at about the mid-point of the Delaware Canal.

Two avenues of approach to Bulls Island are described below. Map 3 may suggest other approaches more convenient for you.

From the east or west on the Pennsylvania Turnpike: Leave the turnpike at Exit 28 for Trenton and Route 1 North toward Interstate 95. After paying the toll, follow Route 1 North more than 6 miles to I-95 North. Once you are on I-95 heading north, follow the directions in the next paragraph.

From the north or south on Interstate 95: Take Exit 1 in New Jersey for Route 29. (If you are coming from Pennsylvania, this exit occurs immediately after crossing the Delaware River.) As you exit, fork right for Route 29 North toward Lambertville. Follow Route 29 North more than 16 miles, in the process jogging left to remain on Route 29 (Main Street) through Lambertville and again bearing left to remain on Route 29 in Stockton and after passing Prallsville Mills. In short, follow Route 29 about 16 miles to the entrance on the left to the D&R Canal State Park, Bulls Island Recreation Area. As you enter Bulls Island Recreation Area, you will cross the Delaware & Raritan path, so you may want to park in the first lot on the right. The feeder canal itself is straight ahead a few

MAP 3—Delaware Canal, Delaware & Raritan Canal, and Lehigh Canal

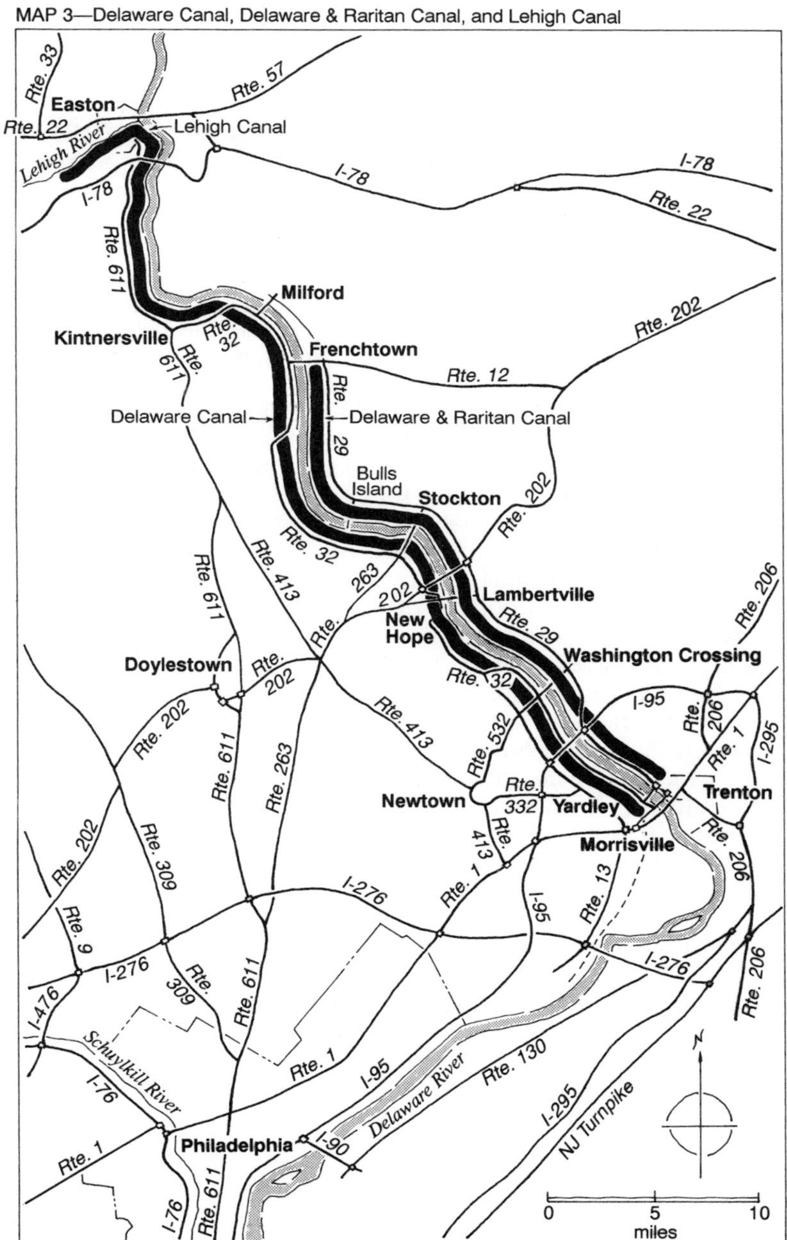

dozen yards, and beyond that is another parking area and the footbridge to the Pennsylvania side of the Delaware River.

AUTOMOBILE DIRECTIONS TO PARKING LOTS IN THE IMMEDIATE VICINITY OF INTERSTATE 95: Although Bulls Island, to which directions are provided above, is a central location within the canal system, you may prefer the convenience of two parking lots—one near the Delaware Canal in Pennsylvania and the other adjacent to the Delaware & Raritan Canal in New Jersey—that are near Interstate 95. These two lots are shown on **Map 4** opposite, and directions to reach the lots are provided on the map itself.

INTRODUCTORY WALKING AND BICYCLING CIRCUITS FROM BULLS ISLAND: A glimpse at **Map 6** on page 32 suggests the possibility of crossing the Delaware River from Bulls Island to Lumberville in Pennsylvania, walking or riding north or south on the Delaware Canal towpath, then crossing back to New Jersey and the Delaware & Raritan path at the next bridge. The circuit north to the bridge linking Uhlerstown and Frenchtown is about 18 miles round-trip and makes a good bike ride. The circuit south to the bridge linking Centre Bridge and Stockton is about 7 miles round-trip and makes a good walk. These trips are described in more detail below.

18-mile circuit from Bulls Island to the bridge at Uhlerstown and Frenchtown: Nearly all of this loop follows the canal paths, but for a short distance at the northern end the route follows local roads where cars are present.

From Bulls Island, cross the Delaware River on the old suspension bridge to Lumberville. At the Pennsylvania end of the bridge, turn right. With caution, go 150 yards along the shoulder of the road to Lumberville Lock No. 12, and there cross back over the Delaware Canal to the towpath.

With the Delaware River on your right, follow the towpath north 9 miles to Uhlerstown.* After passing mile post 41 and

---

*As of 1994, a short detour is necessary at the Point Pleasant Aqueduct. Go back a few dozen yards to a bridge across the canal. Go to route 32 and follow it downhill to an intersection at Point Pleasant. Bear right on Route 32 across Tohickon Creek (notice the aqueduct downstream), then turn right again. After crossing the canal, you can get back onto the towpath. And when you get home, please send a postcard to the Governor of Pennsylvania, Harrisburg 17120, urging that funds be released for rebuilding the Point Pleasant Aqueduct.

MAP 4—Showing quick access from Interstate 95 to parking lots near Pennsylvania's Delaware Canal and New Jersey's Delaware & Raritan Canal

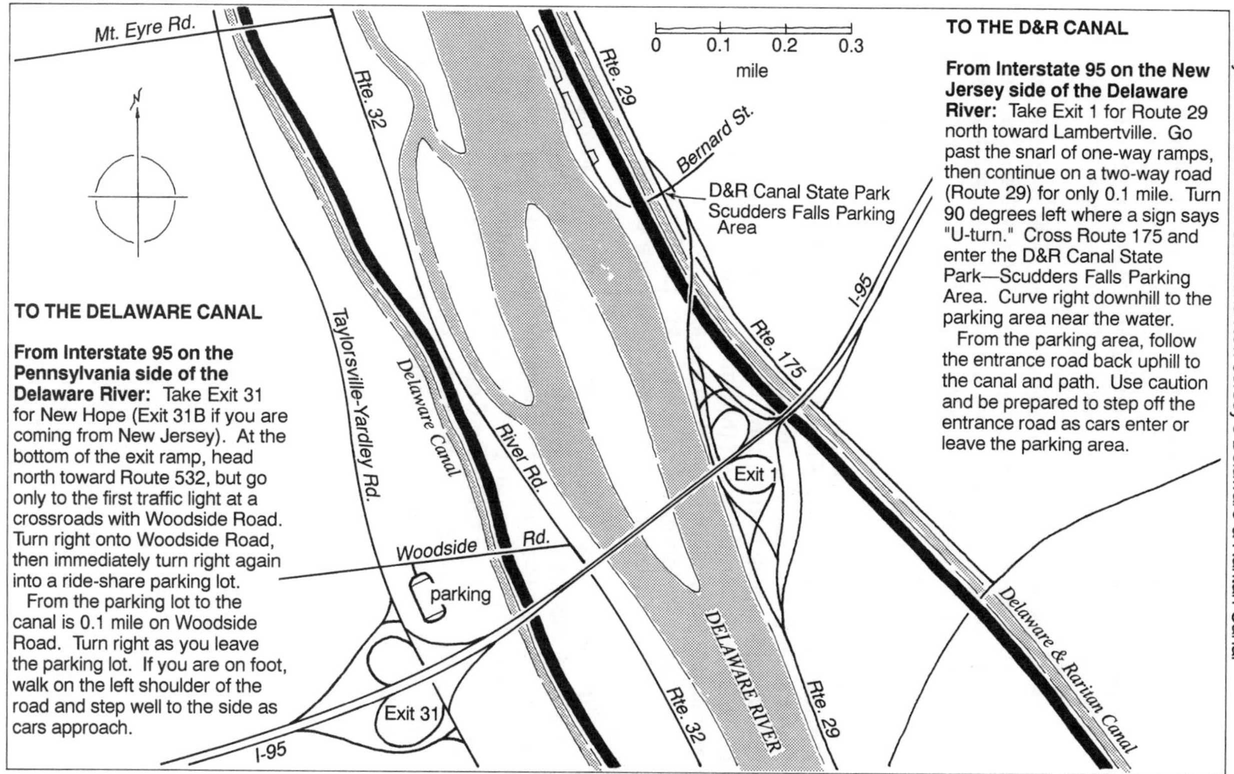

TO THE DELAWARE CANAL

From Interstate 95 on the Pennsylvania side of the Delaware River: Take Exit 31 for New Hope (Exit 31B if you are coming from New Jersey). At the bottom of the exit ramp, head north toward Route 532, but go only to the first traffic light at a crossroads with Woodside Road. Turn right onto Woodside Road, then immediately turn right again into a ride-share parking lot.

From the parking lot to the canal is 0.1 mile on Woodside Road. Turn right as you leave the parking lot. If you are on foot, walk on the left shoulder of the road and step well to the side as cars approach.

TO THE D&R CANAL

From Interstate 95 on the New Jersey side of the Delaware River: Take Exit 1 for Route 29 north toward Lambertville. Go past the snarl of one-way ramps, then continue on a two-way road (Route 29) for only 0.1 mile. Turn 90 degrees left where a sign says "U-turn." Cross Route 175 and enter the D&R Canal State Park—Scudders Falls Parking Area. Curve right downhill to the parking area near the water.

From the parking area, follow the entrance road back uphill to the canal and path. Use caution and be prepared to step off the entrance road as cars enter or leave the parking area.

passing under a covered bridge, turn right at Lock No. 18 and follow Uhlerstown Hill Road away from the steep bluff. At a T-intersection with River Road (Route 32) in front of the Delaware River, turn left and go a few dozen yards to the bridge across the Delaware River. You must walk your bicycle across the bridge on the pedestrian way.

After crossing the Delaware River to Frenchtown in New Jersey, turn right onto the Delaware & Raritan Canal State Park path, which is located just beyond the intersection with River Road a few dozen yards from the bridge. (There is no canal at this point nor anywhere along the New Jersey side of the river north of Bulls Island.) With the Delaware River on your right, follow the path 9 miles south to Bulls Island.

7-mile circuit from Bulls Island to the bridge at Centre Bridge and Stockton: From Bulls Island, cross the Delaware River on the old suspension bridge to Lumberville. To reach the canal towpath that passes under the Pennsylvania end of the bridge, turn right (even though, of course, you will eventually head downstream to the left). With caution, go 150 yards along the shoulder of the road to Lumberville Lock No. 12, and there cross back over the Delaware Canal to the towpath.

With the Delaware River on your left, follow the towpath south 3.5 miles to Centre Bridge, where a stairs ascends to the bridge. Cross the Delaware River to Stockton, New Jersey. From the New Jersey end of the bridge, continue away from the river for 175 yards to the Delaware & Raritan Canal State Park path, which crosses the road some distance beyond the canal itself. Turn left onto the path and follow it north to Bulls Island.

T. AIRY
EXPR
Communities of East and West Mt. Airy
TUESDAY, DECEMBER 31, 1991

...esday, December 31, 1991

...ever by taking nearby day t...

throughout the park explain what happened there.

Visitors can see extensive remains and reconstructions of huts, forts, earthworks, and Washington's headquarters.

Valley Forge National Park is less than an hour away via the westbound Schuylkill Expressway. Valley Forge is open 7 days a week, 8:30 a.m. - 5 p.m. Admission is free during the winter. For directions, call (215) 783-1077.

Museums

The Mercer Museum

The Mercer Museum looks like an old, sprawling castle. It features freestanding, interpretive displays about early American trades and crafts. Visitors can see bath tubs, fishing boats, weapons, musical instruments, printing presses, old kitchen utensils, mining tools — and much more. There is even an old horse-drawn hearse and prisoner's dock and gallows.

The Mercer Museum is located at Pine and Ashland Streets in Doylestown. Hours are Monday-Saturday, 10 a.m.- 5 p.m. and Sunday 12-5 p.m. Admission is $4 for adults, $3.50 for senior citizens, $1.50 for students, free for ages 6 and under. For directions, call (215)345-0210.

The Moravian Pottery & Tile Works

The Moravian Pottery & Tile Works is a national historic landmark operating as a living history museum. Visitors can watch ceramists make tiles during a half-hour, self-guided tour. The same methods have been used since 1900 when Henry Chapman Mercer founded the Tile Works. Red clay is rolled out and cut to form quarry or mosaic tiles, or pressed into copies of Mercer's original molds to form decorative tiles. Some are then fired unglazed or are fired, glazed, and then fired again.

The Tile Works is located on Swamp Road (Route 313) in Doylestown. Open seven days a week, 10 a.m.-5 p.m., with the last tour beginning at 4 p.m. Admission is $2.50 for adults, $2 for senior citizens, children 7 and up, $1. For directions, call (215)345-6722.

The Railroad Museum of Pennsylvania

Located in Strasburg, not far

MAP 5—Lehigh Canal and Delaware Canal: Easton south to Uhlerstown

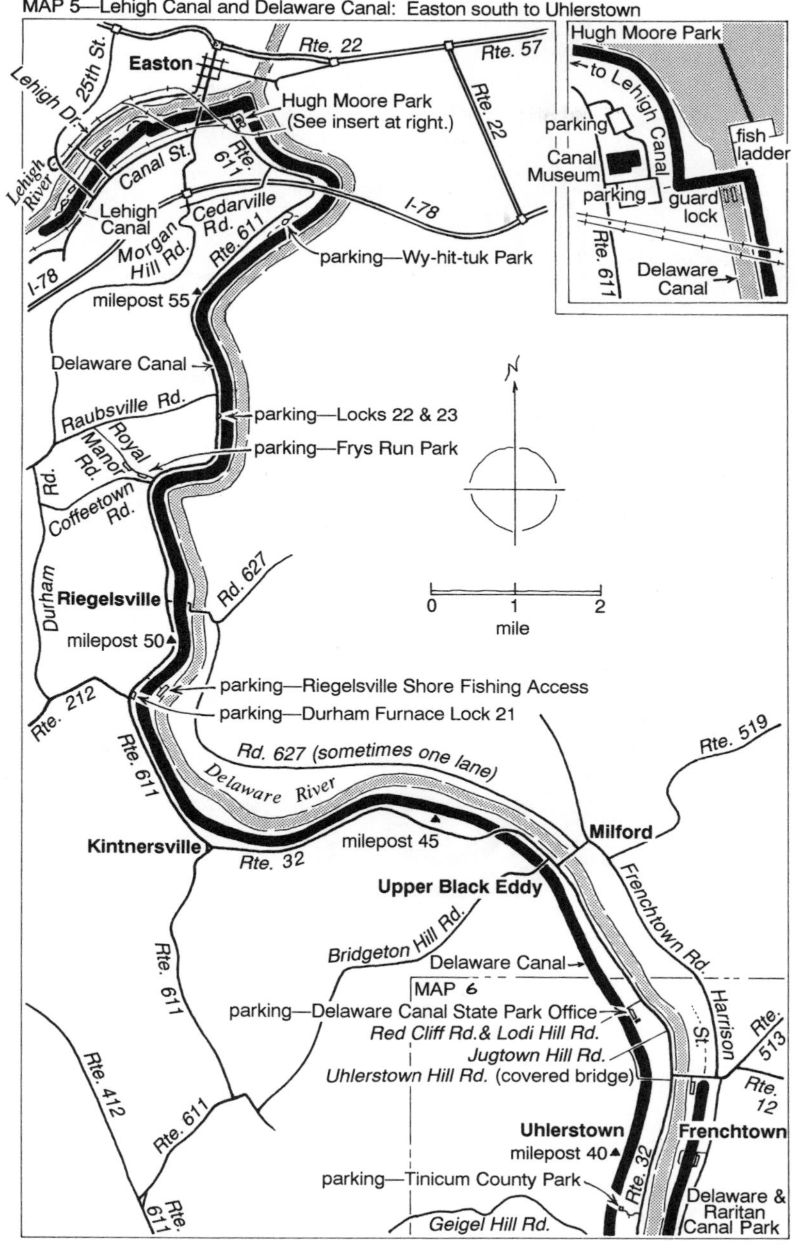

MAP 6—Delaware Canal and Delaware & Raritan Canal:
Uhlerstown and Frenchtown south to New Hope and Lambertville

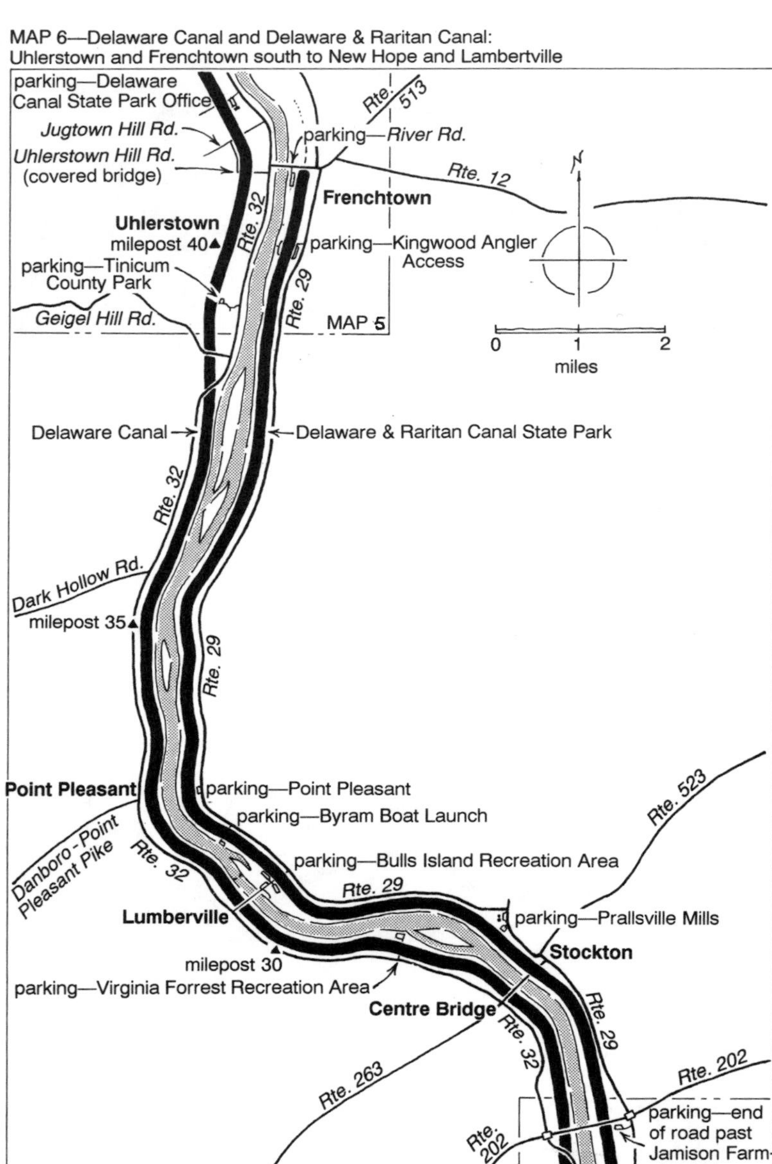

MAP 7—Delaware Canal and Delaware & Raritan Canal:
New Hope and Lambertville south to Morrisville and Trenton

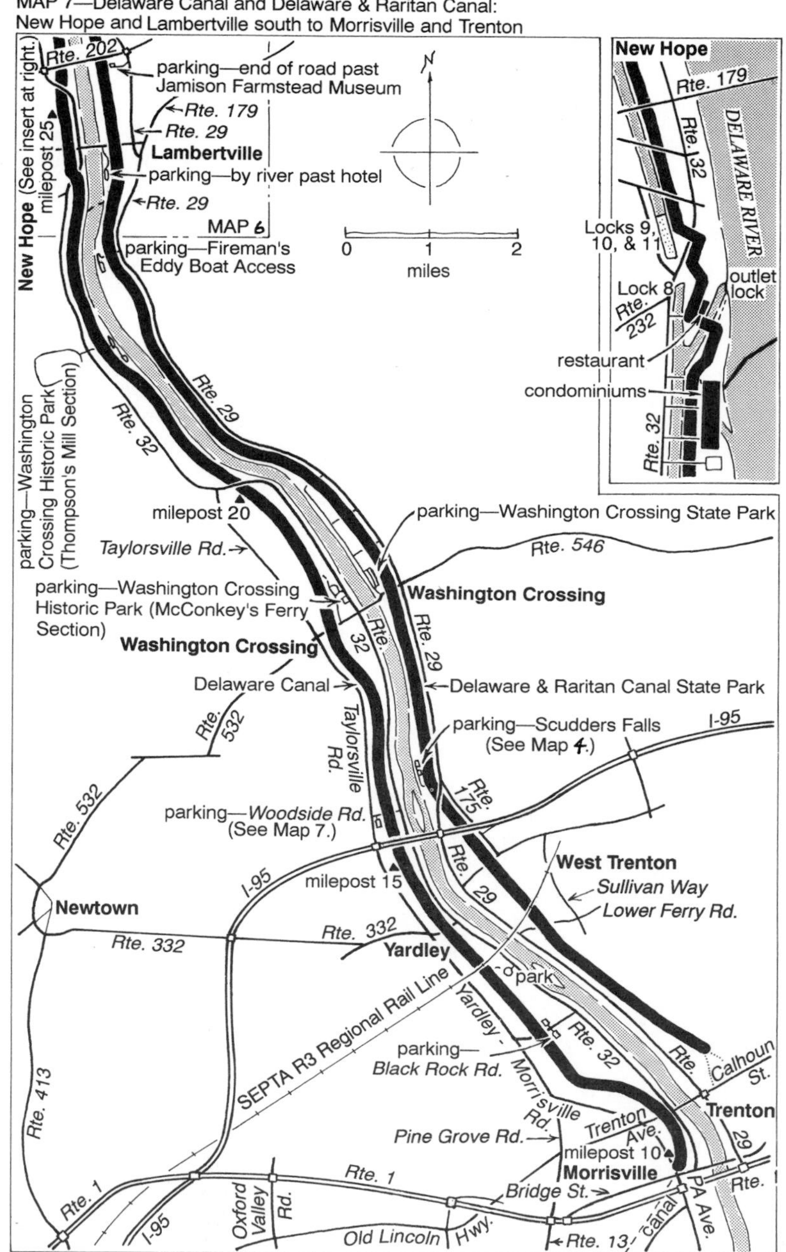

2

HOPEWELL FURNACE NATIONAL HISTORIC SITE FRENCH CREEK STATE PARK

Walking at Hopewell Furnace and hiking, ski touring, and mountain biking at French Creek State Park.

Hopewell Furnace is an outstanding example of an "iron plantation"—a company-owned industrial hamlet typical of American ironworks during the first half of the nineteenth century. The village includes not only the stone furnace but also the appurtenant structures and apparatus: the waterwheel and bellows, the casting house, the office and store, the blacksmith shop, and the tenant houses and ironmaster's residence—all restored and furnished in an historically appropriate manner. The entire complex is shown on Map 8 on page 42. The footpaths and lanes through the village total no more than a mile.

Hopewell Furnace National Historic Site is open daily (except New Year's Day, Thanksgiving, and Christmas) from 9 to 5. Dogs must be leashed. An admission fee is charged March through November. The site is managed by the National Park Service; telephone (610) 582-8773 or, for the hearing-impaired, (610) 582-2093.

For hikers who want a more strenuous outing than is provided by Hopewell Furnace, the national historic site is bordered on three sides by 7,300-acre French Creek State Park. The park's entire network of blazed trails—altogether totaling about 32 miles—is shown on Map 9 on page 45. On an interim, trial basis, some of these hiking trails are also open for mountain biking provided that riders are prepared to dismount fairly frequently in order to walk or carry their bikes over particularly rocky or steep sections. Cyclists must ride single file, yield to other trail users (please dismount as you pass), keep your speed to a moderate, safe pace, and observe posted signs. Mountain biking is not permitted on the property belonging to Hopewell Furnace National Historic Site, which is shown on Map 9 (and also on Maps 10 and 11) by the diagonal lines.

A good day's excursion is to combine a visit to Hopewell

Furnace in the morning with a walk or ride though the surrounding hilly woods at French Creek State Park in the afternoon. One suggested 7-mile hike is shown by the bold line on Map 10 on page 46, and an 11-mile route for mountain biking is delineated on Map 11 on page 47 and discussed starting on page 44.

Because hunting is permitted in some sections of French Creek State Park, hikers and cyclists should wear bright orange jackets or vests unless they have first telephoned the park office to make sure that there is no hunting on the day that they will be in the woods.

French Creek State Park is open daily from 8 A.M. to sunset. The park is managed by the Pennsylvania Bureau of State Parks; telephone (610) 582-9680 for information about the park's various activities, including camping, swimming, boating, fishing, hunting, orienteering, and guided walks.

NEW ORLEANS VICTORY STOVE, Perry Victory Stove, Don't Give Up the Ship Stove, Decatur Flat Front Stove, and Peace Stove: these were just a few of the iron products cast at Hopewell Furnace in the years of patriotic fervor following the War of 1812. As the war receded into the past, new stove motifs appeared: the Flower Pot, Hornet and Peacock, Fox Chase, and Shepherd. By 1832 the iron-making village was producing ninety-eight different stove patterns in cylindrical, oval, square, and other shapes. Some were adapted for burning coal instead of wood. A few models were patented; some bore the name Hopewell, others the names of retailers who supplied their own patterns.

Annual production at Hopewell regularly exceeded three thousand stoves, yet even so the company received more orders than it could fill. In 1841 about 5,000 stoves were sold. During the "long blast" of 1836-37, when the furnace was kept in continuous operation for 445 days, 720 tons of castings were made; all but a few tons were stove parts. During the same period 458 tons of pig iron were produced. At that time Hopewell was at the peak of its prosperity, employing more than 160 miners, woodcutters, colliers, teamsters, molders, and other hands. The village was an "iron plantation"—a single enterprise with its own farms, forests, open pit mines, water source, dwellings, store, and other structures, all supporting the operation of the small stone furnace.

The furnace at Hopewell was built about 1771 at a time when there were more than fifty iron furnaces and forges in Pennsylvania. The furnaces—fat, squat masonry stacks—were hollow and lined with firebrick. Other requisites were water power to operate the bellows, charcoal fuel made from cordwood (the only fuel suitable for cold-blast furnaces), limestone flux to coagulate impurities in the ore, and of course the ore itself. All of these ingredients could be obtained near Hopewell Furnace, which, like other iron-making communities of the day, was located in an extensive tract of forest far from any major city.

Usually furnaces of the late eighteenth and early nineteenth century were built near the bottom of a steep slope (called a bank) so that a bridge, wide enough to accommodate a mule and cart, could run from the crest of the bank to the top of the stack. When a furnace was in operation, iron ore, charcoal, and limestone were carted across the bridge and dumped into the top of the stack, which also served as the chimney. The stack gases were nearly smokeless, but occasionally streams of sparks shot out, and at night a red glow lit the sky. Water-powered bellows provided an intermittent blast of air that, with a heavy, pulsing roar, fanned the furnace fire. At furnaces like Hopewell, the rush of air was called a *cold blast* because the air was not preheated, as it was in the *hot-blast* technology developed later. When a furnace was in blast, the ore was deoxidized in the fire and the molten iron slowly sank to the crucible at the bottom of the stack. Then two or three times a day the lower tap was opened and the liquid iron poured into molds.

The molds might consist of nothing more than short, parallel troughs branching from a central channel dug in the sandy floor of the casting house, which was a barnlike structure built around the furnace. In the early days of iron manufacturing, the main pouring channel and the row of smaller molds were noted to resemble a sow with suckling pigs; hence the term *pig iron* for crude iron. The molds might also consist of patterns pressed into the sand in order to produce *open sand casts*, which were puddles of iron molded only on the lower surface. Early stove panels were made this way, but they tended to be fairly thick and in consequence were extremely heavy and expensive to transport. Open sand casts also, of course, had to be flat. Later, *flask casting*—which requires a two-sided hollow mold—was used to make relatively thin, curved pieces molded on all surfaces.

The proprietors of Hopewell Furnace owned thousands of acres of surrounding forest from which wood for charcoal was cut. Lumbering was done during winter, often by men who worked part-time or seasonally. Cut into 4-foot lengths, the logs were hauled on sleds to charcoal hearths—large circular clearings—scattered throughout the forest. (In many instances, these hearths are still discernible as level, circular platforms at French Creek State Park). There the wood was left to dry until late spring. Colliers then arranged the logs in a circular mass 30 or 40 feet in diameter, with all the pieces standing on end and leaning toward a wooden chimney at the center. Another smaller layer of logs was stacked on top of the first, and a third layer over that, until a rounded heap of wood was built. Then the colliers covered the logs with a layer of leaves and dirt. The chimney was filled with kindling and a fire set at the top.

For as long as two weeks the colliers watched over the mound while the wood smoldered and turned to charcoal. Outbreaks of flame were quickly smothered with dirt. Blue smoke indicated that all was going well, but white smoke was a sign of too much combustion. The rate of charring was controlled by opening and filling air holes. The most dangerous part of the job was "jumping the pit," which entailed climbing on top of the smoking heap and stamping on it to settle the coals and fill in air spaces. Finally, when the charring appeared to be complete, the colliers uncovered the mound a little at a time. The hot charcoal was loaded into metal-lined wagons, which then were hauled to the village and parked in a shed to protect the coals from rain. After the charcoal had cooled, it was added to the supplies stored in the charcoal house near the top of the bank.

Meanwhile, other workers dug iron ore from an open pit mine on the Hopewell property and transported it about 3.5 miles to the furnace. Similarly, limestone was extracted from quarries at Hopewell and carted to the village. Once adequate supplies of charcoal, ore, and limestone were accumulated, the furnace was *put in blast*—that is, ignited for the year. The furnace was kept in blast until the furnace lining deteriorated to the point where it needed to be replaced or until the supplies were exhausted. Usually the first item to run out was charcoal, because it could not be manufactured and replenished during winter.

When the furnace was in blast, workmen known as fillers dumped fresh charges of charcoal, ore, and limestone into the furnace every half hour around the clock. Each charge consisted of about 15 bushels of charcoal, 200 to 300 pounds of ore, and several shovelfuls of limestone. In general, production of a ton of iron consumed 1 or 2 tons of charcoal, 2 tons of ore, and a few hundred pounds of limestone. The daily output at Hopewell was between 3 and 4 tons of iron.

Working in the casting shed, the founder—a man of experience and judgment—occasionally opened the higher of two taps in the furnace to draw off the molten slag that floated on the heavier iron accumulating in the crucible. And by opening the lower tap, the founder could sample the iron itself and to some extent control its quality by calling for changes in the proportion of ingredients and by adjusting the blast of air. Twice each day, when sufficient iron had accumulated to tap the furnace, the founder rang a bell to summon the molders, who then ladled the molten iron into molds that they had prepared since the last casting.

The founder was paid according to the quality and quantity of the iron he produced, and the molders according to the number and intricacy of their castings. For flawed, unusable castings, they received no credit at all. Sometimes women earned money by cleaning the castings and by grinding off stubs of metal where the iron had entered the molds. Similarly, fins of metal produced by the seams in the molds were ground off. Most stove castings were sent unassembled to retailers in the larger towns and cities, although some stoves and other articles were bolted together at Hopewell and sold in the company store.

Aside from the furnace complex (consisting of the furnace itself, the water wheel, bellows, casting house, cleaning shed, bridge, and charcoal house), the other structures at Hopewell Furnace are the company store, the ironmaster's residence, the tenant houses, and the barn for the village draft animals. The store sold food staples and general merchandise to the workers and other residents of the area. The store also served as the company's office, where records were kept detailing orders for iron products, output of the furnace, and each worker's balance of earnings and debits. Workers could also buy produce grown in the village fields, which were leased to sharecroppers. Some employees who lived in the village had their own garden plots, chickens, hogs, and cows.

The ironmaster's residence was called the Big House. A large dining room and kitchen in the basement provided meals (for a fee) to men who were unmarried or working away from home. Visitors present on business frequently dined upstairs in the more formal dining room with the ironmaster and his family and might even spend the night as the ironmaster's guest.

At the peak of Hopewell's prosperity between 1829 and 1839, about twenty tenant houses existed in the village and were leased to workers. Rent was deducted from the tenants' earnings. Some of the houses were small, single-family structures; others were dormitories for single men. Several tenant houses were located near the company's mine. Many workers lived in their own houses near the village and walked to the furnace each day or slept in various outbuildings between shifts.

Although Hopewell as seen today emphasizes the furnace's business as a nineteenth-century stove manufactory, the furnace had been a significant source of cannon, shot, and other iron munitions during the Revolutionary War. Mark Bird, who built the furnace and whose father (also an ironmaster) gave his name to nearby Birdsboro, was a leading patriot. In the autumn of 1777 Mark Bird fitted out three hundred soldiers with uniforms, tents, and provisions at his own expense, and in

February, 1778, he sent a thousand barrels of flour to Valley Forge. Bird owned several furnaces and foundries, and his workers were discharged from the militia during the war so that they could continue to produce munitions.

After the Revolution, however, Bird's fortunes crashed. Large debts owed him by the Continental Congress went unpaid or were discharged in depreciated currency. Hopewell's furnace was flooded and closed. Another of Bird's furnaces burned. Bird borrowed heavily but was unable to repay, so in 1788 his properties were auctioned at a sheriff's sale. "There is no doubt my principle ruin was by the Warr & Depretiation . . . ," Bird wrote in later years.

After a succession of owners during the 1790s, Hopewell was acquired in 1800 by the partnership of Mathew Brooke, his brother Thomas Brooke, and their brother-in-law Daniel Buckley. In various combinations, the descendants of these men continued to operate the ironworks for more than eighty years. The furnace was repaired and improvements made. A stamping mill was constructed in 1805 to crush the slag and to recover bits of iron. A small resmelting furnace was added to increase the output of castings. Between 1800 and 1824 the annual output of iron increased from 311 tons to 857 tons. The blast season was increased from fewer than 235 days to more than 300 days. The proportion of castings—stoves, pots, pans, kettles, mold boards for plows, machine parts, and other domestic, agricultural, and industrial items—surpassed the production of less valuable pig iron. When the Schuylkill Navigation (see Chapter 4) was completed as far as Reading, Hopewell's heavy products could be shipped cheaply to Philadelphia and from there to urban markets as distant as Portsmouth, New Hampshire.

In 1828 the furnace at Hopewell was rebuilt, but ten years later it was outmoded: the hot-blast method of smelting with anthracite was introduced in 1838. Coal was far cheaper than charcoal, and labor costs for iron produced with anthracite were about 20 percent of labor costs for iron made with charcoal. The owners of Hopewell built an anthracite furnace in 1853, but it did not pay; the village was too distant from the coal fields. Production of cast objects ceased, but the village continued to make pig iron, for which there was an insatiable demand because railroads were expanding throughout the country. In 1853 Hopewell actually achieved its greatest output ever: 1,205 tons of pig iron. Even after the rise of large urban iron works in the second half of the nineteenth century, Hopewell remained in operation while production declined. In a final effort to improve the competitiveness of their furnace, the owners in 1880 added a steam boiler to augment the water wheel, and in 1882 they installed a roaster to preheat the ore. But the blast of 1883 was Hopewell's last.

For a period, mining and charcoal-making continued on the Hopewell property in order to supply other furnaces. Quarrying rights were sold to a stone company. Fence posts and rails were cut in the woods. The Big House was used as a summer residence, and the tenant houses were leased. So matters continued until 1935, when the National Park Service decided to restore the crumbling furnace. The U.S. government purchased about 6,000 acres surrounding the village, most of which in 1946 were transferred to the Commonwealth of Pennsylvania to create French Creek State Park. In 1938 Hopewell Village was declared a National Historic Site.

≈ ≈ ≈ ≈

AUTOMOBILE DIRECTIONS: Hopewell Furnace National Historic Site and French Creek State Park are located near Downingtown about 37 miles northwest of downtown Philadelphia and 11 miles southeast of Reading near Pottstown and Birdsboro and the Pennsylvania Turnpike. (See •2 on **Map 2A** on page 7.) Four avenues of approach are described below.

From the east on the Pennsylvania Turnpike: Leave the Turnpike at Exit 23 (the Downingtown exit) for Route 100 serving Pottstown, West Chester, and Hopewell Furnace National Historic Site. After paying the toll, fork right for Route 100 North toward Pottstown. From the top of the ramp onto Route 100 North, go 8.6 miles to a crossroads at a traffic light with Route 23. Turn left onto Route 23 West and go nearly 7 miles to a crossroads with Route 345. Turn right onto Route 345 North and follow it as it twists and turns. After 2.4 miles you will reach the entrance to French Creek State Park on the left; but for Hopewell Furnace you should continue on Route 345 North another 1.4 miles to the entrance on the left at Mark Bird Lane.

From the west on the Pennsylvania Turnpike: Leave the Turnpike at Exit 22 (the Morgantown exit) for Route 10 serving Reading and Morgantown. After paying the toll, fork left for Route 10 South toward Route 23 and Morgantown. From the bottom of the ramp onto Route 10 South, go 0.9 mile to a T-intersection with Route 23 in Morgantown. Turn left onto Route 23 East and follow it 5.4 miles to a crossroads with Route 345. Turn left onto Route 345 North and follow it as it twists and turns. After 2.4 miles you will reach the entrance to French Creek State Park on the left; but for Hopewell Furnace you should continue on Route 345 North for another 1.4

MAP 8—Hopewell Furnace National Historic Site

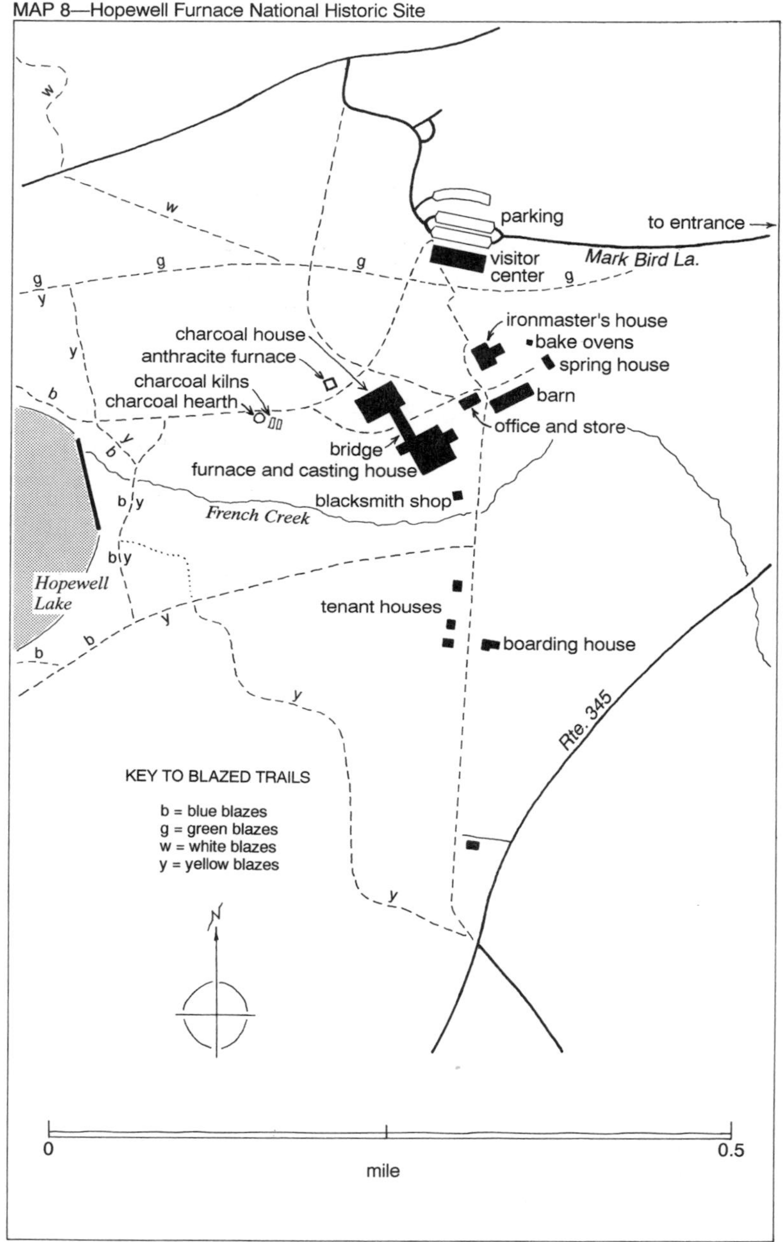

miles to the furnace entrance on the left at Mark Bird Lane.

From the north on Route 100: After going through **Pottstown**, crossing the Schuylkill River, and passing the interchange with **Route 422**, leave Route 100 at the exit for Route 724 West toward Birdsboro. Follow Route 724 West for 6 miles, then turn left and go as straight as possible 1.9 miles to a T-intersection with Route 345. Turn left onto Route 345 South. After 2.7 miles you will reach the entrance to French Creek State Park on the right; but for Hopewell Furnace you should continue on Route 345 South another 0.7 mile to the entrance on the right at Mark Bird Lane.

From the south on Route 100: From the vicinity of **West Chester** follow Route 100 North. After passing the entrance to the Pennsylvania Turnpike, continue 8.9 miles to a crossroads at a traffic light with Route 23. Turn left onto Route 23 West and go nearly 7 miles to a crossroads with Route 345. Turn right onto Route 345 North and follow it as it twists and turns. After 2.4 miles you will reach the entrance to French Creek State Park on the left; but for Hopewell Furnace you should continue on Route 345 North another 1.4 miles to the entrance on the left at Mark Bird Lane.

WALKING AT HOPEWELL FURNACE: **Map 8** opposite shows Hopewell Furnace National Historic Site and, to the west, Hopewell Lake at French Creek State Park.

From the west end of the visitor center, head downhill on the wide path to the charcoal house, the company office and store, the furnace and casting house, and the tenant houses, then return past the barn, spring house, and ironmaster's house.

For Hopewell Lake, a wide path leads west from the charcoal house several hundred yards to the dam. A footpath marked with blue paint blazes crosses French Creek below the dam to reach another wide path that leads east back to Hopewell Furnace.

HIKING AT FRENCH CREEK STATE PARK: Because Hopewell Furnace National Historic Site is surrounded on three sides by French Creek State Park, you may be inclined to leave your car at the furnace parking lot and hike from there. **However, this is not recommended** unless you are completely confident that you will be back before the furnace parking lot closes at 5 P.M. You will have more time and flexibility if, after visiting the furnace, you move your car to one of the lots at French Creek State Park before setting out for a long hike through the woods on the trails shown on **Map 9** opposite. The state park closes at sunset, which during most of the year is much later than 5 P.M.

The bold line on **Map 10** on page 46 shows a 7-mile walk through the eastern part of the state park, which is the best area for hiking because it is more rugged and wild than the western part of the park, where the park's various activity centers are located. Leave your car at the informal parking area at the intersection of Route 345 and Shed Road. The route, which makes use of several different blazed trails, is not suitable for mountain biking because some sections are too rocky and part of the circuit passes through Hopewell Furnace National Historic Site, where off-road biking is prohibited.

MOUNTAIN BIKING AT FRENCH CREEK STATE PARK: As of 1994, mountain biking is permitted on some trails on an interim, trial basis. The bold line on **Map 11** on page 47 shows an 11-mile mountain biking route that avoids most wet areas where bikes can damage the trails. The route also makes use of the park's roads (be prepared for cars) to climb steep grades—a feature which some bikers may scorn, but most, I think, will appreciate. Still, there are many places where you will have to dismount. Go slow.

For the route shown on Map 11, park in one of the small lots near the western end of Hopewell Lake. Start by following the paved park road to Brush Hill. After passing the contact station at the entrance to the Brush Hill campground, turn right into the woods on the green-blazed trail. The route shown on the map will take you across Route 345, along a broad ridge, gradually downhill and around a loop, then back by the way you came.

When you return to Brush Hill, cross the road and again enter the woods on the green-blazed trail, which is soon joined by blue blazes. Follow the green and blue blazes, but when the green trail splits to the left, stay on the blue-blazed trail, which eventually leads downhill to the west, along a gravel road, across a paved road, around a meadow, and again down to a paved road.

Turn right onto the paved road. After passing several houses, turn left to follow a paved road steeply uphill to the Hopewell Fire Tower. At the far end of a loop at the end of the road, continue straight into the woods on a narrow trail, then straight through a trail junction and downhill on the blue-blazed trail, which emerges from the woods near your starting point.

MAP 9—French Creek State Park

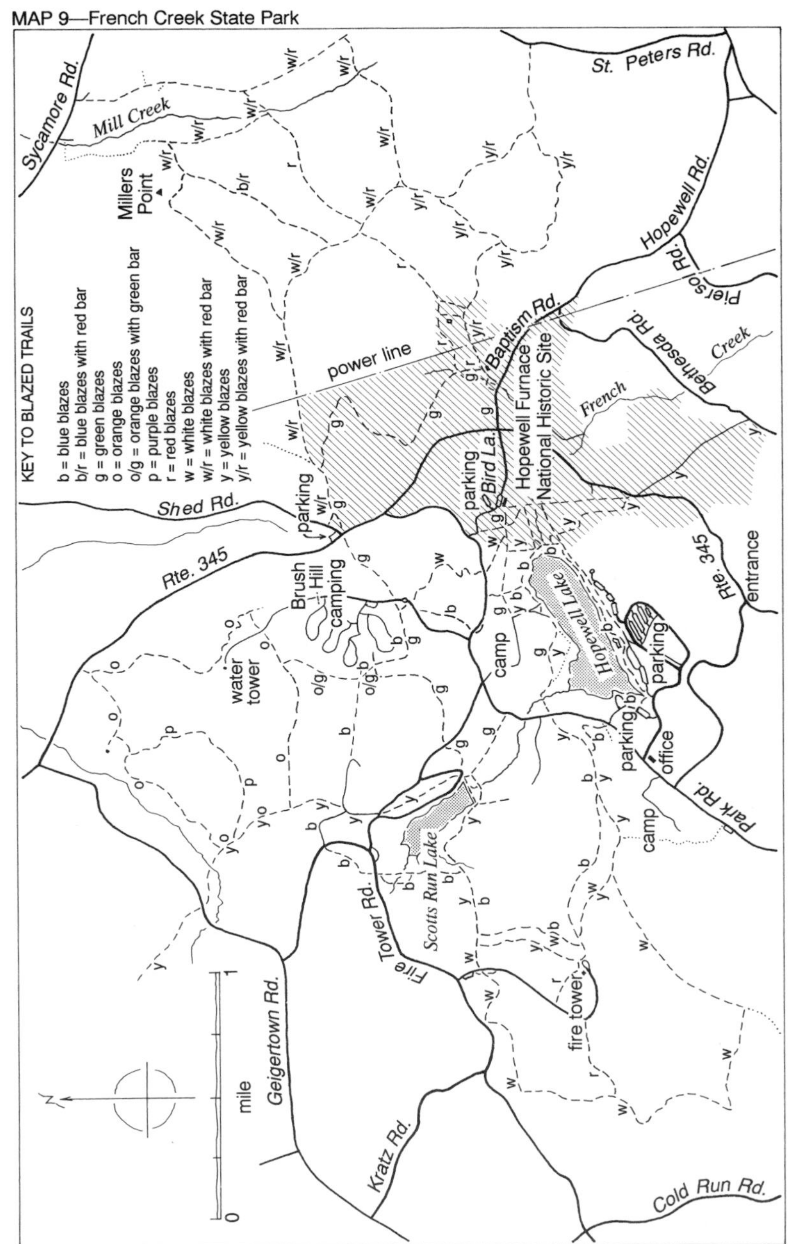

MAP 10—French Creek State Park: 7-mile hike

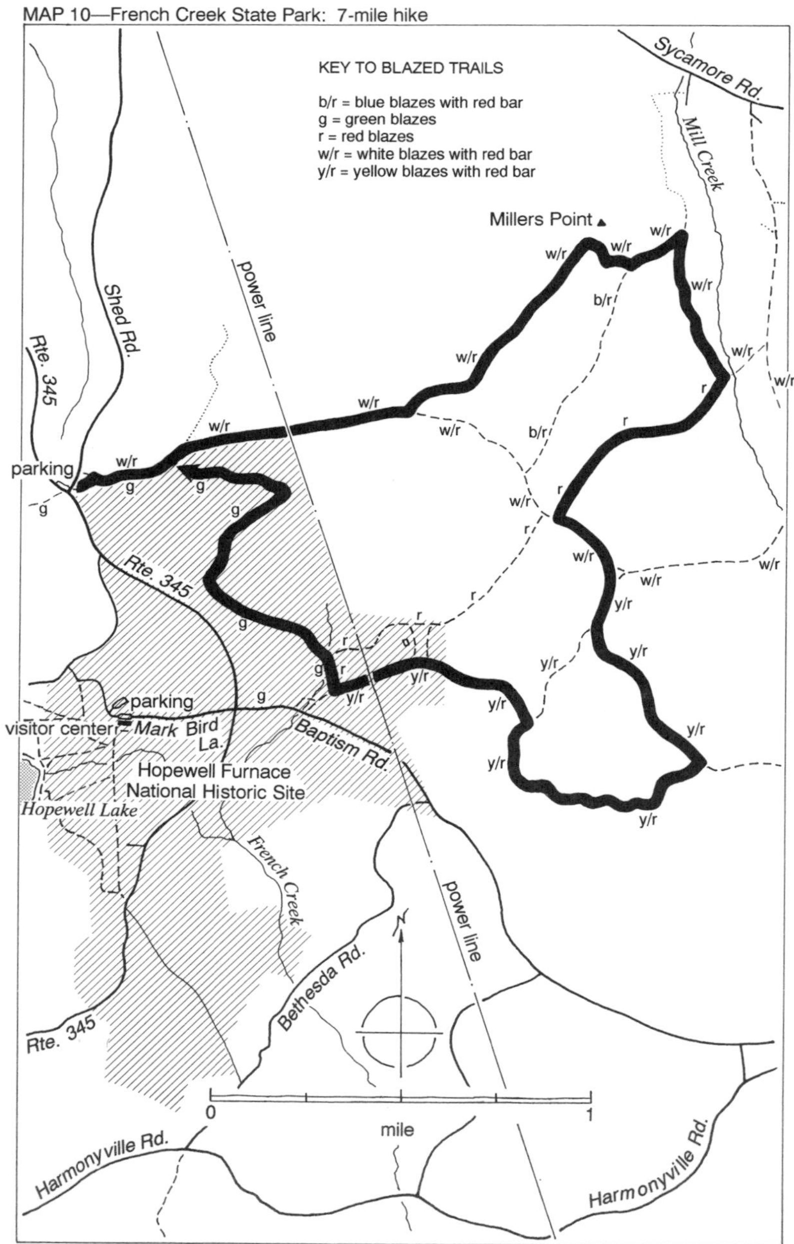

MAP 11—French Creek State Park: 11-mile mountain biking route

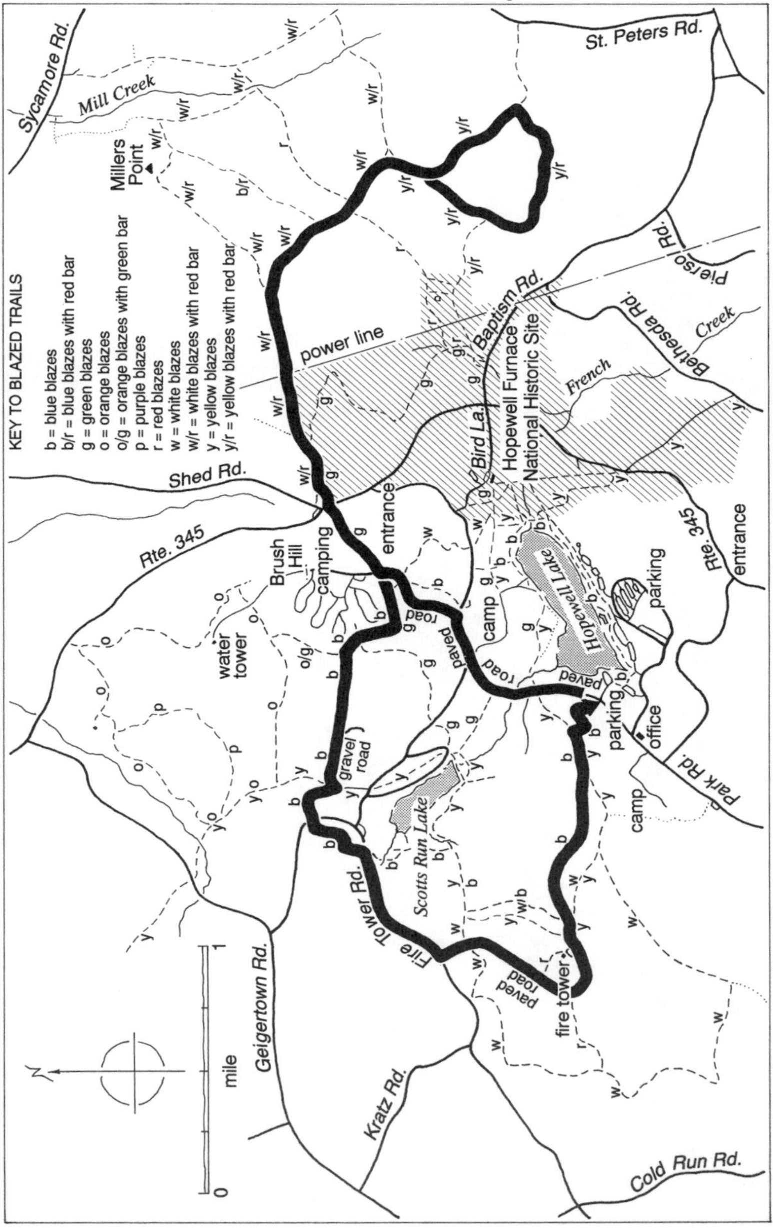

KEY TO BLAZED TRAILS

b = blue blazes
b/r = blue blazes with red bar
g = green blazes
o = orange blazes
o/g = orange blazes with green bar
p = purple blazes
r = red blazes
w = white blazes
w/r = white blazes with red bar
y = yellow blazes
y/r = yellow blazes with red bar

3

VALLEY FORGE NATIONAL HISTORICAL PARK

Walking, ski touring, and bicycling. The national park at Valley Forge is a huge expanse of rolling meadows and wooded hills where the American army under George Washington camped during the winter of 1777-78. The park features reconstructed log huts and earthworks, restored houses where some of the high-ranking officers lived, and an outstanding visitor center. A small fee is charged to tour the Isaac Potts House, which served as Washington's headquarters. Valley Forge also provides the rare opportunity to walk or ride through open countryside which, although no longer farmed, more or less resembles the region's agricultural landscape at the time of the American Revolution.

The bold line on Map 12 on page 59 shows a paved multipurpose path for walkers and bicyclists. The entire round-trip distance, including both spurs to the west, is 8 miles. Bicyclists must ride single file, stay in the bicycle lane, yield to walkers, and keep their speed to a moderate, safe pace. Dashed lines on Map 12 show hiking trails, and of these the most attractive are the Valley Creek Trail at the western end of the park (1.2 miles one-way) and the Schuylkill River Trail along the north bank of the Schuylkill River (3 miles one-way; see the discussion on page 60).

For adult cyclists who are experienced at riding in automobile traffic and who are equipped with helmets, the bold line on Map 13 on page 61 shows the 9.5-mile Encampment Tour, intended primarily for cars but also popular with cyclists who want to see more of the park than is provided by the hike-bike path. The presence of motor vehicles is mitigated by the fact that more than half the Encampment Tour follows one-way roads where most cars are moving fairly slowly. The rest of the route, however, follows two-way roads where traffic is fast and sometimes heavy.

Valley Forge National Historical Park is open daily from dawn until dark. The visitor center is open daily (except Christmas) from 9 to 5. Dogs must be leashed. The park is managed by the National Park Service. The visitor center telephone is (610) 783-1077; the headquarters telephone is (610) 783-1000.

LATE IN AUGUST, 1777, British forces under General Sir William Howe landed at the northern end of Chesapeake Bay. Although Howe had been forced to evacuate Boston in March, 1776, he had returned that summer to take New York, and now, a year later, he planned to seize Philadelphia, the leading city of the colonies and seat of the Continental Congress.

In a series of battles, marches, and counter-marches during September and October, the Continental Army under George Washington was outfought and outmaneuvered. On September 11 the Americans at Chadds Ford on Brandywine Creek failed to stop the northward advance of the British. Feinting first toward Washington's supply depot at Reading, Howe's forces then crossed the Schuylkill River and occupied Germantown and Philadelphia, from which Congress moved west, first to Lancaster and then to York. At Germantown on October 4, the British repulsed an attack by the Americans, who nonetheless remained close enough to Philadelphia to prevent the British from foraging widely. But in mid-November the British compelled the Americans to abandon Fort Mifflin and Fort Mercer on the Delaware River below Philadelphia, thus opening the city to their supply ships.

By mid-December the British were ensconced for the winter in Philadelphia after Howe, early in the month, had made rather tentative efforts to dislodge the main body of the American army from Whitemarsh (site of present-day Fort Washington Park) north of the city. Washington, however, concluded that Whitemarsh was too close to Philadelphia to be a secure winter camp, and on December 11 he moved his army west. By the middle of the month the Americans were on short rations at a temporary encampment at Gulph Mills. There Washington considered several proposals for winter quarters before selecting Valley Forge, to which the troops marched on December 19.

Located about 18 miles from Philadelphia, Valley Forge was too remote for the British to reach with a swift surprise attack, yet close enough for the Americans to harass British units searching for supplies. Based at Valley Forge, Washington's army was in a good position to protect the rest of Pennsylvania, to preserve communications with New Jersey and Maryland, and to minimize the consequences of the loss of Philadelphia. And the terrain surrounding Valley Forge was defensible.

A long, low ridge faced southeast toward Philadelphia; the Schuylkill River protected the north; and attack from the west was barred by Valley Creek and the high hills of Mount Joy and Mount Misery.

Valley Forge itself was an ironworks—or at least had been until a few months prior to the arrival of Washington's army. Owned jointly by David Potts and William Dewees, the forge produced shovels, ax heads, horseshoes, nails, and other such items. On September 18, however, the community was occupied by the British, who burned the forge and a sawmill and damaged a gristmill before moving on to Philadelphia.

When the American forces reached Valley Forge, the army consisted of approximately 12,000 men—that is, less than twenty percent of the crowd that nowadays regularly fills Philadelphia's Veterans Stadium. There were virtually no cattle suitable for eating, and on December 21 an ominous chant of "No meat, no meat" spread through the camp. In order to spur Congress to address his supply problem, Washington wrote that a mutiny might be imminent. Two days later 2,898 men—nearly a quarter of the army—were found to be unfit for duty because they lacked shoes or adequate clothes. Washington wrote Congress that "unless some great and capital change suddenly takes place in the Commissary Department this Army must inevitably be reduced to one or the other of three things: starvation, dissolution or dispersal in order to obtain subsistence in the best manner it can."

Foraging parties were ordered into the countryside to collect food. Joseph Plumb Martin of Connecticut was among those sent out, and in his Revolutionary War memoirs, he described his duty as "plundering—sheer privateering," and as "nothing more nor less than to procure provisions from the inhabitants for the men in the army and forage for the poor perishing cattle belonging to it, at the point of the bayonet." In return for their goods, farmers were given certificates supposedly entitling them to reimbursement and to relief from further requisitions. But even payment in cash was dubious compensation since the army used the debased paper currency issued by the revolutionary government.

Starting February 9, daily markets to which farmers brought supplies were held at the edge of the camp. Washington wrote, "Prices have been affixed by handbills and they are to be strictly observed. However, British currency may prove more attractive to the farmers than our Continental monies and it remains whether patriotism will conquer greed." To prevent commerce with the British, Congress granted the American army authority to try civilians who supplied goods to the enemy, and twenty-one farmers and merchants were in fact convicted at Valley Forge.

Food, clothes, blankets, medicines, and virtually all other materials necessary for the maintenance and refurbishment of the army continued in short supply throughout most of the winter. By February 5 the number of men unable to report for duty because of the lack of shoes or clothes had swelled to 3,989. The troops frequently went without meat, sometimes for as long as a week. Farmers in the vicinity of the camp hid their cattle. The only staple was "firecake," a mixture of flour and water baked on a griddle. The soldiers' pay was several months in arrears.

The shortages did not reflect a general scarcity of goods in Pennsylvania or in other states. Rather, poor transportation and inefficient procurement restricted the flow of supplies. Roads were nearly impassable, and wagon contractors and teamsters were unwilling to work for the wages authorized by Congress. For example, on February 14, one general noted that "the Commissioners have found a quantity of pork in Jersey, of which by a failure of wagons, not one barrel has reached the camp." The Schuylkill River froze late in December and for a few critical weeks was not navigable by boats carrying supplies.

For the mass of the army, the main task after arriving at Valley Forge was to build winter shelters. Before leaving Gulph Mills, Washington had ordered the formation of twelve-man squads. Each squad was to erect its own hut made of logs chinked with clay, and most were completed by the end of January. In the meantime, the men lived in tents where, short of blankets and inadequately clothed for winter, they huddled from the cold. Although the huts were a distinct improvement—they were snug and had clay-lined fireplaces and chimneys—many were poorly ventilated and damp, especially those that had been dug into the earth with a floor as much as 2 feet below the ground outside. General Lafayette termed the huts "little shanties that are scarcely gayer than dungeon cells." When spring arrived, orders were issued to the squads to make the huts as "airy as possible" by removing the chinking from between the logs, and each hut was "purified" daily by burning in it a musket cartridge or a bit of tar. Replicas of some of the huts stand throughout the park.

The huts were built adjacent to the defensive positions assigned to the troops. An inner line of defense ran along the eastern and southern slopes of Mount Joy. By the end of April the inner line consisted of a long dry-moat backed by an earthen berm and secured at each end by redoubts. Very faint remains of some of these entrenchments can still be discerned in the woods below Inner Line Drive. An outer line of defense, which was never fully completed, followed the ridge westward from the site of the present-day visitor center. Crossing the midpoint of this line was Gulph Road, thought to be the most likely approach for the British. Earthworks were also built overlooking a bridge that eventually was constructed across the Schuylkill River.

Most of the army's cannons were massed in the Artillery Park at the center of the camp, where repairs to the gun carriages could be made and from which the cannons could be sent to any point under attack—but attack never occurred. General Howe reported to London that the position of the American army was too strong for him to take during winter weather. By spring the defenses at Valley Forge—and Washington's army itself—were stronger still.

Throughout the winter, disease gripped much of the American army. An estimated two thousand soldiers died of pneumonia, dysentery, typhoid, and typhus, the last two diseases then known as "putrid fever." Sickness was aggravated by inadequate food and clothing and by crowded conditions in the huts. Sanitation was poor. On January 7 Washington ordered "all dead horses in and about the Camp, and all offal, to be burned." He noted the "filth and nastiness" near some of the huts. Five lashes were ordered for "any soldier who shall fail to ease himself anywhere but at a proper Necessary." On February 20 General Joseph Reed noted that "sickness and mortality have spread through the quarters of the Soldiers to an astonishing degree." Hospitals were established in the outlying communities, but the influx of enfeebled troops filled them beyond their intended capacity. Shortages and lack of medical knowledge caused newly arrived patients to be issued blankets and bed straw previously used by men who had died of contagious diseases.

Even relatively healthy soldiers were plagued by scabies, lice, and other vermin. Private Martin described how he and his mates rubbed themselves with a mixture of tallow and sulfur: "We killed the itch and we were satisfied, for it had almost killed us. This was a decisive victory, the only one we had achieved lately." A mocking article in a Tory newspaper noted the large quantity of "meat" to be found crawling on the backs of the Continental soldiers and suggested that it might be a solution for the army's shortage of livestock.

Probably the principal accomplishment at Valley Forge was the development of a new program of military training. The army had been hampered on march and in battle by its inability to move quickly in compact formations. Changing from marching to combat formations, or from one position during battle to another, took an inordinate length of time, and the troops often became confused. Coordination among the forces was difficult because units from different states had been instructed in different systems and formations.

In order to establish a uniform system of drill and maneuver, Washington asked Congress that he be empowered to appoint an experienced officer as inspector general. But to Washington's dismay, a small cabal of Congressional critics foisted on him Major General

Thomas Conway, an Irish-born officer who had served in the French army and to whom Washington was known to be opposed. When Conway arrived at Valley Forge, however, Washington largely ignored him. And after Conway wrote two insulting letters, there was an outpouring of support for Washington, in which those who had pushed Conway forward felt it politic to join. In January Congress sent Conway with Lafayette to Albany, New York, and in May Conway resigned.

Conway was replaced by Friedrich von Steuben, an unemployed Prussian officer who had been recommended to Congress by Benjamin Franklin, America's ambassador in Paris. Von Steuben arrived at Valley Forge on February 23, 1778, and was assigned by Washington to inspect several regiments and to recommend steps to correct whatever deficiencies he found. Favorably impressed with von Steuben's manner, observations, and proposals, Washington appointed him acting inspector general.

Von Steuben's first step was to write a simplified manual of drill procedures to be applied to the entire army. Because von Steuben spoke little English, he wrote his manual in French. As each installment was completed, his aides translated it into English, and from this translation copies were made for the newly-appointed brigade inspectors and passed down to the regimental and company officers. Day by day the troops practiced and learned drills that had been outlined only a day or two before.

As a model for the rest of the army, von Steuben assembled a company of soldiers composed of Washington's guards plus 100 additional men drawn from the various state regiments. Von Steuben personally instructed these men, at times taking a musket in his own hands in the manner of a drill sergeant to demonstrate his simplified manual of arms and routinized procedure for reloading. Squads of "awkward troops" were formed for recruits or other soldiers slow to learn the new maneuvers within the context of their regular units. On April 8 Washington noted, "Our Army, heretofore slovenly and ragged, now is becoming more military."

Von Steuben imposed a standard tempo of marching and a standard stride. He taught the troops to march in columns, to move from columns to combat lines facing the enemy, to wheel in line on the battlefield, and to regroup. He instructed them in the use of the bayonet, for which the British had been feared. (Von Steuben had noted that those Americans who had bayonets used them chiefly as skewers to broil meat.) In short, von Steuben taught the troops to march, shoot, and charge as units, as was required for effective use of the inaccurate muskets and the bayonet. Private Martin commented, "After I had

joined my regiment I was kept constantly, when off other duty, engaged in learning the Baron de Steuben's new Prussian exercises. It was a continual drill."

Some commissioned officers at first were dismayed by von Steuben's attention to detail and his (as they thought) demeaning habit of working directly with the troops. During the inactivity of winter, many officers had applied to go home on furlough, but von Steuben's example prompted them to undertake more responsibility toward their troops.

As spring approached, the army's physical condition, morale, training, and equipment steadily improved. By late February, supplies of food reached the camp more regularly, and by March cattle were being butchered daily. Appointed quartermaster general on March 2, 1778, Major General Nathanael Greene reorganized the army's quartermaster department. New muskets were obtained and old ones repaired. Bayonets—which had been issued to only half the Americans—were manufactured. Teams of draft animals were again assembled. Fresh troops arrived, and as the ranks swelled, part of the army moved to new quarters in front of the old camp. Clothing, shoes, and other supplies came from France and from the states. On May 1 Washington wrote, "Daily this Army looks more like a military force and less like an armed horde." On May 6, 1778, the new alliance with France was celebrated formally by the assembled army.

Soon word reached the camp that the British were preparing to abandon Philadelphia. After half a year they had accomplished virtually nothing, while allowing the Americans to regain and surpass their earlier strength and to forge an effective, well-organized army, which now prepared feverishly to take to the field. On June 18 news arrived that during the night the British had left Philadelphia headed toward New York. By the end of the afternoon, one American division was in pursuit. The rest of the army marched away from Valley Forge the following day, six months exactly after they had limped into their winter encampment.

≈ ≈ ≈ ≈

SEPTA: Bus 99 passes the entrance to Valley Forge National Historical Park. Telephone (215) 580-7800 for current information on schedules, routes, and connections from your starting point. One place to catch Bus 99 is the Norristown Transportation Center, which is served by several other bus routes, the R6 Regional Rail Line from Philadelphia, and the Route 100 trolley through the Main Line suburbs.

Washington's headquarters

AUTOMOBILE DIRECTIONS : Valley Forge National Historical Park is located where the Schuylkill Expressway, the Pennsylvania Turnpike, Route 202, and Route 422 all converge about 18 miles northwest of downtown Philadelphia. (See •3 on **Maps 1 and 2B** on pages 6 and 7.) These different avenues of approach are among those described below. Of course, the turnpike west of Valley Forge is designated Interstate 76, the same as the Schuylkill Expressway. The turnpike east of Valley Forge is Interstate 276.

From Interstate 95 's Exit 7 for Interstate 476 North (the Blue Route): Follow I-476 North to Exit 6B for Interstate 76 West toward Valley Forge, then follow the directions in the next paragraph.

From the east on Interstate 76 (Schuylkill Expressway): Follow the expressway west to Exit 26B for Route 202 South toward West Chester. After getting onto Route 202, exit immediately for Route 422 West toward Pottstown. Follow Route 422 for 1.4 miles, then take the exit for Route 23 West toward Valley Forge. Follow Route 23 a few hundred yards to a crossroads at a traffic light, then head straight into the park. After passing the visitor center, continue straight into the main visitor center parking lot.

From the east or west on the Pennsylvania Turnpike: Take Exit 24 for Interstate 76 East, Route 202, and Interstate 476. At the toll booths, stay in the right-hand lane, then immediately take Exit 25 for Valley Forge. Go about 1.5 miles to an intersection with Valley Forge Road, and there turn left into the park. After passing the visitor center, continue straight into the main visitor center parking lot.

From the north or south on Route 202: Take the exit for Route 422 West toward Pottstown and follow it for about 1.5 miles to the exit for Route 23 West toward Valley Forge. Follow Route 23 a few hundred yards to a crossroads at a traffic light, then head straight into the park. After passing the visitor center, continue straight into the main visitor center parking lot.

From the west on Route 422: After crossing the Schuylkill River, take the exit for Route 23 and Valley Forge. At the top of the exit ramp, turn right. Go a few dozen yards to a crossroads at a traffic light, then head straight into the park. After passing the visitor center, continue straight into the main visitor center parking lot.

MAP 12—Valley Forge National Historical Park: 8-mile hike-bike multipurpose trail

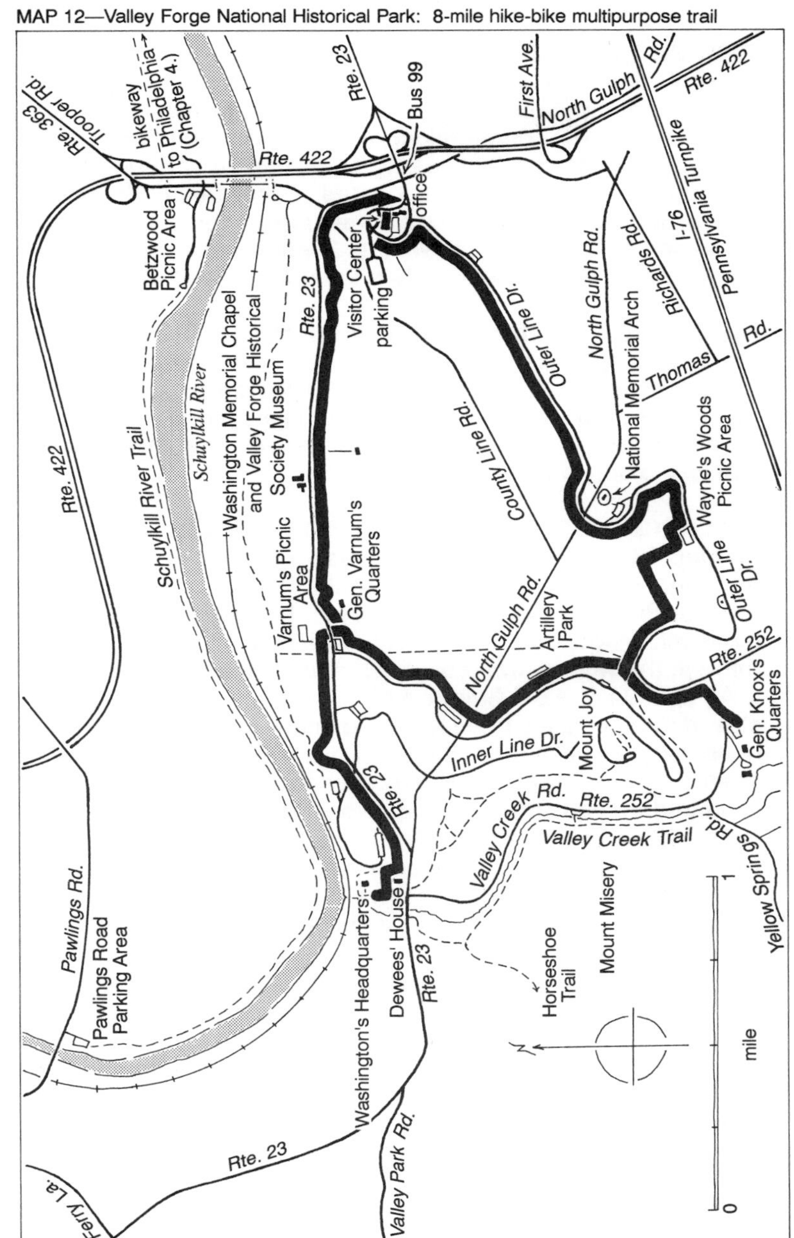

WALKING AND BICYCLING ON THE HIKE-BIKE TRAIL: The bold line on **Map 12** on page 59 shows this 8-mile paved path. From the Valley Forge Visitor Center, follow the multipurpose trail counter-clockwise up and around the building, then sharply right along a broad, grassy ridge where the outer line of defense was located. Continue on the paved path around the park. You may want to skip the spur extending a half-mile southwest to General Knox's quarters, but the spur to Washington's headquarters is well-worthwhile.

BICYCLING ON THE ENCAMPMENT TOUR: The bold line on **Map 13** opposite shows this 9.5-mile route. From the main parking lot below the Valley Forge Visitor Center, simply follow the blue-and-white Encampment Tour signs along the park road. For nearly 3 miles the road is one-way, but the route is two-way at intervals after that.

WALKING ON THE SCHUYLKILL RIVER TRAIL: As shown on **Map 13** opposite, a trail stretches for 3 miles along the northeast side of the river between the Betzwood Picnic Area and the Pawlings Road Parking Area. The path is very pleasant. Wide, level, and paved with rock grit, it winds through the woods and provides frequent views of the river.

As of 1994, the old Betzwood Bridge to the picnic area is closed and not likely to be replaced soon, so a short detour is necessary to reach the Schuylkill River Trail. From the park's main entrance near the visitor center, follow Route 23 East a few hundred yards, then turn right for Route 422 West. Follow Route 422 across the Schuylkill River, then take the exit for Route 363 North toward Audubon and Trooper. **But** at the top of the exit ramp, turn left and follow Route 363 South 0.3 mile to the entrance on the right for Valley Forge National Historical Park, Betzwood Picnic Area.

The Schuylkill River Trail starts at the far end of the picnic area. Walk as far as you want, then return by the way you came.

The Betzwood Picnic Area is also the western terminus of the Philadelphia-Valley Forge Bikeway, described in Chapter 4. The paved bikeway starts near the entrance to the picnic area and stretches nearly 20 miles downriver to the Philadelphia Museum of Art.

MAP 13—Valley Forge National Historical Park:
9.5-mile Encampment Tour for cars and bicycles

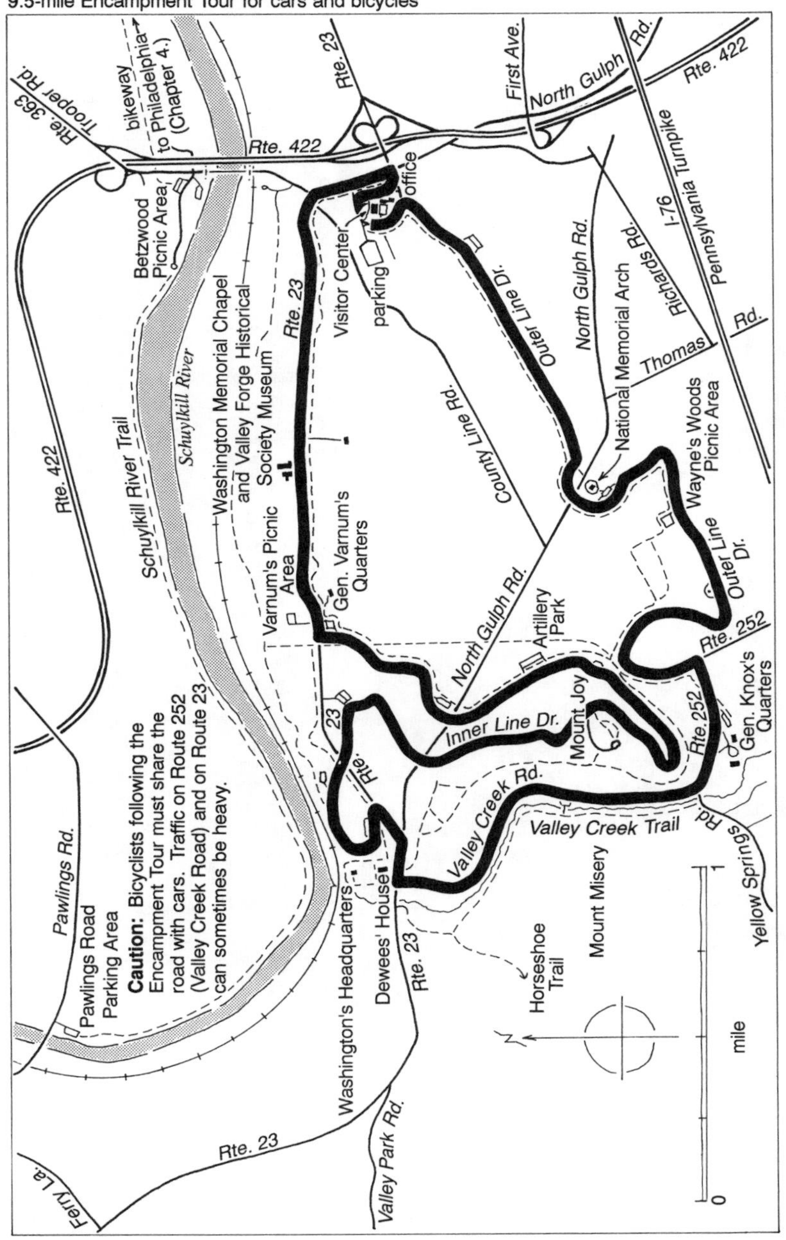

4

THE SCHUYLKILL TRAIL

Philadelphia-Valley Forge Bikeway

Walking, jogging, ski touring, bicycling, and roller-skating. As shown by the bold line on Map 14 on page 69, a 20-mile bikeway follows the northeast bank of the Schuylkill River, connecting the paved riverside paths at Fairmount Park (see Chapter 14) with the Betzwood Picnic Area and trails at Valley Forge National Historical Park (see Chapter 3).

The name "Schuylkill Trail" covers a series of connected bikeways along the river. At present, the Philadelphia-Valley Forge Bikeway is the main segment, although other sections are planned extending the bikeway farther upstream. Incidentally, the paved bikeway that is the subject of this chapter is entirely separate from the unpaved Schuylkill River Trail for hikers at Valley Forge. To avoid confusion, this book will use the name "Philadelphia-Valley Forge Bikeway" to designate the section of paved bikeway discussed here.

Directions for automobile access to the bikeway in Philadelphia start on page 67, and the corresponding cycling or walking directions start on page 68. Automobile directions for access to the bikeway at Valley Forge start on page 68, and the corresponding cycling or walking directions start on page 73.

Although close to the Schuylkill, the Philadelphia-Valley Forge Bikeway does not often provide views of the river—except during late fall, winter, and early spring, when there are no leaves on the trees. Urban sections at Philadelphia, Conshohocken, and Norristown alternate with relatively rural sections and punctuate progress along the trail.

Most of the bikeway follows an old railroad bed and consists of a paved path from which motor vehicles are excluded—although, of course, you still have to watch for cars where roads cross the trail. Until construction of the Philadelphia-Valley Forge section is finished, there are stretches at Manayunk and Shawmont that follow city streets and narrow sidewalks that are not safe for children or other riders who lack experience in traffic. So the first time you go, leave your children at home in order to see for yourself whether the planned improvements have been completed—as is scheduled to occur at Conshohocken and Norristown during the summer of 1994. Until then, the presence of other cyclists and occasional "Bike Trail" signs will help you to navigate the detours.

The bikeway also, of course, provides opportunities for walking and roller-skating, so cyclists must ride single file, yield to other trail users, and keep their speed to a moderate, safe pace.

For walkers and for riders of fat-tired bicycles, the most interesting and picturesque section is the somewhat bumpy 2-mile dirt towpath of the **Manayunk Canal**, which passes old warehouses and mills established when the canal was a working waterway. The canal towpath also passes present-day factories built on the site of earlier works that were powered by water impounded by Flat Rock Dam. For walkers and cyclists who start in Philadelphia at the East Park Canoe House, the distance to Flat Rock Dam and back is 8.8 miles. Because the canal towpath is so bumpy, riders of thin-tired road bikes may prefer a detour along local roads, as shown on Map 15 on page 71.

The Philadelphia section of the bikeway is managed by the Fairmount Park Commission; telephone (215) 685-0000 for information. The Montgomery County section of the bikeway is managed by the county Department of Parks; telephone (610) 278-3555. Finally, the bikeway's access point at Valley Forge is managed by the National Park Service; telephone (610) 783-1000 or (610) 783-1077.

ALTHOUGH FOR THE MOST PART the Philadelphia-Valley Forge Bikeway follows an old railroad bed, the route also provides a look at the Schuylkill Navigation (called by some the Schuylkill Canal), of which the Manayunk Canal was once part.

As its name implies, the aim of the Schuylkill Navigation was to make the river usable by canal boats. Visions of converting the Schuylkill into an inland transportation artery are as old as Pennsylvania itself. William Penn, for example, wrote in 1690 about "a communication by water" linking and including the Schuylkill and Susquehanna. In 1762 Dr. William Smith surveyed a route between these two rivers along Tulpehocken Creek above Reading and Swatara

Creek below Harrisburg. Other surveys were made in the years immediately before and after the American Revolution.

In 1791 and '92, Pennsylvania approved the formation of two private companies to build canals linking the Delaware, Schuylkill, and Susquehanna rivers. Funds were raised by selling shares and later by holding lotteries. In 1794 construction began in earnest, but during the late 1790s some of the principal subscribers for stock defaulted on their obligations to pay installments, and by 1802 work had ceased.

In 1815 the Schuylkill Navigation Company was incorporated. The company's plan was to construct a series of dams in order to maintain a chain of long, deep, slackwater pools in the river itself. The slackwater sections would be linked together by canals, each with one or more locks, as can be seen today at Manayunk, where Flat Rock Dam and the Manayunk Canal were built starting in 1817. By 1825 the Schuylkill Navigation was open from Philadelphia to Mt. Carbon above Pottsville (located well above Reading and not to be confused with Pottstown). The system included 51 miles of river navigation and 58 miles of canals. Canal boats were pulled by mules walking along the towpath bordering the river and canals. There were 18 dams, 23 canals, and 120 locks. Other features included seventeen stone aqueducts to carry the various canals over tributary rivers, a 450-foot tunnel near Auburn, and thirty-one houses for lock keepers. Among the features along the section of river that is passed nowadays by the Philadelphia-Valley Forge Bikeway were a dam and a canal at Conshohocken, a dam and canal at Norristown, and the Catfish Dam and lock below Port Kennedy.

In 1825 the Schuylkill Navigation was linked to the Union Canal at Reading. The Union Canal, which opened in 1827, joined the Schuylkill and Susquehanna rivers, thus completing the project begun late in the eighteenth century to connect the Susquehanna to tidewater on the Delaware.

The Schuylkill Navigation Company earned income not only by charging tolls but also by selling water power. For example, in 1821 the company platted the industrial town of Manayunk and established a series of mill sites between the canal and river. For power, water was fed to each mill and allowed to fall from the canal level to the river level. The canal also, of course, provided an inexpensive and convenient means to transport raw materials and finished products to and from the mills. However, Schuylkill coal dwarfed all other cargo.

Before the advent of railroads, the Schuylkill Navigation Company prospered, but in 1842 the Philadelphia & Reading Railroad was completed to Mount Carbon. The canal company responded to competition from the railroad by undertaking a series of expensive improvements. Locks were enlarged and combined (resulting eventually in seventy-one locks), which not only made possible the use of larger boats, but also speeded traffic. Two million tons of cargo—the most ever carried on the waterway in one year—were transported in 1859. In 1864 the Schuylkill Navigation struck a deal with the Philadelphia & Reading Railroad to split the coal traffic according to a fixed ratio (45 percent for the waterway, 55 percent for the railroad). But in 1869 a miners' strike, low water, and then a flood depleted the resources of the navigation company, which in 1870 leased its holdings to the railroad.

The Philadelphia & Reading Railroad kept the waterway in operation but did little to maintain it. In 1872 the upper reaches of the river and canal system were abandoned, in part because of the accumulation of silt from the washing of coal. The next section of waterway as far downstream as Port Clinton was closed in 1888.

In 1902 the operation of the canal and river system was returned to the Schuylkill Navigation Company, but by 1925 the shipment of Schuylkill coal by water had altogether ceased. Commercial traffic downstream from Manayunk stopped in 1931. Still, however, the navigation company hung on, earning revenue from the generation of electricity at its dams and from tolls paid by excursion boats, for which some sections of the river and canal system were maintained. Finally, however, in 1949 the Schuylkill Navigation Company conveyed its physical assets to the Commonwealth of Pennsylvania, and since then some canals and locks have been filled and some dams removed.

As for the Philadelphia & Reading Railroad, much of the Philadelphia-Valley Forge Bikeway lies immediately adjacent to the Reading tracks, which are still very much in use. The bikeway itself occupies the old railbed of the Schuylkill Secondary, formerly a commuter line that was redundant with the adjacent tracks and so was abandoned in sections during the 1970s. In connection with the national bicentennial in 1976, the Sierra Club advocated the creation of a riverside trail linking Independence Hall and Valley Forge. The first 2.5 miles of bikeway extending northwest from Shawmont were opened in 1978. During the 1980s, 11 miles of railbed in Montgomery County were converted to bikeway in cooperation with the Philadelphia Electric Company, which had bought the right-of-way from Conrail for electric transmission lines. There are plans to extend the bikeway upstream from Valley Forge to Mont Clare and eventually as far as Reading or Pottsville, and also downstream from the Philadelphia Museum of Art to the Delaware River in the vicinity of the airport and the John Heinz National Wildlife Refuge at Tinicum (Chapter 17).

≈ ≈ ≈ ≈

SEPTA: In Philadelphia the Wissahickon Transfer Center, which is served by several bus routes, lies immediately adjacent to the bikeway. (As of 1994, the bikeway here is merely a sidewalk next to Ridge Avenue and Main Street into Manayunk.)

The Norristown Transportation Center, served by the R6 Regional Rail Line from Philadelphia, the Route 100 trolley through the Main Line suburbs, and several bus routes, also lies immediately adjacent to the bikeway 4.5 miles from its western end.

The R6 Regional Rail Line itself parallels the bikeway between Shawmont and Norristown, with stops at Spring Mill and Conshohocken. Telephone (215) 580-7852 for information about taking your bicycle on the train.

Telephone (215) 580-7800 for current information on schedules, routes, and connections from your starting point.

≈ ≈ ≈ ≈

AUTOMOBILE DIRECTIONS TO THE TRAIL IN PHILADELPHIA: The large parking lot for the Canoe House off Kelly Drive in eastern Fairmount Park is a convenient place to start on the Philadelphia-Valley Forge Bikeway. Four avenues of approach are described below.

From downtown Philadelphia: Follow the Benjamin Franklin Parkway northwest toward the Philadelphia Museum of Art. Just before reaching the art museum, fork right for Kelly Drive and follow it north along the river 2.7 miles to a large parking lot on the left.

From the north or south on Interstate 95: Take Exit 17 for Interstate 676 West toward central Philadelphia. After passing the exit for Broad Street, leave I-676 at the exit for the museum area and Benjamin Franklin Parkway. At the top of the exit ramp, turn right. Go 100 yards, then turn left onto the Benjamin Franklin Parkway and move to the right-hand lanes. Just before reaching the art museum, fork right for Kelly Drive and follow it north along the river 2.7 miles to a large parking lot on the left.

From the east or west on Interstate 76 (Schuylkill Expressway): Get off I-76 at Exit 32 for Lincoln Drive and Kelly Drive. (If you are coming from the west, the exit is on the left.) After crossing the Schuylkill River, curve tightly left for Kelly Drive. At the bottom of the exit ramp, follow Kelly Drive 1.9 miles to the large parking lot on the right.

From the south on Route 1: Follow Route 1 (City Avenue) north. After passing the exits for Interstate 76 (Schuylkill Expressway) and after crossing the Schuylkill River, curve tightly left for Kelly Drive. At the bottom of the exit ramp, follow Kelly Drive 1.9 miles to the large parking lot on the right.

BICYCLING OR WALKING FROM PHILADELPHIA TOWARD VALLEY FORGE: The bikeway more or less parallels the Schuylkill River, as shown by the bold line on **Map 14** opposite. From the Canoe House parking lot, follow the paved path north, with the Schuylkill River on your left and Kelly Drive on your right. Continue straight past the Falls Bridge and from there simply follow the sidewalk or bikeway. After passing the bus transfer center at Wissahickon Creek, follow the path alongside Ridge Avenue for a few hundred yards, then fork left downhill onto Main Street through Manayunk. After 0.8 mile, turn left onto Lock Street in Manayunk, and there join the Manayunk Canal towpath.* After passing Flat Rock Dam, continue upriver, following the bikeway all the way through Shawmont, Conshohocken, and Norristown to the Betzwood Picnic Area at Valley Forge National Historical Park. As noted in the introduction to this chapter, there may sometimes be detours marked by "Bike Trail" signs.

For a discussion and map of Valley Forge, see Chapter 3. Located on the northwest side of the Schuylkill River, the Betzwood Picnic Area at Valley Forge is separated from the main body of the park by a condemned bridge that eventually will be replaced. As of 1994, a shuttle bus that leaves the Betzwood Area hourly on the hour carries cyclists and their bicycles around to the main Valley Forge park.

≈ ≈ ≈ ≈

AUTOMOBILE DIRECTIONS TO THE TRAIL AT VALLEY FORGE : Valley Forge is located where the Schuylkill Expressway, the Pennsylvania Turnpike, Route 202, and

---

*Some bicyclists—particularly those riding thin-tired road bikes—find the towpath too bumpy and so prefer to stay on Main Street, then go uphill on Leverington Street to Umbria Street. Turn left and follow Umbria 1.6 miles to a hairpin turn downhill onto Shawmont Avenue. This alternative route is shown on **Map 15** on page 71.

MAP 14—Philadelphia-Valley Forge Bikeway

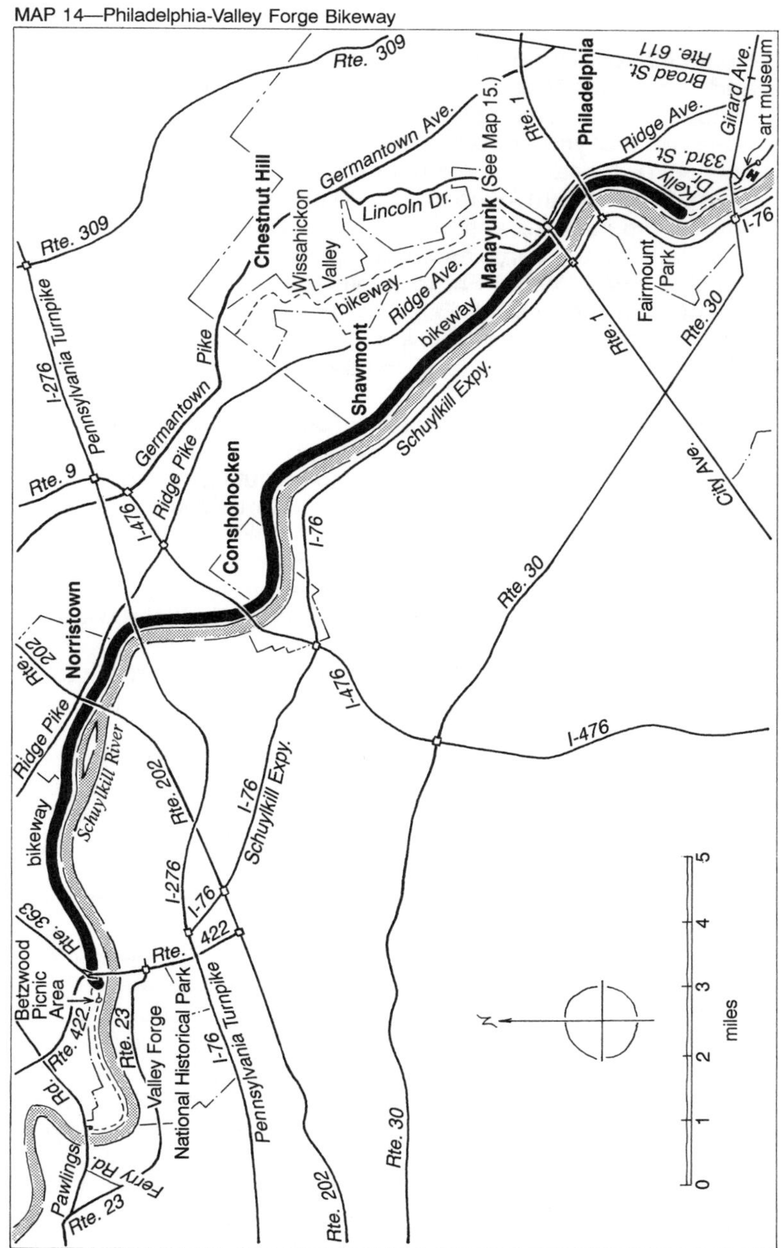

Route 422 converge. (See •4 on **Maps 1 and 2B** on pages 6 and 7, and also **Map 14** on page 69.) These different avenues of approach are among those described below. **Please note**, however, that you are being directed *not* to the main part of the national historical park, but rather to the Betzwood Picnic Area, where there is immediate access to the bikeway. Also, of course, the turnpike west of Valley Forge is designated Interstate 76, the same as the Schuylkill Expressway. The turnpike east of Valley Forge is Interstate 276.

From Interstate 95 's Exit 7 for Interstate 476 North (the Blue Route): Follow I-476 North to Exit 6B for Interstate 76 West toward Valley Forge, then follow the directions in the next paragraph.

From the east on Interstate 76 (Schuylkill Expressway): Follow the expressway west to Exit 26B for Route 202 South toward West Chester. After getting on Route 202, exit immediately for Route 422 West toward Pottstown. Follow Route 422 for 2.0 miles. Take the exit for Route 363 North toward Audubon and Trooper, **but** at the top of the exit ramp, turn left and follow Route 363 for 0.3 mile to the entrance on the right for Valley Forge National Historical Park, Betzwood Picnic Area.

From the east or west on the Pennsylvania Turnpike: Take Exit 24 for Interstate 76 East, Route 202, and Interstate 476. After paying the toll, take Exit 26A for Route 202 South toward West Chester. Pass an exit for Warner Road, then immediately exit onto Route 422 West toward Pottstown. Follow Route 422 for 2.0 miles. Take the exit for Route 363 North toward Audubon and Trooper, **but** at the top of the exit ramp, turn left and follow Route 363 South 0.3 mile to the entrance on the right for Valley Forge National Historical Park, Betzwood Picnic Area.

From the north or south on Route 202: Take the exit for Route 422 West toward Pottstown and follow it for about 2 miles to the exit for Route 363 North toward Audubon and Trooper. **But** at the top of the exit ramp, turn left and follow Route 363 South 0.3 mile to the entrance on the right for Valley Forge National Historical Park, Betzwood Picnic Area.

From the west on Route 422: As of 1994, the Betzwood Bridge is condemned and not likely to be replaced soon, so a short detour is necessary. After crossing the Schuylkill River, take the exit for Route 23. At the top of the exit ramp, turn left onto Route 23 East and go a few dozen yards, then turn right

MAP 15—Philadelphia-Valley Forge Bikeway: alternative routes through Manayunk

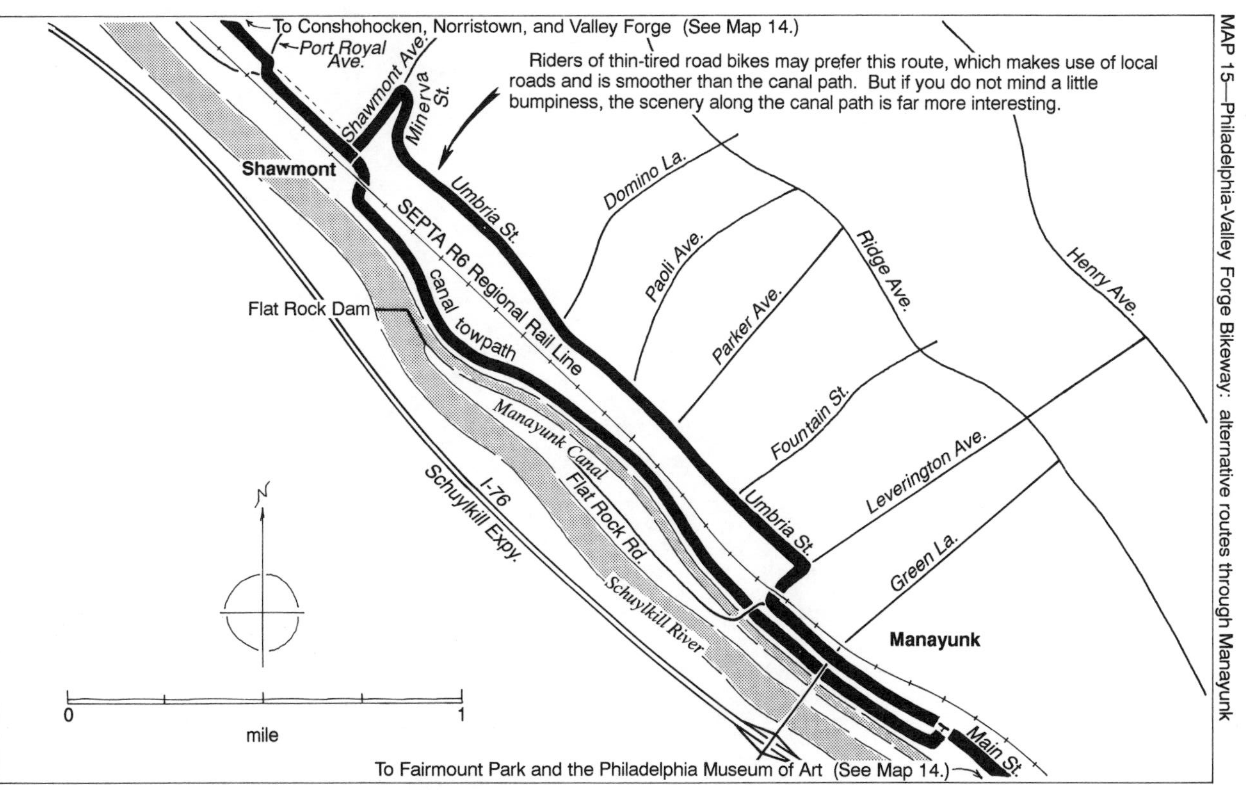

for Route 422 West. After crossing the Schuylkill River again, take the exit for Route 363 North toward Audubon and Trooper. **But** at the top of the exit ramp, turn left and follow Route 363 South 0.3 mile to the entrance on the right for Valley Forge National Historical Park, Betzwood Picnic Area.

BICYCLING OR WALKING FROM VALLEY FORGE TOWARD PHILADELPHIA: The bikeway is located only a few dozen yards from the entrance to the Betzwood Picnic Area. The paved path more or less parallels the Schuylkill River, as shown by the bold line on **Map 14** on page 69. Follow the bikeway through Norristown, Conshohocken, and Shawmont to the end of the Manayunk Canal Towpath at Lock Street.* As noted in the introduction to this chapter, there may occasionally be detours marked by "Bike Trail" signs.

From Lock Street, follow Main Street south through Manayunk for 0.8 mile. At Ridge Avenue, follow the sidewalk or path downhill only 0.2 mile. After passing the bus transfer station at Wissahickon Creek, bear right to follow the path next to Kelly Drive. Continue straight past the Falls Bridge. The paved path follows the Schuylkill River through Fairmount Park to the Philadelphia Museum of Art.

For a discussion and map of the Fairmount Park bike trails along both sides of the Schuylkill River, see Chapter 14. And for a discussion and maps of the Wissahickon Valley trails, see Chapter 11. The Philadelphia-Valley Forge Bikeway links with the Wissahickon trails where Ridge Avenue crosses Wissahickon Creek.

---

*Some bicyclists—particularly those riding thin-tired road bikes—find the towpath too bumpy and so, after passing through Shawmont, prefer to turn uphill onto Shawmont Avenue, then make a hairpin turn to the right onto Minerva Street, which leads to Umbria Street. Follow Umbria for about 1.6 miles, then turn downhill onto Leverington Street and left onto Main Street through Manayunk. This alternative route is shown on **Map 15** on page 71.

5

MILL GROVE

Audubon Wildlife Sanctuary

Walking. John James Audubon's first home in America is now an outstanding museum and 170-acre wildlife refuge where a network of trails—shown by the dashed lines on Map 16 on page 82—provides the opportunity to walk through woods and meadows overlooking Perkiomen Creek and Mine Run. The blazed Green Trail is about 1 mile long; other trails total another mile. Bicycles are not permitted on the trails at Mill Grove.

Various paintings, drawings, and an original edition of *The Birds of America*—the four huge volumes of engraved, hand-colored, life-sized prints that are the basis of Audubon's reputation—are on display in the stone, eighteenth-century house (or museum). Two of the rooms on the second floor are furnished in the style of the early 1800s.

The refuge grounds are open Tuesday through Sunday from 7 A.M. to dusk. The house is open Tuesday through Saturday from 10 to 4 and Sunday from 1 to 4. The property is closed every Monday plus Thanksgiving, Christmas, and New Year's Day. Dogs and picnicking are prohibited.

Mill Grove is managed by the Montgomery County Department of History and Cultural Arts; telephone (610) 666-5593.

"MILL GROVE was ever to me a blessed spot. . . ," wrote John James Audubon, describing in later years his life there as a young man in 1804-05. "For one year I was as happy as the young bird that, having left its parents' sight, carols merrily while hawks watch it for easy prey."

At the age of eighteen, Audubon had been sent from France to America by his father, probably to escape conscription into Napoleon's army. Although born in 1785 in Haiti to the French-Creole mistress of a French sea captain, merchant, and planter, Audubon had been raised in his father's household in France by the captain's indulgent wife.

> My stepmother who was devotedly attached to me completely spoiled me, hid my faults, boasted to everyone of my youthful merits, and—worst of all—said frequently in my presence that I was the handsomest boy in France. All my wishes and idle notions were at once gratified. She went so far as actually to grant me *carte blanche* at all the confectionery spots in the town, and also in the village of Couëron, near Nantes, where we spent summers and eventually moved from the center of the city.
>
> My father was of quite another, much more valuable turn of mind as to my welfare. He believed that the stores of the mind and not the power of gold coins render a man happy. . . . My father, long a seaman, and then in the French Republican Navy, wished me either to follow in his footsteps or to become an engineer. I studied drawing, geography, mathematics, fencing and the like, and also music for which I had considerable talent. Mathematics was hard dull work, I thought. Geography pleased me more. I was quite enthusiastic for dancing, and also for becoming commander of a corps of dragoons some day.
>
> My father was mostly absent on duty, so that my mother let me do much as I pleased. Instead of applying closely to my studies I preferred to go with my friends in search of birds' nests, or to fish and shoot. I usually made for the field, my little basket filled with good eatables for lunch at school, but to burst with nests, eggs, lichens, flowers, and even pebbles from the shore of some rivulet by the time I came home at evening.

Audubon grew up undisciplined, spoiled, charming when he wanted to be, and at times given to telling fanciful lies about himself. He failed his examinations for officer's training. In later years he told his wife that he was the Lost Dauphin, Louis XVII, son of Louis XVI and Marie Antoinette, and that he had been spirited out of prison as a child.

When Audubon was sent to America, he stayed briefly with Miers Fisher, a wealthy Quaker. Fisher was business agent for Audubon's father regarding Mill Grove, a farm that the captain had bought as an investment in 1789. Audubon's father had asked Fisher to place his son (who at that time was named Jean Jacques, not John James) in a suitable household where he could learn English. Fisher responded by offering to have the young man stay with him at Urie, Fisher's handsome estate near Pennypack Creek. Although Audubon later described Fisher as "kindly" and "good and learned," the sedate Quaker and young Frenchman did not get along. According to Audubon:

> [Fisher] was opposed to music of all descriptions, and dancing, and indeed to most of my amusements. He could not bear me to carry a gun or fishing-rod. At last I reminded him that it was a duty to install me on the estate to which my father had sent me.

Audubon's father had not sent his son to Mill Grove, which at that time included a gristmill and 285-acre farm, but Fisher complied with the young man's wishes, apparently glad to get rid of him. Audubon lived briefly with a family near Mill Grove, then later moved to Mill Grove itself as a boarder in the household of the farm's caretaker. Yet Audubon conducted himself as though he were the farm's owner: a young gentleman residing at his country seat.

> At Mill Grove I was presented to the caretaker and tenant farmer, William Thomas, also a Quaker. He was to dole out what was considered sufficient to a young gentleman's quarterly allowance. . . .
>
> I pursued my simple and agreeable studies in Pennsylvania with as little concern about the future as if the world had been made for me. My rambles invariably commenced at break of day. To return, wet with dew, bearing a feathered prize, was and ever will be the highest enjoyment. Hunting, fishing, drawing and music occupied my every moment. Cares I knew not, and I cared naught about them. My neighbor and future father-in-law, William Bakewell of Fatland Ford plantation, a recent arrival from England, an excellent man and a great shot, often hunted with me. I was pleased to believe that his daughter Lucy looked upon me with some favor. His son Thomas was skating with me one morning on the Perkiomen, that first winter. He challenged me to shoot at his hat as he tossed it in the air while I passed at full speed. Accepting with great pleasure I went off like lightening—up and down—until the trigger was pulled. Down on the ice came the hat, as completely perforated as a sieve. He repented (alas! too late) and was afterward severely reprimanded by Mr. Bakewell.

Fatland Ford is located on the east side of Pawlings Road a quarter mile south of the entrance to Mill Grove. The Bakewells moved there after Audubon's arrival at Mill Grove, but the young Frenchman, mindful of the protracted war between France and England, at first refused to call on them, telling Mrs. Thomas that he did not wish to know anyone of the English race. But when he later met Mr. Bakewell while hunting, Audubon found the Englishman to be pleasant company and later, visiting at Fatland Ford, took an instant liking to his daughter. By the time Audubon returned to France in 1805, he and Lucy were engaged without their parents' approval. Audubon's father asked his business agent for information on the Bakewells, "their manner, conduct, means, and reason for being in that country. . . . Tell these good people that my son is not at all rich and that I can give him nothing if he marries in his present condition." The Bakewells, well-to-do gentry, were equally skeptical. Later, however, the parents agreed that their children could marry when they were older and John James was capable of supporting himself and a family.

During his stay at Mill Grove, Audubon joined in a venture he thought would make him rich. With the aid of Francis Dacosta, who had replaced Miers Fisher as business agent, John James and William Thomas reopened an abandoned lead mine on the property. The mine, however, produced only violent disagreements between Audubon and Dacosta, who had acquired a half-interest in Mill Grove.

To the extent that Audubon did any serious work at Mill Grove, it was his drawing:

> When, as a little lad, I first represented birds on paper, I was under the impression that each sketch was a finished picture, because it possessed some sort of a head and tail and two sticks of legs. Oh! what bills and claws I did draw, to say nothing of a perfectly straight line for a back, and a tail stuck in, any way—like an unshipped rudder, and with never a thought of abutments to keep it from falling backward or forward. Many persons praised them to the skies. But my father constantly impressed upon me that nothing in the world possessing life and animation was easy to imitate, as I would gradually learn. I listened less to the others, and more to him; and his kind words and deep interest in my improvement became my law. My first collection of drawings—all stiff, unmeaning profiles—are such as one found in most such works. My next, begun in America, were from birds hung by a string tied to one foot, that I might show every portion as the wings lay loosely spread. In this manner I made some pretty fair signs for poulterers.
>
> While watching the Peewees [Phoebes] and their graceful attitudes a thought struck my mind like a flash of light. Nothing, after all, could ever answer my enthusiastic desire to represent Nature, alive and moving, except to copy her in her own way. I began again. On I went, forming, literally, hundreds of outlines of my favorites, the Peewees. How good or bad I cannot tell, but I fancied I had mounted a step on the high pinnacle before me. I continued for months, simply outlining birds as I observed them, either alighted or on the wing. But I could finish none of my sketches. I lay many different species on the table or on the ground in attitudes for sketching. Alas! They were *dead*, to all intents and purposes, and neither wing, nor leg, nor tail could I place according to my wishes. Next I tried fastening threads to raise or lower head, wing or tail, until I had something like life before me. Yet much was still wanting. When I saw the living birds I felt the blood rush to my temples. Almost in despair I spent about a month without drawing—deep in thought and daily in the company of the feathered inhabitants of Mill Grove.
>
> I cogitated as to how far a manikin of a bird would answer. I labored with wood, cork and wires to form a figure, one so grotesque that when set up it was like a tolerable-looking Dodo. A friend roused my ire by laughing at it immoderately, assuring me that if I wished to represent a tame gander it might do. I gave it a kick, broke it to atoms, walked off, and thought again.
>
> Young as I was, and impatient, I let my desire fill my brains with many plans. Not infrequently I dreamed I had made a new discovery. One morning long before day I leaped out of bed, ordered a horse to be saddled, mounted it, and went off at a gallop towards Norristown, about five miles

> away. Not a door was yet open. I went to the river, took a bath, returned to the town, entered the first open shop, bought wire of different sizes, leaped on my steed and was soon again at Mill Grove. I really believe my tenant's wife thought I was mad. On being offered my breakfast, I told her I only wanted my gun. I was off to the creek, shot the first Kingfisher I met, carried it home by the bill, sent for the miller, and had him bring me a piece of soft board. When he returned with it he found me filing sharp points on wire, ready to show him what I meant to do.
>
> I pierced the body to fix in on the board, passed a second wire above the upper mandible to hold the head in a pretty fair attitude, and with finer wires arranged the feet according to my notions. Even common pins came to my assistance. The last wire delightfully elevated the tail, and at last—there stood the *real* Kingfisher. The lack of breakfast was not at all in my way. No, indeed! I outlined the bird with the aid of compasses, then colored and finished it without a thought of hunger. My honest miller stood by, delighted to see me so pleased. This was what I shall call my first drawing actually from Nature, for even the model's eye was still as if full of life when I pressed the lids aside with my fingers.

Such is Audubon's account of how he came to devise his "wire armature" for posing freshly-killed birds in life-like positions—although it should perhaps be added that by the time this memoir was written, Audubon had become a skilled raconteur and self-promoter of his art. Hence the deft put-down of other, competing bird artists' drawings as no better than his juvenile work: "stiff, unmeaning profiles." In any case, for the rest of his life Audubon used his wire method to pose birds for drawing.

Audubon returned to Mill Grove from France in 1806 in company with Ferdinand Rozier. The fathers of Audubon and Rozier had established their sons in business as informal partners. They were empowered to settle business differences with Dacosta and to sell Mill Grove, which they did. The partners then spent half a year in a sort of apprenticeship at an importing firm in New York before moving to Kentucky to start a general store in Louisville. In 1808 Audubon traveled to Fatland Ford, married Lucy Bakewell, and returned with her to Louisville.

Two years later, while Audubon and Rozier were in their store, a stranger walked in carrying two large volumes. It was Alexander Wilson (discussed in Chapter 6), who was in Louisville collecting bird specimens and selling orders for his *American Ornithology*, of which the first two volume had been completed. Each bird was portrayed in a color plate and described in the accompanying text. Audubon was about to purchase a set when Rozier, ever the more frugal and business-oriented of the partners, told him that he was foolish to buy someone else's pictures when his own were so much better.

Some biographers date the inception of Audubon's own monumental project, *The Birds of America*, from this encounter with Wilson. In any event, after successive business reverses, Audubon spent the period between 1820 and 1826 traveling and drawing birds. Lucy took a series of positions in Louisiana households as governess and teacher while her husband earned money as he traveled by doing chalk portraits, by painting business signs and murals, and by teaching arithmetic, drawing, dancing, fencing, and even swimming.

In 1826, after he had failed to find a publisher or patron in America, Audubon took some 450 watercolor drawings of birds to England, where he was immediately acclaimed a genius. In a series of exhibits, his work was shown throughout Great Britain. Having secured William Home Lizars of Edinburgh as engraver (later replaced by Robert Havell of London after Lizars' colorists went on strike), Audubon worked continuously and brilliantly for twelve years, monitoring the engravers and colorists, writing text, promoting his project, and traveling to find and draw more birds. He was not only the principal artist and author, but also his own publisher, and in that capacity he had to sign up subscribers, press them for payment if they fell behind, replace them if they dropped out, and distribute the finished prints, which at first were not bound. Eventually, whenever he had to be out of England, Audubon left his son Victor in charge in London. When Audubon was in America, he traveled widely and constantly, sometimes with his son John, who was becoming a good artist in his own right, and with other assistants whom he hired. Audubon financed these trips himself, although the federal government helped by putting ships at his disposal for trips along the coast of South Carolina and Florida and again for a bird-finding journey from the Mississippi Delta to Texas.

Printed in double elephant-size folios (an open volume measures 40 by 52 inches) and containing 435 life-sized plates, each individually colored, the four volumes of *The Birds of America* appeared between 1827 and 1838. A fifth volume of text—the *Ornithological Biography*—appeared in 1839. This work was followed by a popular edition of smaller prints in seven volumes and then by *The Viviparous Quadrupeds of North America*, written in collaboration with John Bachman and completed by Audubon's sons after their father's death in 1851. Audubon's original life-sized bird watercolor drawings were sold by his widow to the New York Historical Society, which still owns them.

As for Mill Grove, it was acquired by Samuel Wetherill of Philadelphia in 1813 and remained in the Wetherill family until its sale to Montgomery County in 1951.

≈ ≈ ≈ ≈

SEPTA: Bus 98 runs to a crossroads in the village of Audubon, where Park Avenue from the north and Pawlings Road from the south intersect with Egypt Road. However, from there you still have to walk 0.5 mile south on Pawlings Road (there is no sidewalk) in order to reach the entrance to Mill Grove. (See the insert at the bottom of **Map 16** on page 82.)

Telephone (215) 580-7800 for current information on schedules, routes, and connections from your starting point. One place to catch Bus 98 is the Norristown Transportation Center, which is served by the R6 Regional Rail Line from Philadelphia, the Route 100 trolley through the Main Line suburbs, and several bus routes.

AUTOMOBILE DIRECTIONS: Mill Grove is located in the village of Audubon about 20 miles northwest of downtown Philadelphia. (See •5 on **Map 1** on page 6 and also the insert at the lower right corner of **Map 16** on page 82.) Nearby is Valley Forge, where the Schuylkill Expressway, the Pennsylvania Turnpike, Route 202, and Route 422 converge. (See **Map 2B** on page 7.) These different avenues of approach are among those described below. Of course, the turnpike west of Valley Forge is designated Interstate 76, the same as the Schuylkill Expressway. The turnpike east of Valley Forge is Interstate 276.

From Interstate 95 's Exit 7 for Interstate 476 North (the Blue Route): Follow I-476 North to Exit 6B for Interstate 76 West toward Valley Forge, then follow the directions in the next paragraph.

From the east on Interstate 76 (Schuylkill Expressway): Follow the expressway west to Exit 26B for Route 202 South toward West Chester. After getting on Route 202, exit immediately for Route 422 West toward Pottstown. Follow Route 422 for 2.0 miles. Take the exit for Route 363 North toward Audubon and Trooper. From the top of the exit ramp, go only 0.1 mile, then turn left onto Audubon Road at a traffic light. Follow Audubon Road 1.2 miles to an intersection with Pawlings Road. The entrance to Mill Grove is straight ahead on the far side of the intersection.

From the east or west on the Pennsylvania Turnpike: Take Exit 24 for Interstate 76 East, Route 202, and Interstate 476. After paying the toll, take Exit 26A for Route 202 South toward West Chester. Pass an exit for Warner Road, then immediately exit onto Route 422 West toward Pottstown.

MAP 16—Mill Grove and Audubon Wildlife Sanctuary

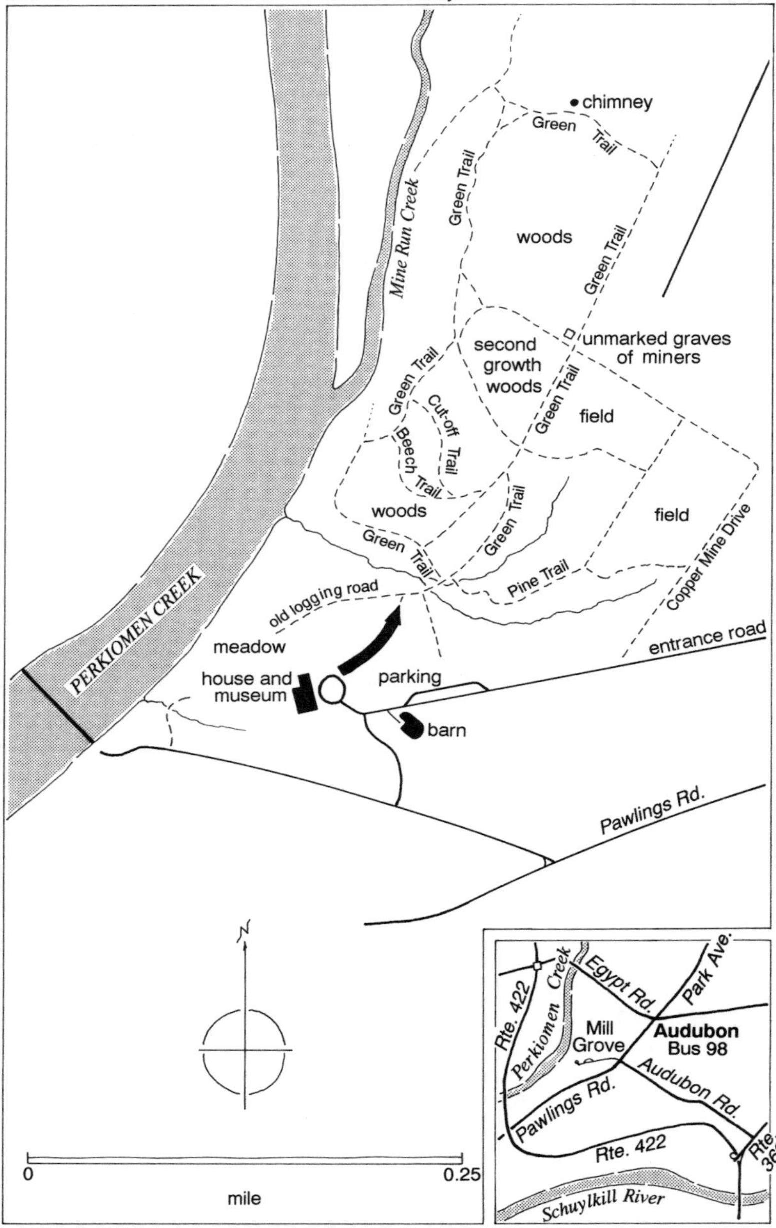

Follow Route 422 for 2.0 miles. Take the exit for Route 363 North toward Audubon and Trooper. From the top of the exit ramp, go only 0.1 mile, then turn left onto Audubon Road at a traffic light. Follow Audubon Road 1.2 miles to an intersection with Pawlings Road. The entrance to Mill Grove is straight ahead on the far side of the intersection.

From the north or south on Route 202: Take the exit for Route 422 West toward Pottstown and follow it for about 2 miles to the exit for Route 363 North toward Audubon and Trooper. From the top of the exit ramp, go only 0.1 mile, then turn left onto Audubon Road at a traffic light. Follow Audubon Road 1.2 miles to an intersection with Pawlings Road. The entrance to Mill Grove is straight ahead on the far side of the intersection.

From the west on Route 422: Take the exit for Oaks and Audubon. At the bottom of the exit ramp, fork right for Audubon and go 1 mile to the intersection of Egypt Road and Pawlings Road at a traffic light. Turn right onto Pawlings Road and go 0.4 mile to the entrance to Mill Grove on the right.

WALKING AT MILL GROVE: First, do not miss the opportunity to see the small but outstanding Audubon museum in the Mill Grove house. The meadow sloping down to the river is also attractive.

The trailhead for the network of paths shown on **Map 16** opposite is located in front of the Mill Grove House at a gap in a stone wall.

6

EVANSBURG STATE PARK

Walking. Evansburg State Park, which includes more than 20 miles of blazed trails shown on Map 17 on page 92, occupies both banks of Skippack Creek north of Norristown. Trails near the river—including the 5-mile Skippack Creek Loop Trail shown by the bold line on Map 18 on page 94—traverse high, steep bluffs and low, bottomland woods (sometimes very muddy). Many of the trails farther back from the river pass through overgrown fields or skirt cropland that is leased to local farmers, thus providing a pleasant mix of scenery. Within the park are many old farmsteads, including the visitor center, which from the riverside trail can be reached via the Old Farmstead Trail.

Because hunting is permitted in some sections of Evansburg State Park, hikers should wear bright orange jackets or vests unless they have first telephoned the park office to make sure that there is no hunting on the day that they will be in the woods.

Evansburg State Park is open daily from 8 A.M. to sunset. Off-road bicycling is prohibited. The park is managed by the Pennsylvania Bureau of State Parks; telephone (610) 489-3729 for information about the park's various activities.

WHAT ORNITHOLOGICAL DISTINCTION is shared by Philadelphia, Nashville, Savannah, and Ipswich, Massachusetts? They are the only U.S. municipalities whose names have been given to birds: the Philadelphia vireo, the Nashville warbler, and the Savannah and "Ipswich" sparrows. Perhaps Ipswich should be ousted from this select set, inasmuch as the American Ornithologists' Union has determined that the Ipswich bird is merely a pale race of the Savannah breed. As for the Baltimore oriole, it and the city were both named for the Lords Baltimore, the colonial proprietors of Maryland. Mark Catesby, an eighteenth-century naturalist, called the oriole the "Baltimore-Bird" because its colors were the same as those of the Baltimores' heraldic flag.

Bird artist John James Audubon was the subject of Chapter 5, and bird identification is the subject of Chapter 7. This chapter too is wholly birdtalk, focusing on the rainy-day pastime of bird names. After all, as a word, *titmouse*, for example, is worth a curious smile, and although a titmouse is easy to identify, how many birders know what *titmouse* means? Why is a petrel so called? And what about *killdeer, turnstone, nuthatch,* and other peculiar bird names?

Although many American Indian place names (Wissahickon and Conshohocken, for example) were adopted by the Europeans, the settlers and early ornithologists made a clean sweep when it came to naming—or rather renaming—North American birds. In a few cases where the same species (brant, for instance) were found on both side of the Atlantic, use of the European name was a matter of course. More often, however, the settlers simply re-used the names of Old World birds for similar-looking—but actually different—New World species. The English, for example, have given the name *robin* to various red-breasted birds in India, Australia, and North America. More often still, the use of general names like *wren* was extended to American birds, with the addition of qualifying words to identify individual species (house wren, Carolina wren, and so forth). However, scientific classification has sometimes placed whole categories of American birds in entirely different families than their European namesakes, as in the case of American warblers. The only North American birds in the same family as the European warblers are the gnatcatcher and kinglets—not at all what are called warblers here. Finally, in relatively rare instances, American birds have been given unique and colorful new names based on their behavior, appearance, and song, as, for instance, the yellow-bellied sapsucker, canvasback, and whip-poor-will.

Early American ornithologists seem to have been quite casual about naming birds. Alexander Wilson (1766-1813), who is generally regarded as the father of American ornithology, once shot a bird in a magnolia tree; hence, magnolia warbler for a bird whose preferred habitat is low, moist conifers. Usually, however, Wilson named birds according to the locality where his specimens were collected. He named the Nashville warbler and the Savannah sparrow, but not the Philadelphia vireo. (It was named by naturalist Charles Lucien Jules Laurent Bonaparte, Prince of Canino and Musignano, a nephew of Napoleon Bonaparte and—judging from his moniker—presumably an authority on names.)

Wilson lived in the Philadelphia area when he was not traveling up and down the Atlantic seaboard and along the Mississippi frontier looking for new species of birds. On several long journeys he gathered bird specimens and enrolled subscribers for his nine-volume *American*

Ornithology, most of which was written in the last seven years of his life. For a brief period in 1794-95, after he had emigrated from Scotland, Wilson lived and worked as a weaver at Joshua Sullivan's house and mill on Pennypack Creek (Chapter 13) just downstream from Pine Road. Later he was a schoolmaster near Bristol and Philadelphia. Entirely self-taught, he became an encyclopedist, bird artist, and naturalist. After his death his work was overshadowed by Audubon's superior, life-sized drawings, but Wilson was in many ways the greater pioneer, depicting 264 species of birds, of which 49 were not previously known.

Not surprisingly, many of the geographic names given to birds by early ornithologists bear no relation to the species' breeding territory or winter range. The Savannah sparrow, for example, is found throughout North America and might just as well have been named for Chicago or Seattle or even Anchorage. Among the Tennessee, Connecticut, and Kentucky warblers (all named by Wilson), only the last is at all likely to be found in its nominal state during the breeding season, and none winter north of Mexico. But probably the greatest geographical misnomer among bird names is our native turkey, after the supposed region of its origin. The name was first applied to the guinea cock, which was imported from Africa through Turkey into Europe and with which the American bird was for a time identified when it was first introduced to Europe in about 1530.

Some bird names, although seeming to refer to specific geographic areas, are actually far broader in their historical meaning. *Louisiana* in Louisiana heron refers to the vast territory of the Louisiana Purchase, even though the bird is usually found only in coastal areas. The species was first collected on the Louis and Clark expedition and was named by Wilson. *Arcadia*, as in Arcadian flycatcher, is an old French name for Nova Scotia, but the term was used generally to suggest a northern clime, as was also *boreal* in boreal chickadee, from the Greek god of the north wind, Boreas.

In addition to birds named *by* early ornithologists and explorers, there are birds named *for* them by contemporary and later admirers of their work. Wilson, for example, is memorialized in the name of a petrel, a phalarope, a plover, a warbler, and also a genus of warblers. Audubon is honored by Audubon's shearwater and "Audubon's" warbler, a form of the yellow-rumped warbler. There was a measure of reciprocity about this last bird name: in 1837 John Kirk Townsend, a Philadelphia ornithologist and bird collector, named "Audubon's" warbler, and a year or two later Audubon returned the favor with Townsend's solitaire. Then there are species named for ornithologists' wives, daughters, and relatives, as in Anna's hummingbird and Virginia's, Lucy's, and Grace's warblers. Some birds bear human names connected to no one in particular. Guillemot (French for "little William"), magpie (in part based on Margaret), martin ("little Mars"), and parakeet ("little Peter") are thought to be pet names or affectionate tags that have become attached to various species.

Color is probably the dominant theme in bird names. Plumages cover the spectrum, ranging from the red phalarope through the orange-crowned warbler, yellow rail, green heron, blue goose, indigo bunting, purple gallinule, and violet-crowned hummingbird. For stripped-down straightforwardness there are names like bluebird and blackbird. For vividness there are color designations like scarlet tanager, vermilion flycatcher, lazuli bunting, and cerulean warbler. To improve our dictionary skills, there are color-based names like fulvous tree duck, ferruginous hawk, flammulated owl, and parula warbler. For unpoetry, there is hepatic tanager, so called because of the liver-colored, liver-shaped patch on each cheek. For meaninglessness there is the clay-colored sparrow. (What color is that? Answer: buffy brown, at least on the rump.) Some bird names less obviously denote basic hues: vireo (green), oriole (golden), dunlin ("little dull-brown one"), canvas-back (for its speckled gray and white back), brant (thought by some to mean "burnt," referring to the dusky black plumage), and waxwing (whose red-tipped secondary wing feathers recalled to someone the color and substance of sealing wax). A great many bird names pair color with some specific body part, as in redhead, goldeneye, yellowlegs, and so forth.

Shape or other distinctive features often are reflected in bird names. The profile of the bufflehead suggests an American buffalo. The loggerhead shrike has a disproportionately large head. Shovelers have long, broad bills. The word *falcon* is derived from a Latin term for "sickle," suggesting the bird's curved talons. From head to toe, there is a body part that is some bird's nominal identity: tufted titmouse, horned lark, eared grebe (*grebe* itself may come from a Breton word for "crest"), ruffed grouse, pectoral sandpiper (for the air sack under its breast feathers), short-tailed hawk, stilt sandpiper (for its comparatively long legs), rough-legged hawk (for its feathered tarsi), sharp-shinned hawk (it has), semi-palmated sandpiper (for its partially webbed feet), and Lapland longspur (for the elongated claw on the hind toe).

Some names indicate size, from *great* and *greater* to *little, lesser,* and *least*. Symmetry would seem to demand a *greatest*, but perhaps that need is filled by *king*, which occasionally refers to stature. The king rail, for example, is the largest of the rails. But sometimes *king* is simply a compliment to a bird's raiment or a reference to distinguishing plumage on its crown, as in the ruby-crowned and golden-crowned kinglets ("little kings"). *Gallinule* itself suggests size, being derived from Latin for "little hen." *Starling* is from the Anglo-Saxon word for bird; with the addition of the diminutive suffix *-ling*, it simply means "little bird." *Titmouse* similarly is a combination of Icelandic and Anglo-Saxon meaning "small bird." The base word *tit* for *bird* also appears in bushtit and wrentit.

A few names, like that of the gull-billed tern, make explicit comparisons with other birds. The hawk-owl has a long slender tail that gives this bird a falcon-like appearance. The lark bunting sings on the wing like a skylark, the curlew sandpiper has a downwardly curved, curlew-like bill. The swallow-tailed kite has a deeply forked tail like a barn swallow. The turkey vulture has a head that somewhat resembles that of a turkey. And *cormorant* is derived from French for "sea crow."

Many bird names refer to distinctive behavior. Woodpeckers, sapsuckers, creepers, and wagtails all do what their names suggest. Turnstones do indeed turn over small stones and shells while searching for food. *Black skimmer* describes the bird's technique of sticking its lower bill into the water while flying just above the surface. *Shearwater* similarly suggests the bird's skimming flight. Frigatebirds (also called man-o'-war-birds) were named by sailors for the birds' piratical habit of pursuing and robbing other birds, as do also parasitic jaegers. *Duck* is derived from Anglo-Saxon for "diver." *Nuthatch* is from "nut hack," referring to the bird's technique of wedging a nut into a crevice and then hacking it into small pieces. *Vulture* is akin to Latin *vellere*, "to pluck or tear." Although many people associate *loon* with the bird's lunatic laugh, as in "crazy as a loon," more likely the word is derived from a Norse term for "lame," describing the bird's awkwardness on land—a result of its legs being very near its tail. There is, however, at least one North American bird that is named for its mental capacity: the booby. Seamen who raided the isolated colonies thought the birds stupid because they were unaccustomed to predators and inept at protecting themselves. The dotterel (whose name is related to "dolt" and "dotage") is another nominally foolish bird. Ernest A. Choate, in his fascinating *Dictionary of American Bird Names*, and Edward S. Gruson, in *Words for Birds*, discuss these and other names.

Some birds, such as the whooping crane, clapper rail, piping plover, laughing gull, mourning dove, warbling vireo, and chipping sparrow, are named for how they sound. Similarly, the comparative volume of their vocalizations is the theme that distinguishes between mute, whistling, and trumpeter swans. *Oldsquaw* suggests this duck's noisy, garrulous voice. The catbird mews and the grasshopper sparrow trills and buzzes like the insect. Gruson, however, says that the grasshopper sparrow is named for its diet, as are the goshawk (literally, "goosehawk") and oystercatchers, flycatchers, and gnatcatchers. The saw-whet owl is named for the bird's endlessly repeated note, which is supposed to suggest the sound of a saw being sharpened with a whetstone. The bittern, whose name ultimately is traceable to its call, has a colorful assortment of descriptive folk names, including "bog-bumper," "stake driver," "thunder pumper," and "water belcher." The evening grosbeak and vesper sparrow both tend to sing at dusk. Finally, of course, many birds' songs or calls are also the basis for their names, including the bobolink, bobwhite, bulbul, chachalaca, chickadee, chuck-will's-widow, chukar, crow, cuckoo, curlew, dick-cissel, godwit, killdeer, kittiwake, owl, pewee, phoebe, pipits, towhee, veery, whip-poor-will, and willet. *Quail* (like "quack") and *raven* are thought originally to have been imitative of bird calls.

Habitat is a major theme of bird names, as with the surf scoter, sandpiper, seaside sparrow, waterthrush, marsh hawk, meadowlark, wood duck, mountain chickadee, and field, swamp, and tree sparrows. Then there is the *kind* of tree or shrub, as in spruce and sage grouse, willow ptarmigan, pinyon jay, cedar waxwing, myrtle warbler, pine siskin, and orchard oriole. The barn, cliff, cave, tree, and bank swallows are named for their preferred nesting sites. As for *prairie warbler*, the name is simply a misnomer; the bird is common east of the Mississippi and usually is found in brushy, scrubby areas.

Several bird names are associated with human figures. Knots, which frequent shores and tidal flats, are said to be named for Canute (or Cnut), King of the Danes. To demonstrate to the sycophants of his court that he was not omnipotent, Canute vainly ordered the tide to stop rising. Petrels are thought to be named for Saint Peter, who walked on the water at Lake Genneserath; when landing in the water, petrels dangle their feet and hesitate for an instant, thus appearing to stand on the waves. Cardinals, of course, are named for the red robes and hats of the churchmen. Similarly, prothonotory warblers have the golden raiment of ecclesiastical prothonotories. The bizarre and contrasting pattern of the harlequin duck suggests the traditional costume of Italian pantomime.

Finally, there is the ovenbird, almost unique among North American birds for being named after the appearance of its nest, which is built on the forest floor and resembles a miniature, domed brick oven. "Basketbird" and "hangnest" are folk names referring to the pendulous nests of orioles.

≈ ≈ ≈ ≈

SEPTA: Buses 91 and 93 pass through Evansburg State Park on Ridge Pike . However, reaching the park's trails involves walking about half a mile on roads that lack sidewalks.

Ask the driver to get off the bus at the intersection with Grange Road. Follow North Grange Road a few hundred feet northeast, then turn left downhill onto Old Baptist Road, which will bring you into the park at the lower-left corner of **Map 17** on page 92.

For your return, you should flag the bus if you expect it to stop at Grange Road.

Telephone (215) 580-7800 for current information on schedules, routes, and connections from your starting point. Buses 91 and 93 originate at the Norristown Transportation Center, which is served by the R6 Regional Rail Line from Philadelphia, the Route 100 trolley through the Main Line suburbs, and several bus routes.

AUTOMOBILE DIRECTIONS: Evansburg State Park is located about 20 miles northwest of downtown Philadelphia and 5 miles northwest of Norristown. (See •6 on **Maps 1 and 2C** on pages 6 and 7.) The different avenues of approach described below all lead to the parking lot at Anders Road, which is a convenient place to start on the Skippack Creek Trail Loop shown on **Map 18** on page 94. An even more compelling reason to drive first to the Anders Road parking lot is that—as of 1994—the adjacent bridge over Skippack Creek is in a state of semi-collapse, closed to vehicular traffic but open to pedestrians, **but even foot traffic may be barred if the bridge deteriorates further**. Consequently, if your hike involves crossing the river at Anders Road, start there so that you will know what conditions prevail at the bridge, and so that you will not be unpleasantly surprised toward the end of your planned circuit by finding the bridge closed.

If you want to park in one of the other lots or drive to the park office or visitor center, refer to **Map 17** on page 92 as you approach the park.

From Interstate 95 's Exit 7 for Interstate 476 North (the Blue Route): Follow I-476 North to its end (don't exit; stay in the left-hand lanes). Pick up a turnpike ticket and continue on Route 9 North, which is the Northeast Extension of the Pennsylvania Turnpike. Once you are on Route 9 heading toward Allentown, refer to the **Route 9** directions three paragraphs below.

MAP 17—Evansburg State Park

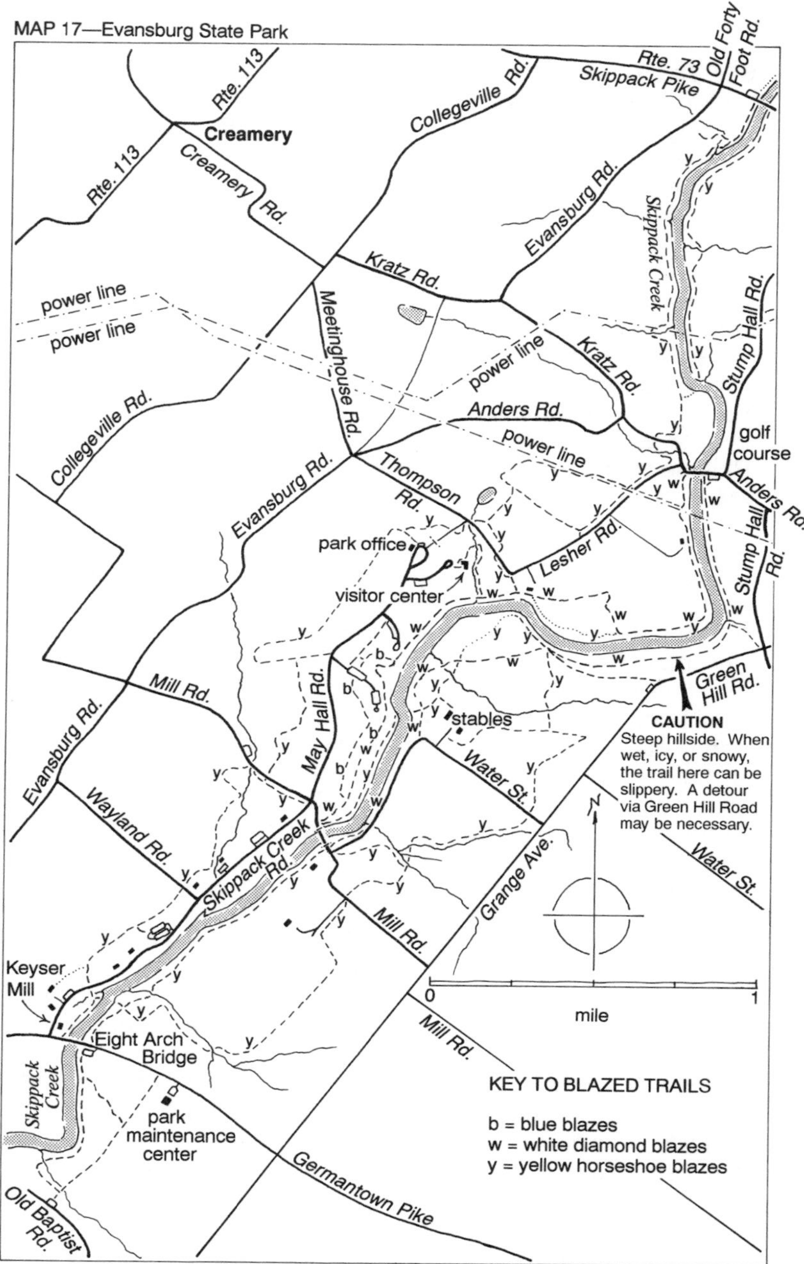

From the east on the Schuylkill Expressway (Interstate 76): Take Exit 28B for Interstate 476 North toward Plymouth Meeting. Follow I-476 North to its end (don't exit; stay in the left-hand lanes). Pick up a turnpike ticket and continue on Route 9 North, which is the Northeast Extension of the Pennsylvania Turnpike. Once you are on Route 9 heading toward Allentown, refer to the **Route 9** directions two paragraphs below.

From the east or west on the Pennsylvania Turnpike: Take the main east-west turnpike to the juncture with Route 9, which is the turnpike's Northeast Extension. If you are coming from the east, the juncture with Route 9 is adjacent to Exit 25A for Interstate 476; fork right for Route 9 North. If you are coming from the west, the juncture with Route 9 occurs shortly after Exit 25 for Norristown. Once you are on the Northeast Extension heading toward Allentown, follow the **Route 9** directions in the next paragraph.

From the north or south on Route 9 (Northeast Extension of the Pennsylvania Turnpike): Go to Exit 31 for Lansdale and Route 63. After paying the toll, turn right onto Route 63 West. Go only 0.3 mile, then turn left onto Old Forty Foot Road.

Follow Old Forty Foot Road as straight as possible (at one point jogging right across Skippack Creek) for a total of 3.1 miles to a traffic light at a crossroads with Route 73 (Skippack Pike). Turn left onto Route 73 and follow it 0.4 mile across Skippack Creek, then turn right onto Stump Hall Road and go 1.0 mile to an intersection with Anders Road. Turn right onto Anders Road, then immediately turn left into the parking area.

WALKING: Evansburg State Park is a great place simply to walk at large, using **Map 17** opposite to navigate the park's network of trails. But first, be prepared for mud on the riverside paths. And second, a caveat is in order concerning opportunities to cross Skippack Creek. For example, a glimpse at Map 17 suggests the possibility of walking along both banks of the river and crossing at Germantown Pike in the south and Skippack Pike in the north. However, the handsome and historic Eight Arch Bridge at Germantown Pike has no sidewalk, and automobile traffic is so heavy that crossing on foot is hazardous . Nor is there any reason for hikers who have walked up the west bank to cross the bridge at Route 73, because the trail down the east bank terminates at a horse

MAP 18—Evansburg State Park: 5-mile Skippack Creek Loop Trail (white blazes)

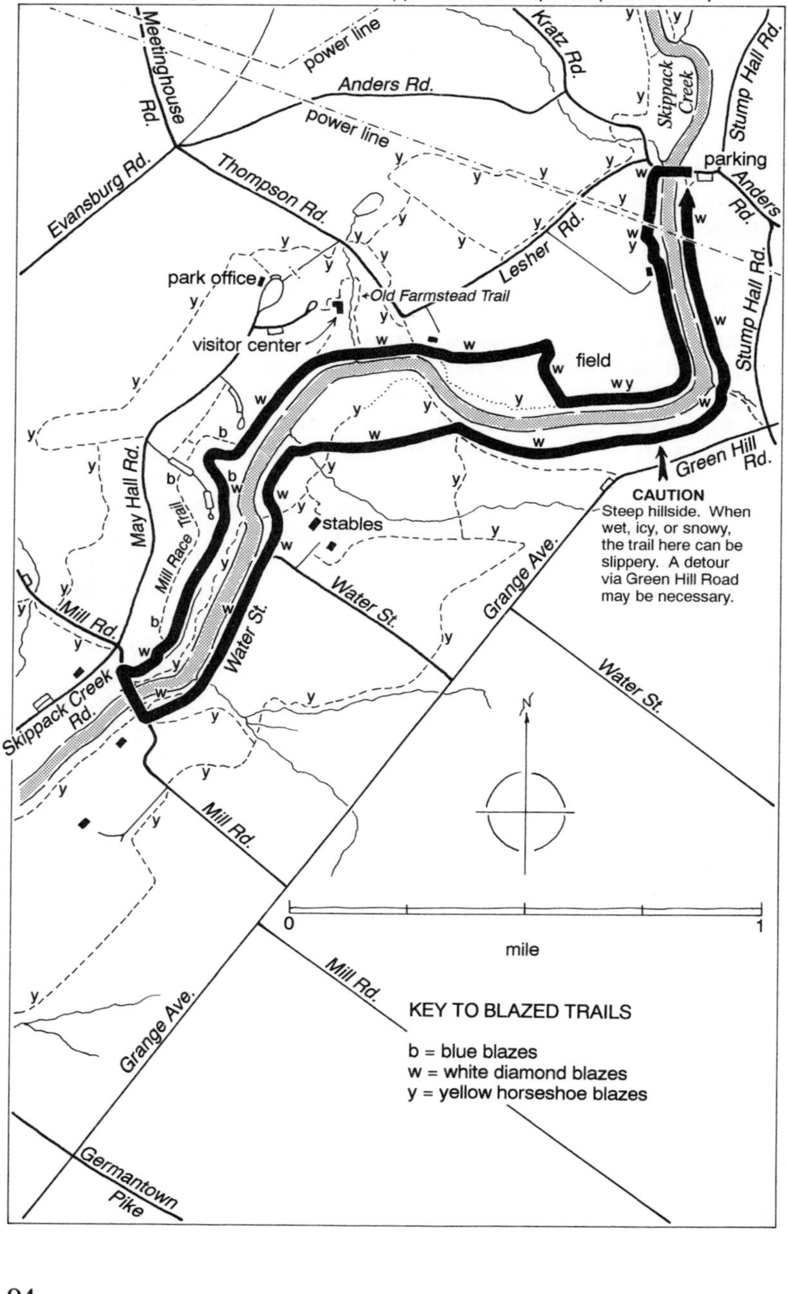

CAUTION
Steep hillside. When wet, icy, or snowy, the trail here can be slippery. A detour via Green Hill Road may be necessary.

KEY TO BLAZED TRAILS

b = blue blazes
w = white diamond blazes
y = yellow horseshoe blazes

ford before reaching Stump Hall Road. In short, the only suitable places for hikers to cross the river are at Mill Road and Anders Road, and even the latter may be closed temporarily or permanently because of the condition of the bridge.

Walking on the Skippack Creek Loop Trail: The bold line on **Map 18** opposite shows this 5-mile circuit, which provides a good introduction to the trails at Evansburg State Park.

With caution, cross the bridge from the Anders Road parking lot, then turn sharply left onto the white-blazed hiking trail. With Skippack Creek on your left, follow the white blazes downstream, sometimes near the creek and sometimes at a distance from the water. As shown on Map 18, periodically you will pass other trails intersecting from the right, of which one—the Old Farmstead Trail—leads to the visitor center in an old farmhouse.

Eventually, after passing some picnic areas atop a high bluff, the white-blazed trail descends gradually to the edge of the bottomland, where the remains of an old mill race are discernible at the foot of the bluff. Continue more or less straight where the blue-blazed Mill Race Trail intersects from the right, then descend the embankment and follow the berm of the mill race to Mill Road.

At Mill Road you can turn left across the bridge in order to continue on the Skippack Creek Loop Trail shown on Map 18. **OR—and this may be advisable when conditions are slippery**—you can turn right and follow the yellow-blazed trail in a loop to the north across Skippack Creek Road, Mill Road, Thompson Road, and Lesher Road and back to your starting point.

For the Skippack Creek Loop Trail, cross the river on the bridge at Mill Road, then turn left onto Water Street. With caution, follow the left shoulder of Water Street next to the river for half a mile. When Water Street bends right, continue straight into the woods on the white-blazed trail. Follow the white blazes through the bottomland and gradually uphill away from the river.

The white-blazed path returns to the edge of Skippack Creek at a five-way trail junction. With caution, follow the white blazes along a steep bluff above the river, **but** if the footing is slippery, you should backtrack to the last trail junction and use the detour noted on the map. Follow either the riverside path or the roads back to the parking lot where you started.

7

PEACE VALLEY PARK
PEACE VALLEY NATURE CENTER

Walking, ski touring, and bicycling. Peace Valley Park in central Bucks County consists of 365-acre Lake Galena and more than 1,100 acres of surrounding land. At the lake's northeastern end is the outstanding Peace Valley Nature Center, which includes a network of foot trails shown on Map 19 on page 105. Bicycles are prohibited on these trails. Altogether totaling about 9 miles, the foot trails provide the opportunity to wander for as little or as long as you like through fields, scrub, and woods. And extending most of the way around the lake is a paved hike-bike path shown by the bold line on Map 20 on page 107. The path is about 5 miles long one way, but nearly a mile at the middle makes use of Creek Road, which also carries local automobile traffic. Bicyclists must ride single file, yield to other trail users, observe stop signs, and keep their speed to a moderate, safe pace.

The trails at Peace Valley are open every day from dawn until dusk. The nature center building, which has exhibits and a store, is open Tuesday through Sunday from 9 to 5. Telephone (215) 345-7860 for information about guided walks and other events and programs sponsored by the nature center. Dogs, even on a leash, are prohibited on the nature center trails.

Peace Valley Park is managed by the Bucks County Department of Parks and Recreation; telephone (215) 348-6114.

PEACE VALLEY PARK and Peace Valley Nature Center, located 3 miles northwest of Doylestown, together have a great variety of natural habitats: meadows and lawn; cultivated, weedy, and overgrown fields; hedgerows and impenetrable brambles; upland and bottomland deciduous woods; pine woods; ponds and streams; and (at Lake Galena) mud flats, shallows, and deep water. Because of this diversity, Peace Valley is among the better places in the Philadelphia region to see a wide assortment of birds. More than 260 species of waterfowl, land birds, and migrating shorebirds have been recorded here—or about 80 percent of all species that occur regularly in eastern Pennsylvania.

Even for fledgling birders, identifying the many species that nest in the Philadelphia region or pass through during migration is easier than might at first be thought. Shape, size, plumage, and other physical characteristics are distinguishing field marks. Range, season, habitat, song, and behavior are other useful keys to identifying birds.

Range is of primary importance for the simple reason that many birds are not found throughout North America or even the eastern United States, but only in certain regions such as the Atlantic and Gulf coasts. For example, cedar waxwings and Bohemian waxwings closely resemble each other, so it helps to know that the latter is not seen in Pennsylvania. Good field guides provide range maps based on years of reported sightings and bird counts. Of course, bird ranges are not static: some pioneering species, such as the glossy ibis and house finch, have extended their ranges during recent decades. Other birds, such as the ivory-billed woodpecker, have lost ground and died out.

Season is related to range, since migratory birds appear in different parts of their ranges during different times of year. The five species of spot-breasted thrushes, for instance, are sometimes difficult to distinguish from each other, but usually only the hermit thrush is present in eastern Pennsylvania during the winter. In summer the hermit thrush is rare near Philadelphia, but the wood thrush is common and indeed nests at Peace Valley. Swainson's thrush and the gray-cheeked thrush are seen during migration in spring and fall. Again, the maps in most field guides reflect this sort of information, and a detailed account of seasonal occurrence is contained in *A Field List of the Delaware Valley Region*, published by the Delaware Valley Ornithological Club. A similar annotated list of birds seen at Peace Valley Park is available at the nature center.

Habitat, too, is important in identifying birds. Even before you spot a bird, its surroundings can tell you what species you are likely to see. Within its range a species usually appears only in certain preferred habitats, although during migration some species are less particular. (In many cases, birds show a degree of physical adaptation to their preferred environment.) As its name implies, the marsh wren is seldom found far from cattails, rushes, sedges, or tall marsh grasses; if a wrenlike bird is spotted in such a setting, it is unlikely to be a house wren or Carolina wren or one of the other species commonly found in thick underbrush or shrubbery. Ducks can be difficult to identify unless you tote a telescope; but even if all you can see is a silhouette, you can start with the knowledge that shallow marshes and creeks normally attract few diving ducks (such as oldsquaw, canvasbacks, redheads, ring-necked ducks, greater and lesser scaup, common goldeneye, and buffleheads) and that large, deep bodies of water are not the usual setting for surface-feeding puddle ducks (American black ducks, gadwalls, mallards, common pintails, American widgeons, wood ducks, northern shovelers, and blue-winged and green-winged teals).

Some of the distinctive habitats that different bird species prefer are open oceans; beaches; salt marsh; mud flats; meadows; thickets; various types of woods; and creeks, ponds, and lakes. The area were two habitats join, called an *ecotone*, is a particularly good place to look for birds because species peculiar to either environment might be present. For example, both meadowlarks and wood warblers might be found where a hay field abuts a forest. All good field guides provide information on habitat preference that can help to locate a species or to assess the likelihood of a tentative identification.

Song announces the identity (or at least the location) of birds even before they are seen. Although some species, such as the red-winged blackbird, have only a few songs, others, such as the mockingbird, have an infinite variety. Some birds, most notably thrushes, sing different songs in the morning and evening. In many species the basic songs vary among individuals and also from one part of the country to another, giving rise to regional "dialects." Nonetheless, the vocal repertory of most songbirds is sufficiently constant in timbre and pattern to identify each species simply by its songs.

Bird songs, as distinguished from calls, can be very complex. They are sung only by the male of most species, usually in spring and summer. The male arrives first at the breeding and nesting area after migration. He stakes out a territory for courting, mating, and nesting by singing at prominent points around the area's perimeter. This wards off other males of his species and simultaneously attracts females. On the basis of the male's display and the desirability of his territory, the female selects her mate. Experiments suggest that female birds build nests faster and lay more eggs when exposed to the songs of males with a larger vocal repertory than others of their species, and the relative volume of their songs appears to be a way for males to establish status among themselves.

In a few species, including eastern bluebirds, Baltimore orioles, cardinals, and white-throated sparrows, both sexes sing, although the males are more active in defending their breeding territory. Among mockingbirds, both sexes sing in fall and winter, but only males do in spring and summer. Some birds, such as canaries, have different songs for different seasons.

Birds tend to heed the songs of their own kind and to ignore the songs of other species, which, after all, do not compete for females nor, in many cases, for the same type of nesting materials or food. In consequence, a single area might include the overlapping breeding territories of several species. From year to year such territories are bigger or smaller, depending on the food supply. Typically, most small songbirds require about half an acre from which others of their species are excluded.

Bird calls (as distinguished from songs) are short, simple, sometimes harsh, and used by both males and females at all times of year to communicate alarm, aggression, location, and existence of food. Nearly all birds have some form of call. Warning calls are often heeded by species other than the caller's. Some warning calls are thin, high-pitched whistles that are difficult to locate and so do not reveal the bird's location to predators. Birds also use mobbing calls to summon other birds, as chickadees and crows do when scolding and harassing owls and other unwanted visitors. Birds flying in flocks, like cedar waxwings, often call continuously. Such calls help birds migrating by night to stay together.

The study of bird dialects and experiments with birds that have been deafened or raised in isolation indicate that songs are genetically inherited only to a very crude extent. Although a few species, such as doves, sing well even when raised in isolation, most birds raised alone produce inferior, simplified songs. Generally, young songbirds learn their songs by listening to adult birds and by practice singing, called *subsong*. Yet birds raised in isolation and exposed to many tape-recorded songs show an innate preference for the songs of their own species. Probably the easiest way to learn bird songs is to listen repeatedly to recordings and to refer at the same time to a standard field guide. Most guides describe bird vocalizations with such terms as *harsh, nasal, flutelike, piercing, plaintive, wavering, twittering, buzzing, sneezy,* and *sputtering*. Played slowly, bird recordings demonstrate that the songs contain many more notes than the human ear ordinarily hears.

Shape is one of the first and most important aspects to notice once you actually see a bird. Most birds can at least be placed in the proper family and many species can be identified by shape or silhouette, without reference to other field marks. Some birds, such as meadowlarks, are chunky and short-tailed, while others, such as catbirds and cuckoos, are elegantly long and slender. Kingfishers, blue jays, tufted titmice, Bohemian and cedar waxwings, and cardinals are among the few birds with crests.

Bird bills frequently have distinctive shapes and, more than any other body part, show adaptation to food supply. The beak can be chunky, like that of a grosbeak, to crack seeds; thin and curved, like that of a shrike, to tear at flesh; long and slender, like that of a hummingbird, to sip nectar from tubular flowers; or some other characteristic shape depending on the bird's food. Goatsuckers, swifts, flycatchers, and swallows, all of which catch flying insects, have widely hinged bills and gaping mouths. The long, thin bills of starlings and meadowlarks are suited to probing the ground. In the Galapagos Islands west of Ecuador, Charles Darwin noted fourteen species of finches, each of which had evolved a different type of beak or style of feeding that gave it a competitive advantage for a particular type of food. Many birds are nonetheless flexible about their diet, especially from season to season when food sources change or become scarce. For example, Tennessee warblers, which ordinarily glean insects from foliage, also take large amounts of nectar from tropical flowers when wintering in South and Central America.

In addition to beaks, nearly every other part of a bird's body is adapted to help exploit its environment. Feet of passerines, or songbirds, are adapted to perching, with three toes in front and one long toe behind; waterfowl have webbed or lobed feet for swimming; and raptors have talons for grasping prey.

Other key elements of body shape are the length and form of wings, tails, and legs. The wings may be long, pointed, and developed for swift, sustained flight, like those of falcons. Or the wings may be short and rounded for abrupt bursts of speed, like those of accipiters. The tail may have a deep fork like that of a barn swallow, a shallow notch like that of a tree swallow, a square tip like that of a cliff swallow, or a rounded tip like that of a blue jay.

Size is difficult to estimate and therefore not very useful in identifying birds. The best approach is to bear in mind the relative sizes of different species and to use certain well-known birds like the chickadee, sparrow, robin, kingfisher, and crow as standards for mental comparison. For example, if a bird resembles a song sparrow but looks unusually large, it might be a fox sparrow.

Plumage, whether plain or princely, muted or magnificent, is one of the most obvious keys to identification. Color can occur in remarkable combinations of spots, stripes, streaks, patches, and other patterns that make even supposedly drab birds a pleasure to see. In some instances, like the brown streaks of American bitterns and many other species, the plumage provides camouflage. Most vireos and warblers are various shades and combinations of yellow, green, brown, gray, and black, as one would expect from their forest environment. The black and white backs of woodpeckers help them to blend in with bark dappled with sunlight. The bold patterns of killdeers and some other plovers break up their outlines in much the same manner that warships used to be camouflaged before the invention of radar. Many shorebirds display countershading: they are dark above and light below, a pattern that reduces the effect of shadows and makes them appear an inconspicuous monotone. Even some brightly colored birds have camouflaging plumages when they are young and least able to avoid predators.

For some species, it is important *not* to be camouflaged. Many seabirds are mostly white, which in all light conditions enables them to be seen at great distances against the water. Because flocks of seabirds spread out from their colonies to search for food, it is vital that a bird that has located food be visible to others after it has landed on the water to feed.

To organize the immense variation in plumage, focus on different basic elements and ask the following types of questions. Starting with the head, is it uniformly colored like that of the red-headed woodpecker? Is there a small patch on the crown, like that of Wilson's warbler and the ruby-crowned kinglet, or a larger cap on the front and top of the head, like that of the common redpoll and American goldfinch? Is the crown striped like the ovenbird's? Does a ring surround the eye, as with a Connecticut warbler, or are the eye rings perhaps even joined across the top of the bill to form spectacles, like those of a yellow-breasted chat? Is there a stripe over or through the eyes, like the red-breasted nuthatch's, or a conspicuous black mask across the eyes, like that of a common yellowthroat or loggerhead shrike? From the head go on to the rest of the body, where distinctive colors and patterns can also mark a bird's bill, throat, breast, belly, back, sides, wings, rump, tail, and legs.

Finally, what a bird *does* is an important clue to its identity. Certain habits, postures, ways of searching for food, and other behavior characterize different species. Some passerines, such as larks, juncos, and towhees, are strictly ground feeders; other birds, including flycatchers and swallows, nab insects on the wing; and others, such as nuthatches and creepers, glean insects from the crevices in bark. Woodpeckers bore into the bark. Vireos and most warblers pick insects from the foliage of trees and brush.

All of these birds may be further distinguished by other habits of eating. For example, towhees scratch for insects and seeds by kicking backward with both feet together, whereas juncos rarely do, although both hop to move along the ground. Other ground feeders, such as meadowlarks, walk rather than hop. Despite the children's song, robins often run, not hop. Swallows catch insects while swooping and skimming in continuous flight, but flycatchers dart out from a limb, grab an insect (sometimes with an audible smack), and then return to their perch. Brown creepers have the curious habit of systematically searching for food by climbing trees in spirals, then flying back to the ground to climb again. Woodpeckers tend to hop upward, bracing themselves against the tree with their stiff tails. Nuthatches walk up and down trees and branches head first, seemingly without regard for gravity. Vireos are sluggish compared to the hyperactive, flitting warblers.

Many birds divide a food source into zones, an arrangement that apparently evolved to ensure each species its own food supply. The short-legged green heron sits at the edge of the water or on a low overhanging branch, waiting for its prey to come close to shore. Medium-sized black-crowned and yellow-crowned night herons hunt in shallow water. The long-legged great blue heron stalks fish in water up to two feet deep. Swans, geese, and many ducks graze underwater on the stems and tubers of grassy plants, but the longer necks of swans and geese enable them to reach deeper plants. Similarly, different species of shorebirds take food from the same mud flat by probing with their varied bills to different depths. Various species of warblers that feed in the same tree are reported to concentrate in separate areas, such as the trunk, twig tips, and tree top. Starlings and cowbirds feeding in flocks on the ground show another arrangement that provides an even distribution of food: those in the rear fly ahead to the front, so that the entire flock rolls slowly across the field.

Different species also have different styles of flight. Soaring is typical of some big birds. Gulls float nearly motionless in the wind. Buteos and vultures soar on updrafts in wide circles, although turkey vultures may be further distinguished by wings held in a shallow V. Some other large birds, such as accipiters, rarely soar but instead interrupt their wing beats with glides. Kestrels, terns, kingfishers, and burrowing owls can hover in one spot. Hummingbirds, like oversized dragonflies, can also hover and even fly backward. Slightly more erratic than the swooping, effortless flight of swallows is that of swifts, flitting with wing beats that appear to alternate (but do not). Still other birds, such as the American goldfinch and flickers, dip up and down in wavelike flight. Some species, including jays and grackles, fly dead straight. Among ducks, the surface-feeding species launch themselves directly upward into flight, seeming to jump from the water, but the heavy diving ducks typically patter along the surface before becoming airborne.

Various idiosyncrasies distinguish yet other species. The spotted sandpiper and northern waterthrush walk with a teetering, bobbing motion. Coots pump their heads back and forth as they swim. The eastern phoebe regularly jerks its tail downward while perching, but wrens often cock their tails vertically. Herons and egrets fly with their necks folded back; storks, ibises, and cranes fly with their necks outstretched. Still other birds have characteristic postures while sitting or flying or other unique habits that provide a reliable basis for identification.

≈ ≈ ≈ ≈

AUTOMOBILE DIRECTIONS: Peace Valley Park is located about 25 miles north of downtown Philadelphia near Doylestown, the seat of Bucks County. (See •7 on **Maps 1 and 2D** on pages 6 and 7.) Several avenues of approach are described below, all leading to the nature center, which is located on Chapman Road near the northeastern end of the park.

From Philadelphia and the south on Route 611: Route 611 is the northward extension of Broad Street. Follow Route 611 North, in the process passing the entrance to the Pennsylvania Turnpike at Willow Grove. From there, continue north on Route 611 about 12 miles, toward the end of which Route 611 turns into a limited-access highway bypassing Doylestown. Leave Route 611 at the exit for Route 313 (Swamp Road). At the top of the exit ramp, turn left onto Route 313 West toward Dublin. Go 2.1 miles, then turn left onto New Galena Road toward Peace Valley. Go 0.7 mile, then turn left again onto Chapman Road toward the Peace Valley Nature Center. Follow Chapman Road downhill 0.3 mile, then turn left into the nature center parking lot just beyond a stop sign.

From the east or west on the Pennsylvania Turnpike: Leave the turnpike at Exit 27 for Willow Grove and Route 611. After paying the toll, fork right for Route 611 North toward Doylestown. From the top of the exit ramp, follow Route 611 North about 12 miles, toward the end of which Route 611 turns into a limited-access highway bypassing Doylestown. Leave Route 611 at the exit for Route 313 (Swamp Road). At the top of the exit ramp, turn left onto Route 313 West toward Dublin. Go 2.1 miles, then turn left onto New Galena Road toward Peace Valley. Go 0.7 mile, then turn left again onto Chapman Road toward the Peace Valley Nature Center. Follow Chapman Road downhill 0.3 mile, then turn left into the nature center parking lot just beyond a stop sign.

From the north on Route 611: You will know that you are

MAP 19—Peace Valley Nature Center

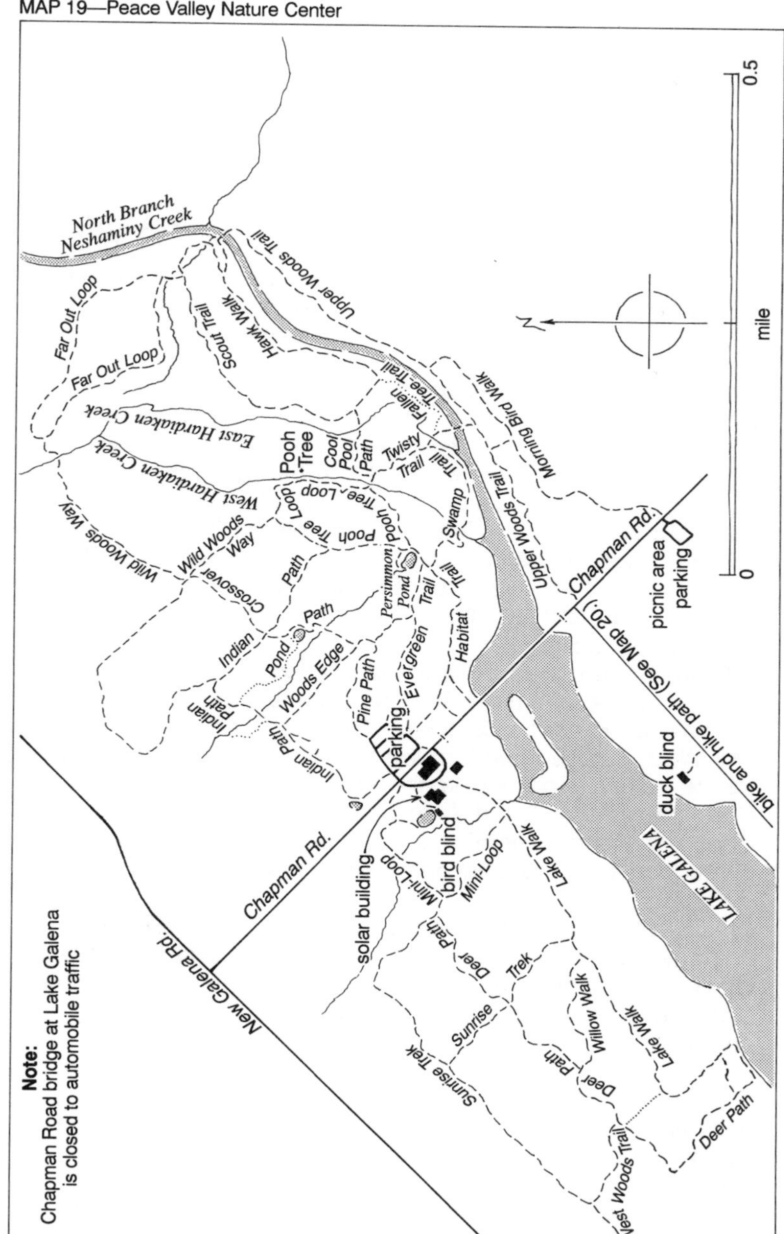

approaching Peace Valley when Route 611 enters Plumstead Township. After passing through Plumstead Village, continue downhill on Route 611 for about 1.3 miles, then—at an obscure intersection marked by high electric transmission lines overhead—turn right onto Curly Hill Road. Follow Curly Hill Road 1.6 miles to a T-intersection, and there turn right onto Route 313 West (Swamp Road). Go only 0.2 mile, then turn left onto New Galena Road toward Peace Valley. Go 0.7 mile, then turn left again onto Chapman Road toward the Peace Valley Nature Center. Follow Chapman Road downhill 0.3 mile, then turn left into the nature center parking lot just beyond a stop sign.

From the south on Route 202: Follow Route 202 North to Route 611 North near Doylestown. From the bottom of the exit ramp off Route 202, follow Route 611 North 1.6 miles to the exit for Route 313 (Swamp Road). At the top of the exit ramp, turn left onto Route 313 West toward Dublin. Go 2.1 miles, then turn left onto New Galena Road toward Peace Valley. Go 0.7 mile, then turn left again onto Chapman Road toward the Peace Valley Nature Center. Follow Chapman Road downhill 0.3 mile, then turn left into the nature center parking lot just beyond a stop sign.

From the north on Route 202: Follow Route 202 South to an intersection at a traffic light with Route 313 (Swamp Road) on the outskirts of Doylestown. Turn right and follow Route 313 West 4 miles, then turn left onto New Galena Road toward Peace Valley. Go 0.7 mile, then turn left again onto Chapman Road toward the Peace Valley Nature Center. Follow Chapman Road downhill 0.3 mile, then turn left into the nature center parking lot just beyond a stop sign.

WALKING AT PEACE VALLEY NATURE CENTER: Map 19 on page 105 shows the nature center's extensive trail network. Use caution at stream crossings. If water is flowing over the stepping stones, or if the stones are covered with snow or ice, do not cross.

THE HIKE AND BIKE PATH: The bold line on **Map 20** opposite shows the route from the nature center around the lake to the park's north entrance. Most of the 5-mile route consists of a paved path closed to motor vehicles, but for nearly a mile near the middle, the route follows Creek Road, which is open to local automobile traffic.

MAP 20—Peace Valley County Park: Hike and Bike Path

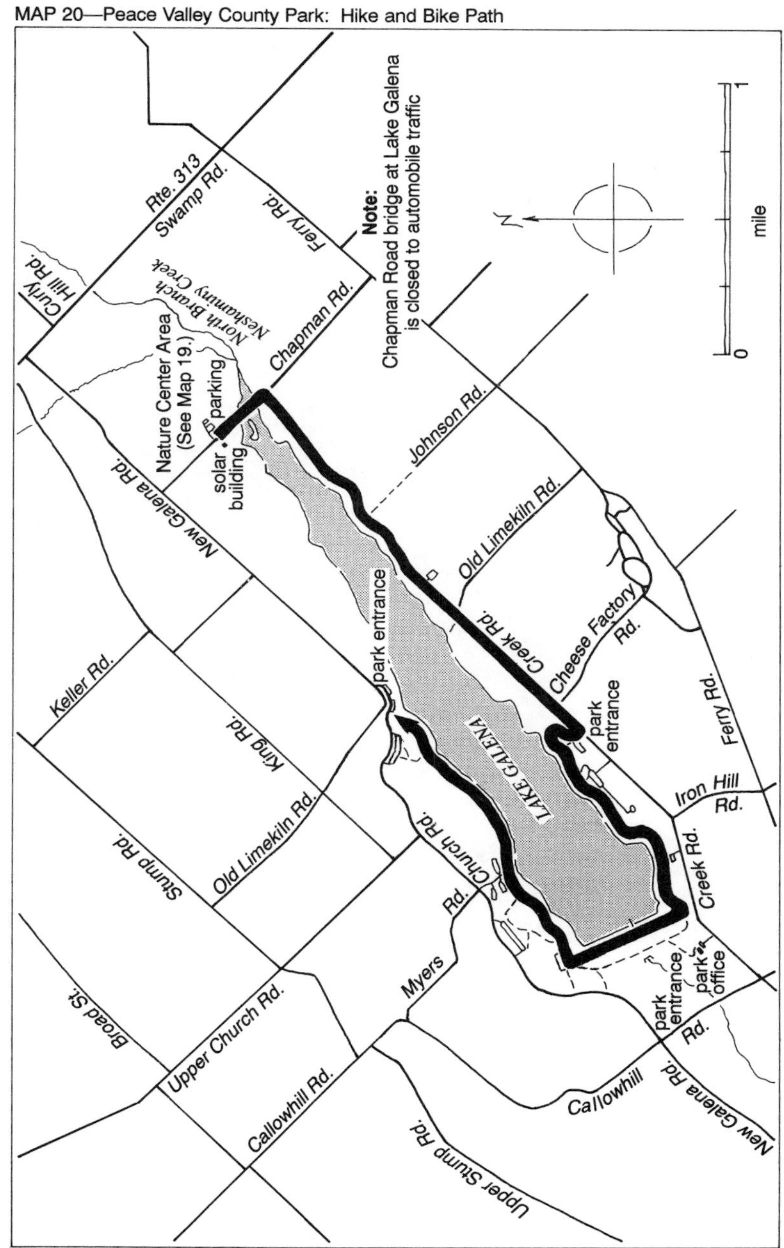

8

TYLER STATE PARK

Walking, jogging, ski touring, and bicycling. The 7.5-mile circuit shown by the bold line on Map 21 on page 117 follows narrow, paved country roads that are closed to motor vehicles—except for the cars of a few park residents who are accustomed to driving very slowly and sharing the road with hikers and cyclists. The park's special charm is that about one quarter of its 1,700 acres is cropland cultivated by local farmers who annually bid for agricultural leases. Similarly, eighteenth- and nineteenth-century farmhouses within the park are occupied and maintained by tenants. Here, then, is a rare opportunity to walk or bicycle on old, tree-lined lanes though woods, meadows, and farm fields. If you have an infant or small child, the paved paths are an excellent promenade for buggies and strollers. Bicyclists must ride single file, yield to other trail users, keep their speed to a moderate, safe pace, and stay on paved paths.

Tyler State Park is open daily from 8 A.M. to sunset. Dogs must be leashed. The park is managed by the Pennsylvania Bureau of State Parks; telephone (215) 968-2021 for information about fishing, boating, ice skating, and canoe rental.

Also within the park is Tyler Hostel, which provides overnight accommodations to members of national and international hosteling groups; telephone (215) 968-0927. The park's Spring Garden Mill—an old flour and feed mill—serves as the Langhorne Players Theater, which operates during the late spring, summer, and early fall; telephone (215) 860-0818. The theater is located on Route 332 west of the intersection with Routes 413 and 532.

IF BY NOW you have taken several of the excursions outlined in this book, you probably have noticed the wide variation in landforms presented by parks in the Philadelphia region. At Peace Valley several watercourses that frequently are dry between rainfalls weave though the woods at the bottom of a broad, shallow valley. In sharp contrast, Wissahickon Creek in Philadelphia has cut a deep yet narrow valley through the highlands at Chestnut Hill and Upper Roxborough. At Morris Arboretum, Tyler State Park, and Ridley Creek State Park, gently winding rivers flow through a rolling landscape, as is typical of southeastern Pennsylvania's Piedmont Province. The Schuylkill River has carved a large valley through the region, and the Delaware River has worn an even wider course, sometimes creating broad floodplains that in places are left well above the river's present course. At the John Heinz National Wildlife Refuge at Tinicum, a meandering tidal creek flows across flat terrain. These varied streams and settings are good examples of different stages in the erosional process by which running water cuts into an elevated region and over the ages carves a variety of characteristic landforms and landscapes.

Although the process of erosion is ceaseless, it of course speeds up during periods of peak flow. Most erosion in the Philadelphia region is attributable to a relatively few heavy rains each year and—even more so—to less frequent but spectacular flood rains. Although these infrequent events may seem freakish, over millions of years they are commonplace and may be said to occur with regularity.

Going hand in hand with erosion—or really as a necessary precursor to it—is the process of weathering, by which a region's rocky foundation is, near the surface, broken down into smaller and smaller pieces that can be carried away by water, which is itself a powerful weathering agent. For example, through *frost action*, water can enter cracks in the rocks and split them apart when the water freezes, eventually reducing rocks near the surface to crumbly fragments. This is the chief form of *physical weathering*, but there are other physical processes, including penetration into rock fissures by roots of trees and other plants, which as they grow pry the rocks apart.

As rocks are reduced to smaller fragments by physical processes, *chemical weathering* becomes increasingly important, and again water is a major agent. Through *hydrolysis*, water reacts with minerals in the rocks, creating clay and freeing some elements which are carried away in solution. Through *carbonation*, carbon dioxide in soil (where it is produced by bacteria) or in the air combines with water to form a weak acid called carbonic acid, which dissolves limestone. Through *oxidation* some minerals, of which iron is the chief, react with oxygen in air and in water, thus contributing to the disintegration of the parent rock of which the oxidized minerals were formerly part. Working together, physical and chemical weathering convert bedrock to soil or to an intermediate, crumbly substrate called *saprolite*, on which the process of erosion discussed below can then work.

Wherever rain falls on land, any downward-pitched trough, even though at first shallow or insignificant, is self-aggrandizing, collecting and channeling the water that flows off a broad area, as may be seen at Tyler State Park where some horse trails worn across the tops and slopes of hills have turned into gullies that collect rainwater sweeping downhill across meadows and fields. Even in the absence of such troughs, rainwater flowing in sheets down a "smooth" hillside tends to organize itself into runnels that in turn erode little rills, some of which may eventually develop into gullies that carry away the runoff. Initially, many minor watercourses are dry between rains, but some may be fed seasonally by melting snow or even continuously by springs or the outflow from wetlands or even glaciers where precipitation is stored for a period before continuing its journey to the sea.* Gradually, the gullies and ravines deepen with erosion, and once they penetrate the water table, they are fed by a steady seepage of groundwater. Now and again steep slopes may simply slump downhill, or a steep embankment may collapse directly into a stream, where the loosened material is easily carried away.

As a stream extends itself by developing tributaries, its erosive power rapidly increases. The larger drainage area concentrates more water in the main channel downstream, where stream energy is swelled by the greater mass of moving water. The increase in energy is more than directly proportional to stream volume. As the volume increases, an ever-smaller fraction of the river's energy is consumed in overcoming friction with the streambed, and in consequence the speed of the river increases and so does its ability to carry fine clay, silt, and sand in suspension, to abrade and wear down rocks, and to push and role pebbles and cobbles downstream.

Obviously, the ocean constitutes a base level below which a river cannot erode.** Nonetheless, the current continues to erode the bank laterally wherever the stream is deflected by each slight turn. This tendency to carve wider and wider curves is present along the entire stream but is accentuated in the lower, older reaches, where the processes of erosion have been operating for a longer time than in the upper reaches. As the river approaches the ocean, downward cutting is

---

* The most recent incursion of continental ice to extend southward from eastern Canada into New England, New York, and northern Pennsylvania receded about 10,000 or 12,000 years ago, and during the two or three millennia of melting, rivers like the Susquehanna and Delaware were far more voluminous and more erosive than they are today.

** Submarine canyons, like those along the edge of the Continental Shelf, are not an exception to this principle. Such canyons were carved by rivers when the level of the sea was lower.

no longer possible, but sideward cutting can continue as long as there is flow. Gradually, a meandering course develops as the river snakes back and forth, eroding first one side of the valley and then the other. When sinuosity becomes so extreme that the curves loop back on themselves, the current will intercept the channel farther downstream, cutting off the looping meander. Thus, as millennia pass, the river migrates in an ever-changing course over a broad floodplain, leaving behind abandoned channels here and there.

At the mouth of the river where it empties into an ocean or estuary, a distinctive geologic feature forms. As the current dissipates in the standing water, the capacity of the stream to carry material in suspension is reduced and then eliminated, so that the river's load of sand and silt is dropped and forms a delta, as has occurred at Darby Creek at Tinicum. Because the current slows gradually, the deposits tend to be sorted, with larger, heavier particles dropped first. After the delta has extended itself a considerable distance in one direction, a flood may cut a new and shorter channel to open water, causing the former course to be abandoned, at least for a period. Deltas typically have several channels or sets of channels among which the stream shifts as deposits are concentrated first in one and then in another. Meanwhile, the countless gullies and ravines at the river's headwaters continue to fan outward like the branches of a growing tree. As the tributaries extend themselves, the watershed becomes larger and larger. A growing river may even intercept and divert to itself (or *capture*) streams that previously took a different course to the sea. Material eroded from areas far up a river's many tributaries is redeposited farther downstream, then re-eroded over and over again as the river's capacity to carry sand and silt in suspension fluctuates with the volume of runoff.

According to one conceptual model of stream erosion developed in the nineteenth century by William M. Davis, examining the variables of stream gradient, valley depth, valley width, and number of meanders will indicate the stage of development that has been reached by any stretch of river. In the earliest stage, gullies and ravines eat into the elevated land surface. Because the dominant direction of cutting is downward, the gullies and ravines are steep-sided and V-shaped, and even after they join to form larger valleys, the gradient of the streambed is steep compared to navigable waterways. Rapids are common. There are only minor flats in the valley bottom. The ratio of valley depth relative to width is at its maximum. Such a stream was said by Davis to be in *youth.*

As a stream's elevation approaches base level, the gradient diminishes and downward cutting slows. Bends in the course of the stream become accentuated, meanders start to develop, and the width of the valley increases relative to its depth. Sideward cutting produces a continuous floodplain. Such a stream is said to be in *maturity*.

Finally, when downward cutting has become so slow as virtually to cease and the stream is as close to base level as it can get, sideward cutting may eventually produce a nearly flat and featureless valley, much wider than it is deep, across which the river meanders from side to side. The gradient is low, and the broad bottomland is marked only by the scars, swamps, and lakes left by former channels. Perhaps a few rock hummocks and hills—more resistant to erosion than were their surroundings—are left rising above the low valley floor. This stage of river development is *old age*. The ultimate (and largely theoretical) expression of old age is what Davis called a *peneplain*, meaning "almost a plain" and denoting a surface of regional extent and low elevation, with only small variations in relief, produced by long-continued fluvial erosion. Most geologists today, however, think that even if other geologic events (such as fluctuations in sea level and movements in the earth's crust) did not occur, prolonged erosion would create a landscape in which low, rolling hills occupy far more of the region than Davis postulated, especially where vegetation protects the land surface.

Of course, never does all of a river reach old age. The gullies and ravines at the river's headwaters remain youthful as they continue to spread out and consume the upland. The river is also likely to have a mature midsection.

The terms *youth, maturity,* and *old age* can also be applied to an entire region to describe the extent to which it has been acted upon by stream erosion. As an upland region experiences the headward erosion of a stream system, more and more of the landscape is given over to a branching system of gullies, ravines, and valleys. Eventually, the upland lying between different stream branches or even different watersheds is cut away until the divide changes from a wide plateau to a narrow ridge, and then to a low, rounded rise. Meanwhile, the valleys slowly widen and develop broad, flat floodplains. For as long as an area is mostly upland, it is said to be in youth. During the period that valley walls and slopes occupy most of the landscape, the region is said to be in maturity. And when most of the landscape is given over to bottomland, the area is said to be in old age. Of course, the terms *youth, maturity,* and *old age* do not describe the actual age of a river or landscape, but only its stage of erosional development—and even so, the terms are rather inexact. Nonetheless, the analogy to a living organism is helpful if one's main goal is to understand the general tendency or sequence of stream erosion in the absence of various other factors and forces mentioned below.

Chief among these complicating factors is the effect produced by varying degrees of resistance to erosion among the different kinds of rocks that underlie a river's watershed. It is a common thing for rivers to show a profile passing from youth to maturity to old age (at this last stage, complete with a wide valley and meandering course), then to re-enter a relatively narrow valley with a steep gradient before once again transitioning to an older landscape. This pattern may occur several times along a single river, and in each case the sections characterized by a wide valley and meandering course are in areas of relatively unresistant rock compared to what is found next downstream. As a local example, the Wissahickon Valley in Montgomery County has a relatively gentle profile compared to the youthful gorge downstream in Philadelphia. This anomaly is traceable to the fact that the downstream section flows through an area of hard crystalline rock that is more resistant to erosion than the sandstone, shale, and limestone that underlie the upstream section. In theory, prolonged erosion should eventually eliminate such anomalies by wearing away even the resistant rocks that cause them.

The varying degrees of resistance to erosion among different kinds of rocks also affects stream patterns. Where differences in resistance are minimal, a river, if viewed from the air, tends to branch out into tributaries like a tree viewed in profile. This pattern is called *dendritic*. But where some rocks are more easily eroded than others, the stream pattern will reflect this fact. For example, a *trellis pattern*—like a grape vine strung on parallel wires or a fruit tree espaliered to a garden wall—is characteristic of areas where alternating hard and soft beds of rock have been tilted or folded by movements in the earth's crust and then partially eroded away. Where the hard layers intersect the land surface, they remain as high ridges. Where the softer layers intersect the surface, they are eroded into valleys by streams that sometimes manage to link from one valley to the next. Stream patterns can also reflect the tendency of some rocks to split into rectilinear joints, as does sandstone.

Finally, tectonic movements in the earth's crust can, for protracted periods, cause the land to rise at rates less than, equal to, or greater than the countervailing rate of erosion, thus retarding or even renewing the sequence of erosion outlined in this discussion. Some such movements may be isostatic adjustments by which pieces of the crust, which are "floating" on softer layers below, rise as the surface is worn away, much as an iceberg would rise if only the part above water were subject to melting. Another theory is that crustal plates, spreading from rifts in the ocean basins, sometimes slide under the continental margins and raise the land even as it erodes. Careful studies have shown that if present rates of erosion are applied to the past, the Appalachian Mountains should have been worn away long ago, but upward movement has enabled them to endure despite erosion. Whatever the cause for the uplift occurring in Pennsylvania, one result is that the general contours of the land surface—especially in areas of middling relief like the Piedmont Province near Philadelphia—are far more stable than the ongoing process of stream erosion would indicate.

≈ ≈ ≈ ≈

AUTOMOBILE DIRECTIONS: Tyler State Park is located in Bucks County just west of Newtown and about 20 miles northeast of downtown Philadelphia. (See •8 on **Map 1** on page 6.) As discussed below, the Pennsylvania Turnpike and Interstate 95 provide convenient avenues of approach.

From the east or west on the Pennsylvania Turnpike: Leave the turnpike at Exit 28 for Trenton and Route 1 North toward Interstate 95. After paying the toll, follow Route 1 North more than 6 miles to I-95 North. Once you are on I-95 heading north, follow the directions in the next paragraph.

From the north or south on Interstate 95: Leave I-95 at Exit 30 for Route 332. At the top of the exit ramp, turn onto Route 332 West toward Newtown. Go nearly 5 miles, in the process passing straight through intersections where Route 413 joins from the left, where Route 532 joins from the left, and where Route 332 turns left. Finally, at an intersection and traffic light where Route 413 North and Route 532 North veer right, turn left into the entrance for Tyler State Park. Follow the entrance road 0.3 mile to a crossroads, and there continue straight into the parking lot for the Plantation Picnic Area.

WALKING AND BICYCLING: The bold line on **Map 21** on page 117 shows the 7.5-mile route described below. For a shorter excursion, you can easily cut off part of the circuit by using one of the other lanes shown on the map. Although the route recommended here is closed to most automobile traffic, be alert for occasional vehicles going to and from houses in the park.

From the lower end of the parking lot for the Plantation Picnic Area, fork left downhill to follow the asphalt-paved Quarry Trail past a baseball field on the left and a picnic area on the right. Continue downhill through the woods. Bear left at a pair of restrooms, then (after 50 yards) turn right onto Tyler

Drive Trail and follow it past several picnic and parking areas to a low concrete bridge.

Cross Neshaminy Creek on the low bridge, then turn right upstream. Follow the paved Mill Dairy Trail past the Thompson Dairy House, which was built in 1775. At a T-intersection with the Dairy Hill Trail, turn right and follow the paved path downhill, then around to the left along the river and gradually uphill. At a four-way intersection, turn right and follow the Covered Bridge Trail downhill past the youth hostel to Neshaminy Creek and the former site of a covered bridge, which was burned down but may be rebuilt.

From the river, return uphill on the Covered Bridge Trail and follow it straight through the crossroads where the Dairy Hill Trail intersects from the left and the White Pine Trail intersects from the right. Follow the Covered Bridge Trail as it winds downhill past a barn on the left and a house on the right. Turn right at a T-intersection with the Dairy Hill Trail, then turn left at the next intersection onto No. 1 Lane Trail. Again, pass between a barn and a house.

Follow No. 1 Lane Trail as it zigzags past fields and eventually descends into the woods. Pass yet another house and barn. Fork left across a small stone bridge where College Park Trail intersects from the right. After passing a house on the left and then a small parking lot on the right, turn left onto the Stable Mill Trail. There may be some traffic here going to and from the parking lots.

Follow the Stable Mill Trail past two houses, the first of which serves as headquarters for the Pennsylvania Guild of Craftsmen. At an intersection with the Natural Area Trail, continue straight on the Stable Mill Trail.

Eventually, turn left onto the Mill Dairy Trail, then fork right immediately onto the Woodfield Trail. At the next intersection, bear right onto the Mill Dairy Trail and return along Neshaminy Creek to the low bridge. Turn right across the bridge and follow Tyler Drive Trail to the right downstream. At the intersection with the Quarry Trail, turn left, then bear right past the restrooms to go back to your starting point at the Plantation Picnic Area.

MAP 21—Tyler State Park: 7.5-mile circuit

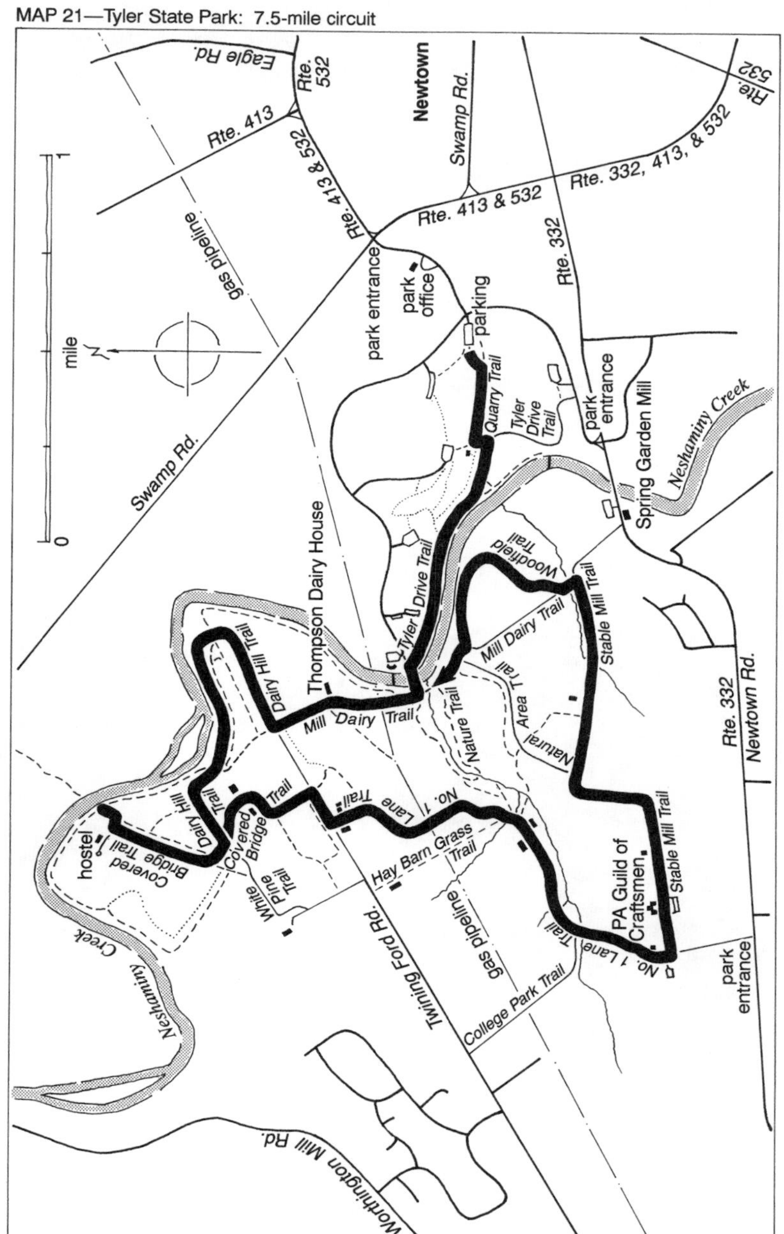

9

WASHINGTON CROSSING HISTORIC PARK, PENNSYLVANIA
WASHINGTON CROSSING STATE PARK, NEW JERSEY

Walking and bicycling. Washington Crossing is, of course, the place where about 2,400 American soldiers under George Washington crossed the Delaware River by boat on Christmas night, 1776, in order to attack and defeat the Hessian garrison at Trenton the next morning. Today visitors can walk back and forth across the Delaware on a handsome old truss bridge that links Washington Crossing Historic Park in Pennsylvania with a corresponding state park in New Jersey, as shown on Map 22 on page 129. The round-trip distance between the two parks' visitor centers is 2.5 miles.

For a longer walk or bicycle ride outlined by the bold line on Map 23 on page 131, the towpath of the Delaware Canal provides a very interesting and attractive way to hike or bike 9 miles round-trip between McConkey's Ferry and Thompson's Mill, which are two different sections of the historic park in Pennsylvania. The dirt towpath is suitable for fat-tired or hybrid bicycles, provided that you are prepared for a somewhat bumpy ride and do not expect to go very fast. If you plan to bring your children, they should be old enough to steer steadily, since if they veer off the towpath, they could plunge into the canal or down the steep embankment into the Delaware River. Cyclists must ride single file, yield to other trail users, and keep their speed to a moderate, safe pace.

The McConkey's Ferry Section features not only the ferry inn (the only surviving structure that stood here at the time of the American Revolution), but also several nineteenth-century structures and the present-day visitor center, which provides exhibits and a film. The Thompson's Mill Section includes the 18th-century Thompson-Neely House and barn, the 19th-century gristmill, Bowman's Hill Tower, and Bowman's Hill Wildflower Preserve, where there are several miles of footpaths.

Washington Crossing Historic Park in Pennsylvania is open

Monday through Saturday from 9 to 5 and on Sunday from noon to 5. It is closed certain holidays, but not Memorial Day, July 4, Labor Day, and most especially Christmas. Bowman's Hill Tower, which provides a panoramic view of the Delaware River and surrounding countryside, is open April through October from 10 to 5 on weekdays and from 10 to 6 on weekends; it is also open on weekends in November. Call beforehand for information regarding times for touring the historic buildings, which are well worth seeing and for which there is an admission fee. Special programs include not only walking tours of the historic buildings at the McConkey's Ferry section, but also an annual candlelight tour early in December and the crossing re-enactment on Christmas Day. The park is managed by The Washington Crossing Park Commission in cooperation with the Pennsylvania Historical and Museum Commission; telephone (215) 493-4076.

Washington Crossing State Park in New Jersey is open daily from 8 A.M. until 4:30 P.M. in winter and until 8 P.M. in summer. The 18th-century Johnson Ferry House, where Washington and his staff are believed to have gathered until all the troops had crossed the river, is usually open Wednesday through Sunday; for specific hours call (609) 737-2515. The visitor center, which has an excellent collection of Revolutionary War artifacts, is open Wednesday through Sunday from 9 to 4:30. Although the focus in this chapter is on the park's historic area, there are also 13 miles of hiking trails and a circuit for mountain biking that are shown on a map available at the visitor center. The park is managed by the New Jersey Division of Parks and Forestry; telephone (609) 737-0623.

FOLLOWING THE OUTBREAK OF FIGHTING between British troops and Massachusetts militiamen at Lexington and Concord on April 19, 1775, the Second Continental Congress convened at Philadelphia in May and appointed George Washington to head the Army of the United Colonies, or Continental Army. On July 2 Washington assumed command outside Boston and eventually forced the British to evacuate the city in March, 1776. Under General Sir William Howe, the British withdrew by ship to Halifax, but five months later they reappeared at New York, where on August 27 they badly defeated the Americans in the Battle of Long Island. On November 20 German mercenaries employed by England captured Fort Washington at the northern end of Manhattan Island. About twenty-five hundred American soldiers were taken prisoner, a loss slightly exceeding the entire American force that later fought at Trenton.

By the end of November 1776, Washington's army was retreating southwestward across New Jersey. Ten thousand British and German soldiers under Major General Cornwallis were in close pursuit. According to a report that Washington sent to Congress on November 23 from Newark, the American army numbered 5,410 troops, counting nearly two thousand men who a week later simply went home when their enlistments expired.

To weaken American resistance still further, General Howe issued a proclamation offering clemency to anyone who signed a statement promising that he would "remain in a peaceable Obedience to His Majesty," King George III. So many people appeared before British officials that the forms on which the loyalty oath was printed ran out. "The conduct of the Jerseys has been most infamous," Washington later wrote to his half-brother John Augustine.

> Instead of turning out to defend their country, and affording aid to our army, they are making their submissions as fast as they can. If they had given us any support, we might have made a stand at Hackensack and after that at Brunswick, but the few militia that were in arms, disbanded themselves . . . and left the poor remains of our army to make the best we could of it.

On December 1 Washington directed the seizure of all boats on the Delaware River for 70 miles above Philadelphia. In particular he mentioned Durham boats, which were cargo boats developed for the shallow and sometimes turbulent river. They were 40 to 60 feet long, 8 feet wide, and pointed at each end like chubby, oversized canoes. They could carry up to 20 tons yet even when loaded drew less than 3 feet. The first such boats are supposed to have been built by Robert Durham in the 1740s to transport iron produced at Durham Furnace, located 10 miles below Easton. They were guided by long oars as they floated downstream with the current, but had to be poled laboriously back upstream by men pacing back and forth along the walking rails at the top of each gunwale. Replicas are displayed at Washington Crossing Historic Park in Pennsylvania.

From New Brunswick Washington wrote on Sunday, December 1, 1776, to inform Congress that "we shall retreat to the West side of [the] Delaware."

> I have sent forward Colonel Humpton to collect proper boats and craft at the ferry for transporting our troops, and it will be of infinite importance to have *every other craft*, besides what he takes for the above purpose, secured on the

> west side of the Delaware, otherwise they may fall into the enemy's hands and facilitate their views.

The enemy's views were presumed to be the capture of Philadelphia or the pursuit and destruction of Washington's army. Cornwallis in fact almost caught up with the Americans at Newark and then at New Brunswick, but Howe had instructed him to proceed no farther. Cornwallis sent an aide back to New York to seek permission to attack the American army before it crossed the Delaware into Pennsylvania. After a delay of five days, Howe joined Cornwallis with still more troops. Their combined force left New Brunswick on December 6. At Princeton the American rear guard slowed the British advance, while the rest of Washington's army crossed the Delaware at Trenton on December 7 and 8. The rear guard then raced to the river, where the last troops boarded the Durham boats and rowed to safety just as a Hessian brigade entered the village of Trenton with brass band playing.

At first General Howe considered pushing on to Philadelphia. There were no bridges across the Delaware, so he sent Cornwallis up the river to Coryell's Ferry (present-day Lambertville) to look for boats. None was found: all boats had been removed to the western bank. However, Washington had little reason to believe that this stratagem would stop the British for long. They could bring their attack flatboats overland by wagon from New York or build new boats on the spot. At Trenton Howe had discovered 48,000 feet of lumber already cut into boards. Also, within a day's march of Trenton there were eight fords where the British could wade across the river. If the river froze, as sometimes happened in January, the British could march across. "Upon the whole there can be no doubt that Philadelphia is their object, and that they will pass the Delaware as soon as possible," Washington wrote to Congress.

> Happy should I be if I could see the means of preventing them. At present I confess I do not. All military writers agree, that it is a work of great difficulty, nay impracticable, where there is any extent of coast to guard. This is the case with us and we have to do it with a force small and inconsiderable and much inferior to that of the enemy . . . . Our little handful daily decreasing by sickness and other causes: and without aid, without considerable succours and exertions on the part of the people, what can we reasonably look for or expect, but an event that will be severely felt by the common Cause and that will wound the heart of every virtuous American—the loss of Philadelphia.

In expecting the British to press their advantage, Washington was reasonable, and he was realistic—but he was wrong. He had not, of course, reckoned on General Howe's characteristic lack of energy and initiative. On December 12 the winter's first snow began (until then the weather had been extraordinarily mild), and on the next day the British commander decided to call off the campaign for that year. New Jersey appeared to have been pacified by his program of pardon and reconciliation. After the military reverses suffered by the Americans during the summer and fall, enthusiasm for the Revolution was waning. Also, Howe had intercepted one of Washington's letters and knew that the enlistment of more than half of Washington's remaining force expired on January 1. Howe evidently believed that the rebel army—poorly clothed, ill-equipped, and somewhat demoralized—would by spring dissolve of its own accord. So in New Jersey he distributed his troops in a chain of garrisons stretching from Burlington to Hackensack and returned to New York, where he had an attractive mistress. Cornwallis prepared to sail for England, where his wife was ill. He would come back in the spring "if there is another campaign, which we doubt."

Despite the setbacks of the last half-year—or perhaps because of them—Washington immediately contemplated a counterthrust. He was fully aware that decisive and victorious action was essential if new recruits were to be raised and if the public, the state legislatures, and the various state militia were to support the Revolution. As early as December 13 Washington wrote to Governor Jonathan Trumbull in Connecticut that he was hoping "to attempt a stroke upon the Forces of the Enemy, who lay a good deal scattered and to all appearances in a state of security." The three regiments of Hessian mercenaries garrisoned for the winter at Trenton were a conspicuous target, close at hand. German outposts around the town were attacked daily by American patrols sent across the river. The Hessians were intimidated into staying within the immediate vicinity of the village, except when they went out in large parties, hauling cannons with them. Yet the Hessian commander, Colonel Rall, was so contemptuous of the Americans' military ability that he failed to fortify the town. "Let them come!" he told one of his officers. "We want no trenches! We'll go after them with the bayonet!"

On December 22 John Honeyman, a butcher and cattle dealer who supplied the Hessians with meat, was captured by an American patrol outside Trenton. He was taken to Washington, who interrogated him personally and in private. Washington, in fact, had met Honeyman at Hackensack in November and had hired him as his personal spy, an arrangement that was known to no one else. Honeyman told Washington everything he knew about the German garrison at Trenton, where he had spent the preceding week. At the conclusion of the interview, Washington ordered Honeyman put under arrest, but the prisoner "escaped" that night. By December 24 Honeyman found his way back to Trenton, where he reported his adventure to Colonel Rall. The American army, Honeyman said, was incapable of a large action. It lacked coats, shoes, food, and equipment necessary for a march. By British and German standards, this was largely true. The comforting news confirmed Rall's belief that the Americans could do nothing to harm him. Only the day before he had dismissed as "women's talk" the report by a loyalist that the Americans were readying themselves for a march of several days.

On December 23 Washington had in fact issued orders that the troops were to prepare a supply of cold food for three days. After his conversation with Honeyman, he wrote to Colonel Joseph Reed at Bristol that "Christmas Day at night, one hour before the day, is the time fixed upon for our attempt on Trenton. For Heaven's sake, keep this to yourself, as the discovery of it may prove fatal to us; our numbers, sorry I am to say, being less than I had any conception of; but necessity, dire necessity will, nay must, justify my attack."

The battle plan called for Colonel John Cadwallader to cross the Delaware River at Bristol with about a thousand newly-raised Pennsylvania militia and five hundred regular Continental troops. They were to engage the enemy garrison at Bordentown to prevent help being sent to Trenton. A mile below Trenton, Brigadier General James Ewing was to cross the Delaware with seven hundred Pennsylvanians to block the Hessians if they tried to retreat southward across Assunpink Creek, a tributary of the Delaware River. Washington himself, with twenty-four hundred regulars, was to cross at McConkey's Ferry, 9 miles above Trenton, then march south to attack the town.

Early on Christmas afternoon Washington's troops assembled behind a ridge west of the ferry landing. As soon as darkness fell, the Durham boats, which had been hidden behind Malta Island several miles upstream, were brought down to the crossing point. Late in the day Washington received a letter from Reed saying that General Israel Putnam, the hero of Bunker Hill, refused to bring his troops out from Philadelphia to join the foray into New Jersey because he was afraid loyalists would seize the city if he left. Next Cadwallader reported that his militiamen could not be relied on to fight. Washington replied, "Not withstanding the discouraging accounts I have received from Colonel Reed of what might be expected from the operations below, I am determined, as the night is favorable, to cross the river and make the attack upon Trenton in the morning. If you can do nothing real at least create as great a diversion as possible."

An American officer at McConkey's Ferry wrote in his diary on December 25:

> 6:00 p.m. The regiments have had their evening parade but instead of returning to their quarters are marching toward the ferry. It is fearfully cold and raw and a snow storm is setting in. The wind is northeast and beats in the faces of the men. It will be a terrible night for the men who have no shoes. Some of them have tied old rags around their feet. Others are barefoot, but I have never heard a man complain. They are ready to suffer any hardship and die rather than give up their liberty.

Washington was among the first to cross the river. The big boats were rowed by men from Colonel John Glover's regiment of sailors from Marblehead, Massachusetts. Drifting sheets of ice on the river hit the boats and pushed them downstream. Loading eighteen cannons and their draft horses took longer than expected. It was three o'clock in the morning before the entire force was brought across. The advance toward Trenton, located 9 miles to the south, had been planned to begin at midnight but did not get under way until four o'clock, with only three hours of darkness left.

At Trenton, Colonel Rall had continued to ignore one warning after another. On Christmas he received a letter from the British commander in New Jersey stating that the Americans might attack. That evening one of his sentries on the north side of Trenton was killed by a small Continental force that, without orders from Washington, had crossed the river and fired on a German outpost. Rall assembled his soldiers, forced the raiders to retreat, and then dismissed the incident. That evening, while Rall was drinking and playing cards, Moses Doane, an American loyalist and leader of a band of marauders who preyed on supporters of the Revolution, tried to see the German commander. Doane was denied admittance, but he sent in a note, which Rall put in his pocket unread.

Sleet fell as the Americans advanced toward Trenton in two columns by separate roads. At one point Washington received a message from one of his generals: "Muskets wet and can't be fired." Washington replied, "Tell your General to use the bayonet. The town must be taken." Yet many troops were without bayonets, and few had been trained in their use. The plan appeared to be going awry in other ways also. As dawn came, Washington's troops met the soldiers who had skirmished with the Germans the prior evening. Washington was furious, telling their officer that he may have ruined the impending attack by putting the enemy troops on their guard. Also, unknown to Washington, Cadwallader had taken his troops across the river and then back again when their artillery could not be unloaded because of ice along the New Jersey shore. General Ewing and his militia opposite Trenton did not even attempt the crossing.

Sunrise came at twenty minutes after seven, but it was not until eight o'clock that the attack began. The Americans advanced at a trot from north and east toward the outskirts of the small town of about a hundred and thirty houses. The German guards fell back, shouting the alarm to turn out. The Americans were able to set up their artillery at the ends of the principal streets and to seize many of the houses before the three German regiments were fully formed. After a brief artillery duel, an American charge captured the only two cannons the mercenaries brought into play. Firing from doorways and windows and raking the streets with grapeshot, the Continental troops pushed the Germans back. Described by some historians as a "brawl" or a "kind of large-scale riot," the battle continued in the sleet for about an hour before one of the German regiments broke and fled to the southwest across a bridge over Assunpink Creek. This escape route was soon blocked by the Americans. With his two remaining regiments, Colonel Rall tried to force a way out to the north but was stopped by cannon fire. He ordered his men to fall back and, a moment later, toppled from his horse, mortally wounded. Soon afterward the Germans surrendered. The note that Rall had failed to read the night before was found in his pocket: "Washington is coming on you down the river, he will be here afore long. Doan."

The American victory was unqualified. Although 300 to 400 Germans escaped, about 900 were captured and 106 were killed or wounded. Four Americans were wounded, and several others died—not from bullets but from the cold. Some of the Americans broke into the Germans' supply of rum, but Washington ordered forty hogsheads of liquor to be spilled into the street. The rest of the day was spent ferrying the exhausted army and their prisoners back across the Delaware River between Johnson's and McConkey's Ferry. In the process several more Americans collapsed and died of exposure.

The victory at Trenton galvanized the moribund patriot cause. Cadwallader, reinforced by militia from Philadelphia and believing that Washington was still at Trenton, finally managed to cross the river on December 27. In New Jersey the militia started to turn out. The Hessians abandoned Burlington and Bordentown. After learning that Washington was back in Pennsylvania, Cadwallader urged the Commander in Chief to join him to "keep up the panic." On December 30 Washington again brought his army across to Trenton. On the same day about half of the men whose enlistments expired on January 1 agreed, for a bounty of ten dollars, to serve six weeks more.

After joining forces with Cadwallader, Washington found himself at the head of an army of about five thousand men, more than half of whom were Pennsylvania militia, most without battle experience. By evening on January 2 this army was confronted at Trenton by a force of seven thousand Germans and British regulars who had marched south from Princeton. During the night, with campfires left burning and rags tied to the wheels of their artillery to muffle their movement, the Americans sneaked away. Circling north, they defeated an enemy garrison of twelve hundred at Princeton the next day. The British at Trenton rushed north again, but Washington moved to a strong position at Morristown, where the American army spent the winter. Shaken, the British withdrew from almost all of New Jersey. A Virginia loyalist, after passing through the state, wrote in his diary:

> The minds of the people are much altered. A few days ago they had given up their cause for lost. Their late successes have turned the scale and now they are all liberty mad again. Their recruiting parties could not get a man, . . . now men are coming in by companies . . . . They have recovered their panic and it will not be an easy matter to throw them into that confusion again.

Lord George Germain, the British secretary of state for the Colonies, put it more succinctly: "All our hopes were blasted by the unhappy affair at Trenton."

≈ ≈ ≈ ≈

SEPTA: There is no service to Washington Crossing, but the R3 Regional Rail Line from Philadelphia runs to Yardley. From there you can walk or bicycle 4 miles north to Washington Crossing via the towpath of the Delaware Canal, which is itself a beautiful excursion. (See Chapter 1 for a discussion of the Delaware Canal.)

From the train station in Yardley, descend to Main Street visible in the distance diagonally across the station parking lot. Turn left onto South Main Street and follow it 0.4 mile to an intersection with College Avenue. Turn right and follow East College Avenue a hundred yards. After crossing the canal, double back to the right next to the bridge in order to reach the towpath. With the canal on your left, follow the towpath north to Washington Crossing Historic Park.

Telephone (215) 580-7800 for current information on schedules, routes, and connections from your starting point. And telephone (215) 580-7852 for information about taking your bicycle on the train.

AUTOMOBILE DIRECTIONS: Go first to Pennsylvania's Washington Crossing Historic Park, which is located 27 miles northeast of downtown Philadelphia on the Delaware River below New Hope. (See •9 on **Map 1** on page 6.) The Pennsylvania Turnpike and Interstate 95 provide convenient avenues of approach.

From the east or west on the Pennsylvania Turnpike: Leave the turnpike at Exit 28 for Trenton and Route 1 North toward Interstate 95. After paying the toll, follow Route 1 North more than 6 miles to I-95 North. Once you are on I-95 heading north, follow the directions in the next paragraph.

From the north or south on Interstate 95: Leave I-95 at Exit 31 for New Hope (Exit 31B if you are coming from New Jersey). At the bottom of the exit ramp, turn north toward New Hope, Washington Crossing Historic Park, and Route 532. Go 2.7 miles to a crossroads with Route 532 at a traffic light. Turn right onto Route 532 and go 0.6 mile, then turn left onto Route 32 North. Go only a few hundred yards, then turn left into the parking area opposite the park's visitor center.

WALKING ACROSS THE DELAWARE TO THE JOHNSON FERRY HOUSE AND VISITOR CENTER IN NEW JERSEY: **Map 22** opposite shows this short excursion. From the visitor center at Washington Crossing, Pennsylvania, bear half-left out the front doors. With the river on your left, follow the wide gravel path to the McConkey's Ferry Inn near the end of the bridge. (Most of the historic buildings here date from the nineteenth century, when the community was called Taylorsville. For tours of the buildings, see the park staff at the visitor center.)

With caution, cross Route 532 and follow the walkway on the bridge across the river. At the New Jersey end of the bridge, continue uphill a few dozen yards to the towpath of the Delaware & Raritan Canal. With caution, turn left across the road, then follow a ramp that leads up and across a pedestrian bridge over Route 29. Follow the path to a T-intersection with a park road where—about 100 yards downhill to the left—the Johnson Ferry House is located.

From a stone barn within sight of the Johnson Ferry House, a dirt track called Continental Lane leads uphill to the visitor center at Washington Crossing State Park, New Jersey. Continental Lane is the route followed by the American soldiers as they began their 9-mile nighttime march to Trenton.

Return to Pennsylvania by the way you came.

MAP 22—Washington Crossing Historic Park (Pennsylvania) and Washington Crossing State Park (New Jersey)

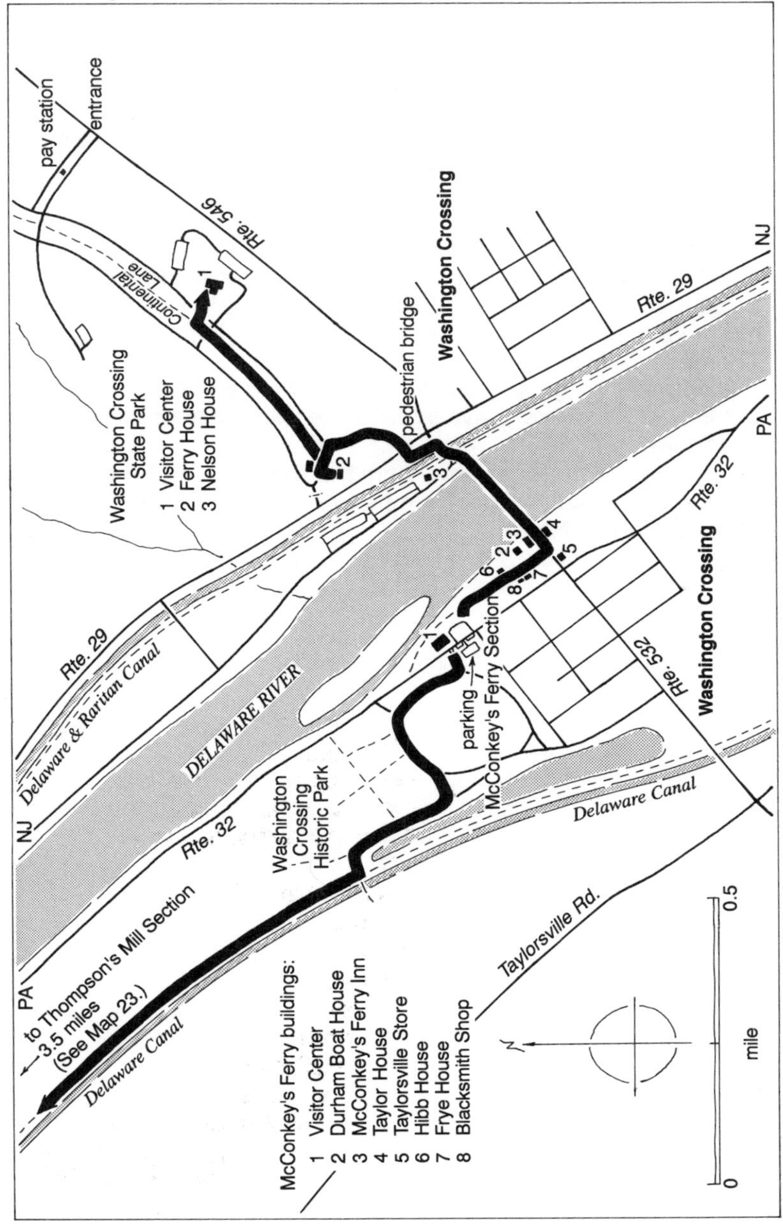

≈ ≈ ≈ ≈

WALKING, BICYCLING, OR DRIVING FROM McCONKEY'S FERRY TO THOMPSON'S MILL: As shown on **Map 23** opposite, Washington Crossing Historic Park in Pennsylvania is divided into two parts. The bold line on Map 23 shows a way to walk or bicycle along the towpath of the Delaware Canal 9 miles round-trip between the two sections of the park. To get started, refer back to Map 22 on page 129, which shows the McConkey's Ferry section at a somewhat larger scale than does Map 23. Although the towpath is closed to motor vehicles, be alert for cars at McConkey's Ferry and Thompson's Mill.

A map showing the many footpaths at the Bowman's Hill Wildflower Preserve is available at the wildflower preserve headquarters.

If you would prefer to drive from the McConkey's Ferry section of the park to the Thompson's Mill section, simply follow Route 32 North.

MAP 23—Washington Crossing Historic Park: From McConkey's Ferry Section to Thompson's Mill Section via the Delaware Canal towpath

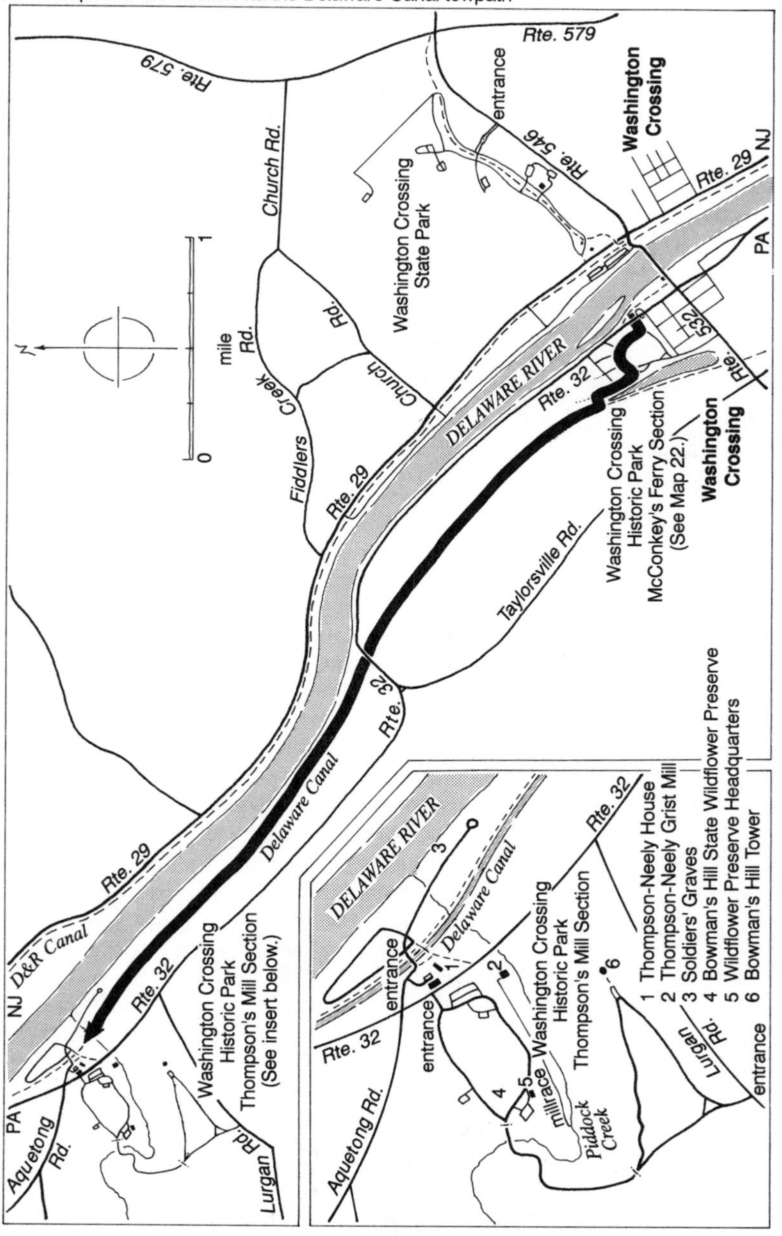

10

MORRIS ARBORETUM of the UNIVERSITY OF PENNSYLVANIA

Walking. Located in Chestnut Hill at the boundary between Philadelphia and Montgomery counties, the Morris Arboretum provides the opportunity to see thousands of varieties of native and exotic trees and shrubs, plus various gardens and other features drawn from the traditions of European and Japanese landscape architecture. Changing exhibits appear in the sculpture garden, and other sculptures are on permanent display.

Gently graded paved paths—shown on Map 24 on page 143 and altogether totaling about 2 miles—wind through the arboretum. If you have an infant or small child, the paths are suitable for buggies and strollers.

The arboretum is open on weekends April through October from 10 to 5, and on weekends November through March from 10 to 4. On weekdays year-round, it is open from 10 to 4. An admission fee is charged. Dogs, picnicking, bicycling, and collecting plant samples are prohibited.

The arboretum is administered by the University of Pennsylvania. Telephone (215) 247-5777 for information about guided tours and educational lectures, programs, and courses.

THE MORRIS ARBORETUM in Chestnut Hill was formerly the country estate of John T. Morris and his sister Lydia, who began to develop Compton (as they called the place) in 1887, six years after John had retired from active management of an iron manufacturing firm founded by his father. From their travels in America, Europe, and Asia, John and Lydia Morris brought back ideas, artworks, garden ornaments, and plants and seeds for Compton. They not only cultivated trees and shrubs from around the world, but also adorned their property with a wide variety of traditional landscape features, including a balustraded,

Italianate overlook, a Roman loggia housing a statue of Mercury (inspired by excavations at Heraculaneum), a small grotto, a sort of Baroque step fountain of gently cascading water, a terrace rose garden, an oak allée, and a swan pond and Tuscan love temple—all within the context of an English-style estate of broad lawns, meadows, artfully scattered trees and copses, and curving wooded margins. At the top of their hill, the Morrises constructed a baronial stone mansion that has since been torn down. The present-day George D. Widener Education Center is the former carriage house.

The Morrises shared the late Victorian fascination with things Oriental. They not only traveled to Japan but also hired a Japanese garden designer, whose work at Compton includes three separate gardens, including a Japanese hill garden featuring a miniaturized landscape made of earth and rocks excavated when the Swan Pond was dug. Charles Sprague Sargent, director of Harvard University's Arnold Arboretum from 1873 to 1927, thought the collection of Asian plants at Compton was outstanding. He sent the Morrises many seeds and seedlings collected for the Arnold Arboretum by Ernest "Chinese" Wilson, a plant explorer who between 1899 and 1918 introduced more than 1,500 foreign plants to America.

John Morris died in 1915 and Lydia in 1931. It was their intention that Compton ultimately become a school and research center for horticulture and botany, and by Lydia's will their 166-acre estate was bequeathed to the University of Pennsylvania. Today the landscape and gardens created by the Morrises can still be seen, meticulously maintained or altogether restored. The allée, for example, was demolished by a windstorm in 1991 but has been replanted, and a large greenhouse for a fernery has been rebuilt. While many outstanding tree specimens planted by the Morrises survive, the plant collection has been vastly enlarged. The arboretum has more than 6,850 varieties of trees and shrubs from the north temperate zone around the world. Each is labeled with a metal tag attached to the trunk or a branch, listing the plant's scientific and common names and its natural range. The Morris Arboretum is thus a perfect place to learn about both native and foreign plants, or just to go for a stroll in a beautiful setting.

≈ ≈ ≈ ≈

Learning to identify trees in not difficult. Every walk, bicycle ride, or automobile trip is an opportunity for practice. Notice the overall forms and branching habits of the trees, and also the distinctive qualities of their twigs, buds, bark, leaves, flowers, and fruits or seeds. These factors are the key identification features that distinguish one species from another. Finally, when using a field guide, check the maps or descriptions that delineate the geographic range within which a tentatively identified tree or shrub is likely to be found.

Some trees, of course, have very distinctive and reliable forms. Familiar evergreens like balsam fir and eastern red cedar have a conical shape, like a dunce cap, although in dense stands the red cedar tapers very little and assumes the columnar form of the Italian cypress, which it somewhat resembles. The deciduous little-leaf linden, imported from Europe and used as a street tree, is also more or less conical in shape, but with wider-spreading lower branches than the evergreens mentioned above. The American elm displays a spreading form like a head of broccoli. A full-bodied egg-shape is characteristic of the sugar maple and beech, although both will develop long, branchless trunks in crowded woods, as do most forest trees competing for light. The vertically exaggerated cigar shape of Lombardy poplar—a form called fastigiate—and the pendulous, trailing quality of weeping willow are unmistakable. (Both Lombardy poplar and weeping willow have been introduced to North America from abroad.)

Branching habit, an important clue to some trees, is observable even at a distance. White pine, for example, has markedly horizontal branches with a slight upward tilt at the tips, like a hand turned with its palm up. Norway spruce (another imported species) is often seen as an ornamental tree dwarfing and darkening a house near which it was planted fifty or a hundred years ago; it is a very tall evergreen—sometimes reminding me of a pagoda—with long, evenly-spaced, festoon-like branches. The slender lower branches of pin oak slant downward, while those of white oak and red oak are often massive and horizontal, especially on mature trees growing in the open. The lower branches of the horse chestnut (yet another European import) also droop but then curl up at the tips in chunky twigs. Elm branches spread up and out like the mouth of a trumpet. The trunk of the mature honey-locust diverges into large branches somewhat in the manner of an elm. Even the reviled *ailanthus* or tree of heaven, which springs up in dense groves of spindly, spiky saplings wherever earth has been disturbed, eventually develops a spreading form somewhat like an elm or honey-locust.

A good botanist or forester can identify trees by their twigs alone—that is, by the end portion of the branch that constitutes the newest growth. During winter the shape, color, size, position, and sheathing of buds are important. For instance, beech buds are long and pointed, tan, and sheathed with overlapping scales like shingles. Sycamore and magnolia buds are wrapped in a single scale. The twigs of horse chestnut are tipped with a big, sticky, brown bud, while those of silver maple, and to a lesser extent red maple, end with large clusters of red buds. Some oaks, such as white oak, have hairless terminal buds, while other species, such as black oak, have hairy end buds.

Aside from buds, other characteristics of twigs are color, thorns, odor, hair, pith, and the size, shape, and position of leaf scars marking where the leaf stems were attached. For example, most maple twigs are reddish brown, but the twigs of striped maple and mountain maple are greenish. Thorns and spines are significant because relatively few trees have them, notably honeylocust, black locust, Hercules club, prickly ash, buckthorn bumelia, devil's walking stick, Osage-orange, American plum, some crabapples, and the many varieties of hawthorn. *Ailanthus* twigs, which show huge leaf scars, have a rank odor when broken open. Most oaks have hairless twigs, although some species such as blackjack oak are distinctly hairy. As for pith, it can be chambered, solid, spongy, or of different colors, depending on the species. Oak, hickory, and tulip trees are common forest species in the Philadelphia region, but only the pith of white oak in cross section forms a star. Finally, the location of leaf scars in opposite pairs along the twigs (as with maples) distinguishes a wide variety of trees and shrubs from those with leaf scars arranged alternately, first on one side and then on the other (as with oaks). All these distinguishing features can best be appreciated simply by examining the twigs of different species.

Bark is not always a reliable clue for identifying trees, as the color and texture of bark change with age or from trunk to branches to twigs. Often the distinctive character of bark is seen only in the trunks of large, mature trees. Bark can be smooth, furrowed, scaly, plated, shaggy, fibrous, crisscrossed, or papery. Some trees, of course, may be clearly identified by their bark. The names *shagbark hickory* and *paper birch* speak for themselves. Striped maple has longitudinal, whitish stripes in the smooth green bark of the younger trees. The crisscrossed ridges of white ash, the light blotches on sycamores, and the smooth gray skin of beech are equally distinctive. Birches and some cherries are characterized by horizontal lenticels like random dashes.

Most people notice leaves, particularly their shape. The leaves of the gray birch are triangular; ginkgo, fan-shaped; catalpa, heart-shaped; sweetgum, star-shaped; beech, elliptical (or actually pointed at each end); and black willow narrower still and thus *lanceolate*. Notice also the leaf margin or edge. Is it smooth like rhododendron, wavy like water oak, serrated like basswood, or deeply lobed like most maples? And how many lobes are there? Tulip trees, for example, have easily recognized four-lobed leaves; maples have three- or five-lobed leaves. Also, are the lobe tips rounded like white oak or pointed like red oak? Or, maybe, as with sassafras and red mulberry, the same tree has leaves that are shaped differently, the most distinctive being those with a single asymmetrical lobe creating a leaf outline like a mitten. In some trees, such as the large-leaf magnolia with its tobacco-like foliage, the sheer size of the leaves is significant. Similarly, sycamores have leaves resembling sugar maples or red maples, but usually bigger and coarser in texture.

Some leaves such as those of the Japanese maple, horse chestnut, and Ohio buckeye are palmately compound, meaning that they are actually composed of leaflets radiating from the end of the stem like fingers from the palm. In the fall the whole compound leaf may drop off the tree as a unit, or the leaflets may fall off individually, and then finally the stem. Other leaves, such as ash, hickory, and sumac, are pinnately compound, being composed of leaflets arranged in opposite pairs along a central stalk. With pinnately compound leaves growing from the top of a branchless trunk, the saplings of *ailanthus* resemble little palm trees. Still other leaves are *bi*pinnately compound, somewhat like a fern. The leaflets grow from stalks that, in turn, spread from a central stalk. Honeylocust, Kentucky coffeetree, and the ornamental imported silktree are examples.

Although the needles of evergreens are not as varied as the leaves of deciduous plants, there are still several major points to look for, such as the number of needles grouped together. White pine has fascicles of five; pitch pine, loblolly pine, and sometimes shortleaf pine have fascicles of three; and jack pine, red pine, Virginia pine, Austrian pine, and sometimes shortleaf pine have fascicles of two. Needles of spruce, hemlock, and fir grow singly, but are joined to the twig in distinctive ways. Spruce needles grow from little woody pegs, hemlock needles from smaller bumps, and fir needles directly from the twig, leaving a rounded pit when pulled off. Spruce needles tend to be four-sided, hemlock flat, and fir somewhere in between. The needles of larch (also called tamarack) grow in dense clusters and all drop off in winter. The needles of bald cypress also drop off—hence its name.

Flowers are a spectacular, though short-lived, feature of some trees and shrubs. Three variables are color, form, and (less reliably) time of bloom. Eastern redbud, with red-purple clusters, and shadbush (also called Allegheny serviceberry), with small, white, five-petaled flowers, are among the first of our native trees to bloom, sometimes as early as late March in the Philadelphia region. As members of the rose family, apples, cherries, plums, peaches, and hawthorns all have flowers with five petals (usually pink or white) in loose, white clusters, typically blooming in April. The blossoms of flowering dogwood, which also appear in April or early May, consist of four white, petal-like bracts, each with a brown notch at the tip, while the flowers of alternate-leaf

dogwood consist of loose, white clusters. These are a few of our native species commonly thought of as flowering trees and shrubs, but the blossoms of other native species are equally distinctive, such as the small but numerous flowers of maples or the tuliplike flowers and durable husks of tulip trees. Unlike most trees, witch hazel—which produces small, yellow, scraggly flowers—blooms in fall or winter.

Finally, the seeds or fruit of a tree are a conspicuous element in summer and fall, sometimes lasting into winter and even spring. Even if a tree is bare, the fruits and seeds (or for that matter, the leaves) can often be found littered on the ground around the trunk. Nobody who sees a tree with acorns could fail to know that it is an oak, although some varieties, such as willow oak and shingle oak (also known as northern laurel oak) are deceptive. Distinctive nuts are also produced by beech trees, horse chestnuts, hickories, and walnuts. Some seeds, like ash and maple, have wings; such winged seeds are termed *samaras*. Others, such as honeylocust, Kentucky coffeetree, and redbud, come in pods like beans and in fact are members of the same general legume family. The seeds of birches, poplars, and willows hang in tassels, while those of sweetgum and sycamore form prickle-balls (as do the shells of horse chestnut and buckeye). Eastern cotton-wood produces seeds that are wind-borne by cottonlike tufts. And, of course, brightly colored berries and fruits are produced by many species, such as crabapples, holly, hawthorn, and hackberry. The female ginkgo has pale pink, globular, and remarkably foul-smelling fruit. Among needle evergreens, spruce and pine cones hang from the twigs, while fir cones stand upright like stubby candles, and the small hemlock cones grow from the twig tips.

In conclusion, the trick to tree identification, like bird identification discussed in Chapter 7, is a gestalt approach that entails considering, either simultaneously or in rapid succession, a wide variety of features of which the ones discussed here—form and branching habit, twigs, buds, bark, leaves, flowers, and fruits or seeds—are the most obvious and the most readily observed. Don't get hung up pondering any single ambiguous or inconclusive feature; move on to consider other clues.

≈ ≈ ≈ ≈

SEPTA: Although it is possible to reach the Morris Arboretum by bus, doing so entails walking nearly a mile from the bus stop (about half of it uphill) before you reach the arboretum's education center, which for most visitors is the place where they *start* walking through the arboretum.

Bus L follows Germantown Avenue/Pike past the intersection

with Northwestern Avenue. Get off at the corner and follow Northwestern Avenue 0.4 mile north past Chestnut Hill College to the entrance to the Morris Arboretum on the right. Where there is no sidewalk, walk well off the road on the grassy shoulder. (See **Map 24** on page 143.) From the entrance, follow the winding drive 0.4 mile uphill to the education center. **Use caution:** walk on the left facing the oncoming traffic and step off the entrance drive as cars approach.

Telephone (215) 580-7800 for current information on schedules, routes, and connections from your starting point. One place to connect with Bus L is Chestnut Hill, which is served by several other bus routes and by the R8 Regional Rail Line.

AUTOMOBILE DIRECTIONS: The Morris Arboretum is located at the northern corner of Philadelphia in the city's Chestnut Hill section. (See •10 on **Maps 1 and 2E** on pages 6 and 7.) Several avenues of approach are described below.

From the north or south on Interstate 95: Take Exit 17 for Interstate 676 West toward central Philadelphia. Stay on I-676 past the exits for Broad Street and the Benjamin Franklin Parkway, then merge with Interstate 76 West (Schuylkill Expressway). Once you are on I-76 westbound, follow the directions in the next paragraph.

From the east or west on Interstate 76 (Schuylkill Expressway): Leave the expressway at Exit 31 for Belmont Avenue and Green Lane on the west side of the Schuylkill River opposite Manayunk. At the bottom of the exit ramp, turn across the river and follow Green Lane 0.9 mile straight uphill through Manayunk to an intersection with Ridge Avenue. Turn left and follow Ridge Avenue 3 miles to an intersection at a traffic light where Spring Lane intersects from the left and Bells Mill Road intersects from the right. Turn right and follow Bells Mill Road 1.4 miles down into the Wissahickon Valley and up the other side to an intersection with Germantown Avenue. Turn left and follow Germantown Avenue downhill 0.7 mile to an intersection with Northwestern Avenue, then turn right and follow Northwestern Avenue 0.4 mile to the entrance to the Morris Arboretum on the right. Follow the winding entrance drive 0.4 mile uphill to the fee station and parking lots.

From the west on the Pennsylvania Turnpike: Leave the Turnpike at Exit 25 for Norristown. After paying the toll, take the first ramp down to the right (it is unmarked); the ramp leads onto **Route 422 (Germantown Pike)** east toward Philadelphia. Follow Germantown Pike east 3.6 miles to an intersection at a traffic light with Northwestern Avenue. Turn left onto Northwestern Avenue and go 0.4 mile to the entrance to the Morris Arboretum on the right. Follow the winding entrance drive 0.4 mile uphill to the fee station and parking lots.

From the east on the Pennsylvania Turnpike: Leave the Turnpike at Exit 26 for Fort Washington. After paying the toll, take **Route 309 South (Fort Washington Expressway)** toward Philadelphia. Go 2.2 miles, then take the exit for Paper Mill Road. At the bottom of the exit ramp, turn right toward Chestnut Hill. Go 1.4 miles to a crossroads at a traffic light with Bethlehem Pike, and there continue straight through the intersection onto Stenton Avenue, which immediately curves right. Follow Stenton Avenue 0.7 to a crossroads at a traffic light where Wissahickon Avenue intersects from the right and Northwestern Avenue intersects from the left. Turn left onto Northwestern Avenue and go 0.1 mile to the entrance to the Morris Arboretum on the left. Follow the winding entrance drive 0.4 mile uphill to the fee station and parking lots.

From the north or south on Interstate 476 (the Blue Route): The southern end of I-476 starts at Exit 7 off Interstate 95 near Chester; the northern end of I-476 starts at Exits 25-25A off the Pennsylvania Turnpike. If you are coming from the south, leave I-476 at Exit 8 for Germantown Pike - East. From the bottom of the exit ramp, follow Chemical Road 0.3 mile, then turn right onto Germantown Pike - East and go 3.3 miles to an intersection at a traffic light with Northwestern Avenue. Turn left onto Northwestern Avenue and go 0.4 mile to the entrance to the Morris Arboretum on the right. Follow the winding entrance drive 0.4 mile uphill to the fee station and parking lots.

If you are coming from the north on I-476, take Exit 7 for Norristown, then—after going only 0.1 mile from the top of the exit ramp—bear right just beyond a traffic light onto Alan Wood Road. Go around the jug handle back to the light, and there turn left, which will put you onto Ridge Pike headed toward Philadelphia. Follow Ridge Pike about 1.6 miles to an intersection at a traffic light with Joshua Road, and there turn left. Follow Joshua Road 0.4 mile, then turn right onto Germantown Pike and go 1.9 miles to an intersection at a traffic light with Northwestern Avenue. Turn left onto Northwestern Avenue and go 0.4 mile to the entrance to the

Morris Arboretum on the right. Follow the winding entrance drive 0.4 mile uphill to the fee station and parking lots.

From the intersection of Bethlehem Pike and Germantown Avenue in Chestnut Hill: Go north on Germantown Avenue 1.4 miles to an intersection at a traffic light with Northwestern Avenue. Turn right and follow Northwestern Avenue 0.4 mile to the entrance to the Morris Arboretum on the right. Follow the winding entrance drive 0.4 mile uphill to the fee station and parking lots.

WALKING: The arboretum's paths and main features are shown on **Map 24** opposite. As of 1994, a few of the paths shown on the map do not exist, but their construction is planned for the near future.

Stop by first at the George D. Widener Education Center, where you can pick up material on the arboretum and its various programs and current exhibits. Located next to the entrance drive, the Widener Center is the building that you passed on your way uphill to the parking lots.

MAP 24—Morris Arboretum of the University of Pennsylvania

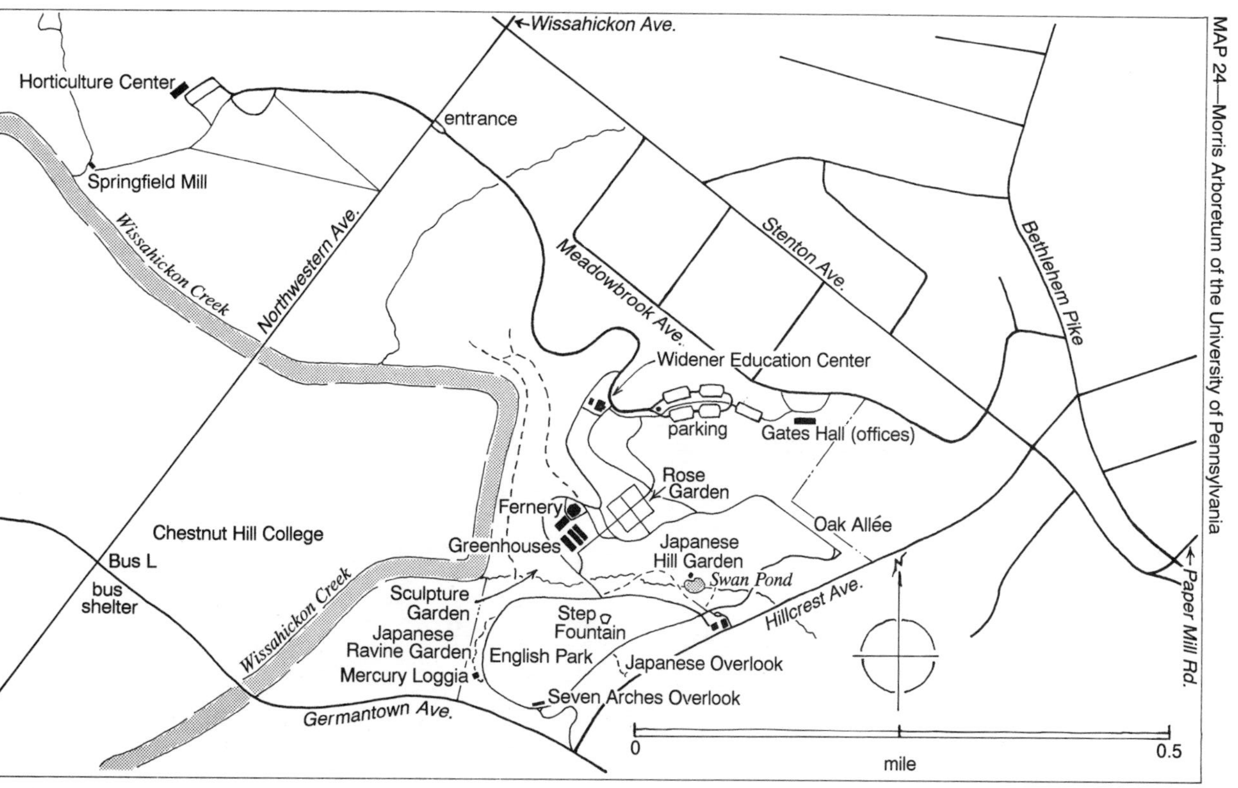

11

WISSAHICKON VALLEY

Walking, jogging, ski touring, and bicycling. With its high wooded bluffs, rock outcrops, and abrupt twists and turns, the gorge carved by Wissahickon Creek as its descends to the Schuylkill River through Philadelphia provides some of the most dramatic scenery in the metropolitan region. The valley combines a picturesque wilderness aura with the ease of a wide and winding carriage road along the bottom of the valley. This nineteenth-century carriage road is one of the outstanding recreational facilities of the East Coast. In addition to the carriage road, which is popular with walkers, joggers, horseback riders, and cyclists, there are dozens of miles of narrow dirt trails along the sides and rims of the valley and tributary ravines.

All but the lowermost segment of the bold line on Map 25 on page 156 shows the carriage road that extends 5.5 miles from the Montgomery County line downstream along Wissahickon Creek to Lincoln Drive near Rittenhousetown. Called Wissahickon Drive or Forbidden Drive, the carriage road is paved with hard-packed rock grit and is closed to cars except for a short stretch below Wises Mill Road at Valley Green Inn. The lowermost segment of the bold line on Map 25 shows a paved bikeway that continues from the end of the carriage road at Lincoln Drive 2 miles down the valley to Ridge Avenue. At Ridge Avenue cyclists can follow the bikeway that runs 4.6 miles along the Schuylkill River to the Philadelphia Museum of Art, as described in Chapter 14. Another option at Ridge Avenue is to join the Philadelphia-Valley Forge Bikeway discussed in Chapter 4.

Maps 26, 27, and 28 on pages 159-161 show the Wissahickon Valley in detail. The most northerly section of the valley shown on Map 26 is the Andorra Natural Area, where the network of trails above the carriage road is closed to bicyclists. For information on guided hikes, workshops, and events at the Wissahickon Valley, stop by the Tree House Visitor Center at Andorra or telephone (215) 685-9285.

All the trails shown on Maps 27 and 28 are open to mountain bikers, hikers, and horseback riders alike—although some of the trails are rugged and passable only on foot.

The park is open from dawn until dark—or even after dark in the case of people walking or jogging on the carriage road or patronizing Valley Green Inn. Dogs must be leashed. Bicyclists must yield to other trail users, keep their speed to a moderate, safe pace, and ride single file—except on the carriage road, where they may ride two abreast. There is enough room on the carriage road for cyclists to give wide berth to walkers and joggers, and they are asked to do so.

The Wissahickon Valley is managed by the Fairmount Park Commission; telephone (215) 685-0000.

Ho! Away for the Wissahickon
For the dance and good stewed chicken.
Catfish! Waffles! Good hot toddy,
Cheers the heart and warms the body.
Swiftly gliding o'er the snow,
Merrily away we go.

THIS SLEIGHING SONG celebrates the Wissahickon Valley of the mid-nineteenth century. Taverns and roadhouses that bordered the Schuylkill River and Wissahickon Creek were popular haunts of the day. There were the Punch Bowl, Robin Hood Tavern, Belmont Cottage, Lions at Falls, and other hostelries along the Schuylkill, and the Indian Rock Hotel, Valley Green Inn, Lotus Inn, Wissahickon Hall, Maple Springs Hotel, and the Log Cabin on the Wissahickon. This last establishment featured the added attraction of two black bears chained to a stagecoach in front of the tavern, as well as a menagerie of owls, foxes, monkeys, and other small animals. Not to be outdone, the nearby Maple Springs Hotel had a bear that was trained to open and guzzle bottles of carbonated mineral water purchased by the customers, and a museum of curiously carved roots and other such objects assembled by the proprietor, Joseph "Whittler" Smith. Writing in 1913 in his book of memoirs, Cornelius Weygandt recalled that when he was a child, "a black bear on a chain at this tavern often drew my vote for a walk down the creek, if Father let us choose which way we should walk."

Contemporary guidebooks, advertisements, and memoirs like those of Weygandt almost invariably mention catfish and waffles as a particular delicacy of the period. Weygandt reported a fishmonger as recalling, "There wasn't a hotel or a tavern or a restaurant anywhere you'd drive or boat out of Philadelphia didn't hang out a sign, 'catfish and waffles,' come March, and keep it hung until long about the Fourth of July." Weygandt himself reminisced:

> "Catfish and waffles" began with fried catfish and a relish. A steak of beef followed, with fried potatoes, generally stewed chicken and the waffles. And after the chicken and the waffles, the coffee. . . .
>
> At one of the Wissahickon roadhouses the proprietor went through the hocus pocus of netting catfish from a great tank full of fish, telling you that they were caught in the creek "only yesterday," and that he would kill and cook for you the fish you had just seen netted. He carried the fish into the kitchen, from which, I suppose, he carried them back to the tank as soon as you were out of the way. There were, doubtless, catfish for all waiting fully fried by the time patrons were likely to drop in.
>
> So famous did this hostelry make its "catfish and waffles" that they became the combination for wedding dinners and brought hundreds of brides and grooms here for that important function. I know of one couple, wedded in 1857, to whom the Wissahickon remained always a place of pure romance because of such a visit. It was not Niagara, to be sure, the Mecca of subsequent generations of lovers, but it was a place of wild beauty, after its quiet fashion. And it could be visited again and again and its old memories renewed of a Sabbath, or of a holiday, even if one could not get a day's vacation when one yearned for it, as in this more hurried and less busy time.

Quantities of catfish formerly were caught in the Schuylkill River and in Wissahickon Creek. Charles V. Hagner, in his *Early History of the Falls of the Schuylkill*, wrote in 1869:

> I have seen men, in one scoop of the dip-net, have it so full of these catfish as to be unable to lift them in the boat, but were obliged to take them out of it with their hands and other contrivances. . . . They came regularly on or about the 25th of May, the run of them lasting some two or three weeks. They were caught in immense numbers during the season, put in artificial ponds made for the purpose, and taken out as wanted during the summer and fall months. Thousands of people resorted to the hotels of the Falls to eat them. . . .

Weygandt recalled the mud "kicking with catfish" when the water was let out of the Germantown reservoir on Paper Mill Run, which flows into Wissahickon Creek. According to some accounts, the name Wissahickon itself is derived from the Delaware Indian term *Wisamikon*, supposedly meaning catfish stream, but others point to *Wissauchsickan*, meaning yellow-colored stream.

When the Wissahickon Valley was purchased by Philadelphia in 1868 for inclusion in Fairmount Park, the taverns—although allowed to remain open—languished and failed nonetheless. "But, alas," says Theo B. White in *Fairmount, Philadelphia's Park*, "with the acquisition of these inns and taverns, the commission imposed temperance. It is quite obvious that beer, wine, and whiskey were normal and desirable companions to a platter of catfish and waffles, and when such was denied, the patronage declined to extinction." Today only Valley Green Inn, built midway up the Wissahickon Valley in 1850, survives as an active eatery (it has a liquor license). Owned by the park commission but privately managed, this excellent restaurant is well worth a visit. Wissahickon Hall, formerly a hotel built near the lower end of the valley in 1849, is now a police station.

During the eighteenth century and continuing into the nineteenth, the Wissahickon Valley and some of the bigger tributaries were an important industrial center. Falling about 100 feet in a distance of 7 miles, Wissahickon Creek provided water power for a series of gristmills, sawmills, paper mills, textile mills, linseed oil mills, carpet and dye works, canneries, and other manufactories. The earliest was Robeson's Wissahickon Mill for producing flour, built at the mouth of the creek about 1686.

In 1683 Francis Daniel Pastorius emigrated from Germany and established Germantown just east of the lower Wissahickon Valley. Pastorius was the agent for the Frankfort Land Company, a group of Frankfort Quakers who bought the tract from William Penn. Also in 1683 the first permanent Mennonite settlement in America was made at Germantown by immigrants from Krefeld on the lower Rhine.

Soon these and other settlers began erecting mills along the upper stretches of Wissahickon Creek and its tributaries. William Rittenhouse, grandfather of the astronomer and clockmaker David Rittenhouse, was not only pastor of the new Mennonite community but also an early industrialist, who in 1690 established the first paper mill in the colonies. By 1850 the mill village had more than 50 buildings. A few structures still stand on Paper Mill Run just above its confluence with Wissahickon Creek. For information on tours of Rittenhousetown, telephone (215) 438-5711. (Access to Rittenhousetown is off Wissahickon Avenue just north of its intersection with Lincoln Drive; see Map 28 on page 161.) Flax mills, textile mills, and fulling and dye works were also established. The settlers from Krefeld in particular produced fine linen cloth that came to be well known throughout the colonies.

Another German hamlet was Krisheim, on what is now Cresheim Creek, a tributary of the Wissahickon. Wises Mill Road, Thomas Mill Road, and Bells Mill Road, all of which lead from the highlands down to the creek at various points along the valley, perpetuate some of the other mill sites and names—although, in fact, the names of the mill owners and access roads constantly changed. For example, in Smedley's 1862 *Atlas of the City of Philadelphia*, Thomas Mill Road is shown as Spruce Mill Lane and Bells Mill Road is Pauls Mill Lane. Livezey Lane recalls the Livezey family, who in 1747 acquired property in the Wissahickon Valley and established a large gristmill. Their house still stands next to the creek on the east bank a half-mile below Valley Green Inn. In 1826 a road from Rittenhousetown to the Schuylkill River was constructed, and in 1850 the Wissahickon Turnpike Company completed what is now Wissahickon Drive.

Manufacturing in the Wissahickon gorge came to an end, however, when the area was acquired for Fairmount Park. By the Act of Assembly of 1868, the park commission was directed to appropriate land to the heights on either side of the valley. During the next fifteen years, all of the mills were torn down in order to protect the purity of the Schuylkill River, which was Philadelphia's water supply.

Although of secondary importance at the time, preservation of the Wissahickon scenery was also a recognized goal. Fanny Kemble, a British actress who married Pierce Butler of Philadelphia, is said to have awakened Philadelphians to the beauty of the area through her poetry and prose descriptions of the valley. (Kemble later divorced Butler and returned to England, where during the Civil War she wrote articles against slavery, which she had seen up close as a result of living on Butler's appallingly primitive rice plantation in Georgia.) The story writer George Lippard romanticized the region, as did Edgar Allen Poe in a short magazine piece called "Morning on the Wissahickon." With its rocky course, cliffs, tall trees, and gorgelike valley, the Wissahickon appealed to the contemporary taste for picturesque and dramatic wilds popularized by the Hudson River school of artists and other landscape painters of the day. In 1867 Frederick Law Olmsted, who had collaborated with Calvert Vaux to design New York's Central Park, reported to the Fairmount Park Commission that "the Creek Road offers such unparalleled attractions for driving, it is so accessible and convenient of approach and can be secured at this time at a cost so moderate, that no route can at all be compared to it."

After the valley was acquired for the park, the creek road was improved and the toll gates removed. Wissahickon Drive became a place for the fashionable set to see and be seen. T. A. Daly, a journalist, wrote in 1922:

> [I]n a winter when the roads were white, and not too deeply covered, trim sleighs drawn by fast steppers flashed up and down the drive from Ridge Road to Chestnut Hill; and moonlight nights especially were all a jangle of

> silver bells. On fine afternoons from early spring until late fall the sedate carriage-folk of Germantown and Chestnut Hill in their broughams and landaus, the grand ladies shielding their complexions from the sun with tiny parasols and sitting scarcely less erect than their liveried coachmen, took the air and enjoyed the scenery with calm dignity. . . .

Today Wissahickon Drive is still an immensely popular promenade, winding past massive "rustic" masonry bridges that no park commission could possibly afford to build nowadays. Expansion of the park has continued through purchases and gifts. In 1976 and 1981, the Andorra Natural Area was acquired and developed as a nature education center. The Andorra area includes part of an old tree nursery, and in consequence many exotic specimens are scattered throughout the woods.

Also scattered through the park are various historic sites. A tablet set in the rock at the entrance to Wissahickon Drive off Lincoln Drive commemorates the Battle of Germantown on October 4, 1777, just after the British had seized Philadelphia. Part of the action took place in the lower Wissahickon Valley. The British held the southern rim of the gorge. The Pennsylvania militia under General John Armstrong were supposed to advance southward along the Ridge Road (Ridge Avenue today) while other, larger columns attacked the main British force at Germantown farther east. However, the assault was ill coordinated and confused by fog. Although a major battle was fought at Germantown, the attack at the lower Wissahickon never amounted to much. American and British artillery exchanged fire from the heights on each side of the valley while the opposing infantry skirmished on the slopes. Only a few hours after the attack began, the Americans were forced to retreat, leaving behind one of their cannons, in Armstrong's words, on "the horrendous hills of the Wissahickon."

Another plaque on the east side of Wissahickon Creek below Kitchen's Lane (Map 28, page 161) commemorates baptisms by immersion that were held here by followers of Joseph Gorgas, a Seventh Day Baptist who bought the property in the early 1700s. Gorgas's house (called The Monastery) is now part of a stable complex at the rim of the valley. Eventually Gorgas's Baptist Brethren and later Gorgas himself withdrew to the larger semi-monastic community of Seventh Day Baptists at Ephrata, Pennsylvania.

Also in a religious vein is the sojourn in the Wissahickon woods of Johann Kelpius and his following of about forty men. They were German Pietists who emigrated to America in 1694 and settled near the west rim of the Wissahickon Valley at what is now Hermit Lane near the Henry Avenue bridge. Calling themselves the Society of the

Woman in the Wilderness, they awaited the coming of the millennium, which they believed would occur near the end of the century. They built an enormous log house—the Tabernacle of the Mystic Brotherhood—that had an observatory on its roof where they watched for the arrival of the Woman, representative of the spirit of early Christianity, which they sought to emulate in their celibacy and primitive living. Kelpius himself is said to have lived or meditated in a nearby cave. Following the death of Kelpius in 1708, his followers dispersed.

At the foot of Hermit Lane is a bridge leading to Lincoln Drive, where—on the south side of the creek—two taverns, the Log Cabin and the Maple Springs Hotel, formerly stood.

Many of the historic features, trails, and other amenities of the Wissahickon Valley in Philadelphia are maintained by the efforts of the Friends of the Wissahickon. For information about the conservation programs and recreational activities of this group, write to Friends of the Wissahickon, P.O. Box 4068, Philadelphia, PA 19118.

≈ ≈ ≈ ≈

TO ENTHUSIASTS OF GEOLOGY, *Wissahickon* is more than just the peculiar name of a Philadelphia creek. The word identifies a broad band of more-or-less similar rocks extending from Trenton, through Philadelphia, across southeastern Pennsylvania, and into Delaware and eastern Maryland. It was at Wissahickon Creek, where the stream valley has cut deeply into bedrock, that the geologic unit called the Wissahickon Formation was first studied and described.

In Philadelphia the boundary between the Piedmont Province and the Coastal Plain is defined largely by the zone where the hard crystalline bedrock of the Wissahickon Formation dips southeastwardly beneath the thick blanket of Coastal Plain silt, sand, and gravel. At Tinicum (discussed in Chapter 17) the surface of the Wissahickon Formation protrudes upward through the silt and sand at a few points to form incongruous hills, such as Tinicum Island, within the Coastal Plain. Because they are resistant to erosion, the Wissahickon rocks form the dramatic highlands of Roxborough, Chestnut Hill, and Germantown. Cascades and rapids have developed where the Schuylkill River, Wissahickon Creek, and other streams cross the Wissahickon Formation, as is characteristic of the Fall Zone between the Piedmont and Coastal Plain.

Most of the rocks that make up the Wissahickon Formation are metamorphic, meaning that they resulted from the application of great heat and pressure to previously existing rocks. For example, a variety of fairly similar schists were formed by the compression of sedimentary shale, which had been created earlier in an underwater environment by the deposition and consolidation of mud. These schists reflect their sedimentary origin by occurring in distinct layers that were laid down as horizontal beds. Later the beds of shale were tilted and folded by movements in the earth's crust. The pressure that caused this deformation probably also caused the sedimentary shale to change into schist, which is by far the most abundant type of rock within the Wissahickon Formation.

One result of the application of heat or pressure is recrystallization, by which are formed mineral crystals larger than those—and sometimes chemically different from those—that previously existed in the rock. Shale is made of very small mineral fragments, but schist has visible flaky crystals composed of yet other minerals. The crystals in schist are highly foliated, meaning that they occur in parallel sheets formed at right angles to the direction from which pressure was applied. The foliation produces a marked cleavage along which the rock splits apart.

The tendency of crystals to reorient and adjust to directional pressure is more marked in some minerals than in others. Mica, for example, readily reorients to pressure. In the Wissahickon Valley the schist commonly contains shiny, flat crystals of mica, which sometimes can be found on the surface of the ground or in the streambed as mica flakes or even "books" that can be separated into many thin crystal sheets. Chemical analysis shows that the mica is composed of the same elements that previously were present in the minerals found in the sedimentary beds of shale—and before that in the clay from which the shale was formed—except that the elements have been recombined and rearranged by metamorphism into the micaceous minerals abundant in schist. Also, some outcroppings of schist are peppered with dark-red, nearly round crystals of garnet.

Gneiss (which also occurs in the Wissahickon Valley) has crystals larger than schist and results from the metamorphosis of igneous rocks or even some sedimentary rocks. Mobilized by pressure or heat, the minerals have reorganized themselves into distinct light and dark bands of different composition. Gneiss is harder than schist and does not show marked foliation or cleavage.

Quartzite, harder still than gneiss, is another metamorphic rock found in the Wissahickon Valley. This dense rock, usually white, is recrystallized sandstone, originally formed by the deposition and cementing of sand. Like gneiss, quartzite lacks foliation or cleavage. The recrystallized grains interlock like joints of a jigsaw puzzle, making quartzite a very obdurate rock, sometimes seen simply lying on the ground in white chunks after everything else in the vicinity has long since weathered, fragmented, and disintegrated into soil.

Various igneous rocks can also be seen at the Wissahickon Valley. Pegmatite and granite are both light-colored igneous rocks that on close examination have a coarse-grained, speckled quality. Their large crystals and lack of foliation reflect the gradual cooling of molten material called *magma* before it reached the surface of the ground. There are, however, other processes by which a sedimentary or metamorphic rock can be altered by heat or pressure so that it becomes pegmatite or granite.

Pegmatite has particularly large crystals. Quartz, mica, and feldspar can be seen easily, often in crystals 0.5 inch across or larger. As an igneous rock, pegmatite usually occurs in thin veins called *sills* that penetrated as magma between beds of sedimentary rock. Pegmatite also occurs in so-called *dikes* cutting across the grain of the surrounding rock, perhaps as a result of flowing through cracks or fissures in the stone. Sometimes *xenoliths* (literally, "foreign rocks") are embedded within pegmatite. They are sedimentary or metamorphic fragments that were enveloped by the igneous intrusion.

The occurrence of alternating layers of schist and quartzite, all of which have been tilted, folded, and intermixed with other metamorphic and igneous rocks, suggests a scenario for the creation of the Wissahickon Formation. It appears that the Wissahickon zone was covered by a shallow sea in which beds of mud and sand were deposited one after another. That, at any rate, is the type of environment in which mud and sand are deposited today along the continental shelf. Beds of sand are laid down in areas close to shore; mud in areas farther from shore. The alternating layers of mud and sand thus suggests that the water in which this deposition occurred fluctuated in depth. As the sediments accumulated, they were compacted by their own weight and cemented to form shale and sandstone. Then a period of regional compression from the southeast and northwest crumpled the beds of sedimentary rock and changed the shale and sandstone to schist and quartzite. At the same time, intrusions of magma penetrated through faults and fissures in the rock. Erosion has subsequently stripped away overlying material, dissected the formation, and exposed the Wissahickon rocks to view.

The most recent occurrence of regional compression fitting this scenario is the Alleghany Orogeny. (*Orogeny* means the process of mountain making.) This mountain-building event occurred between 320 and 225 million years ago, supposedly when Africa collided with North America, thus producing the Appalachian Mountains in much the same way that the more recent collision of India with Asia has produced the Himalayan Mountains. Obviously, Africa and North America have since moved away from each other (and are still doing so). However, there is overwhelming evidence that the regional compression that produced the Piedmont rocks of southeastern Pennsylvania, including the various Wissahickon rocks, occurred during one or another period of mountain building that preceded the Alleghany Orogeny. If so, the Alleghany Orogeny no doubt squeezed the Piedmont rocks still more and, geologists think, thrust them northwestward to their present position.

In the course of your excursions in the Wissahickon Valley, examine the stone outcroppings that occur frequently along the paths, creek, and slopes to see if you can observe any of the rock types and formations described above. For enthusiasts, Bruce K. Goodwin's *Guidebook to the Geology of the Philadelphia Area*, published by the Pennsylvania Geological Survey, provides a detailed discussion of dozens of specific sites within the valley.

≈ ≈ ≈ ≈

SEPTA: Chestnut Hill, served by the R8 Regional Rail Line and several bus routes, provides good access to the northern end of the Wissahickon Valley. Referring to **Map 27** on page 160, from the top of the stairs at Chestnut Hill West Station, follow Germantown Pike north a hundred yards to Rex Avenue. Turn left onto Rex Avenue and follow it down into the park. **Map 25** on page 156 shows that the R8 Regional Rail Line also provides access to the midsection of the Wissahickon Valley from other stations.

As shown on **Map 28** on page 161, the Wissahickon Transfer Center, which is served by several bus routes, provides good access to the southern end of the Wissahickon Valley. The paved path leading upstream is directly across Ridge Avenue from the transfer center.

Map 28 also shows that Wissahickon Station on the R6 Regional Rail Line provides good access to the southern end of the Wissahickon Valley. If you are bringing your bicycle, Wissahickon Station is the best option. From the station follow Ridge Avenue downhill to the paved path that leads up the valley directly across from the Wissahickon Transfer Center.

Telephone (215) 580-7800 for current information on schedules, routes, and connections from your starting point. And telephone (215) 580-7852 for information about taking your bicycle on the train.

AUTOMOBILE DIRECTIONS: The Wissahickon Valley in Philadelphia runs from the Montgomery County line south past

Chestnut Hill to the stream's mouth at the Schuylkill River near Route 1. (See **Map 25** on page 156.) The directions below guide you to parking lots at Bells Mill Road which provides good access from surrounding roads and also immediate access to the Andorra Natural Area and to the carriage road, walkway, and bikeway at Wissahickon Drive (also called Forbidden Drive). Several avenues of approach are outlined.

There are, of course, other access points and parking lots, notably on Northwestern Avenue at the park's northern end (the lots here are small), on Ridge Avenue at the southern end (again, the lot is small), and on Wises Mill Road and Valley Green Road where they dead-end at the bottom of the valley at approximately the park's midpoint. These and other parking lots are shown on the maps, but I suggest that you start by going to Bells Mill Road. (See •11 on **Maps 1 and 2E** on pages 6 and 7.)

From the north or south on Interstate 95: Take Exit 17 for Interstate 676 West toward central Philadelphia. Stay on I-676 past the exits for Broad Street and the Benjamin Franklin Parkway, then merge with Interstate 76 West (Schuylkill Expressway). Once you are on I-76 westbound, follow the directions in the next paragraph.

From the east or west on Interstate 76 (Schuylkill Expressway): Leave the expressway at Exit 31 for Belmont Avenue and Green Lane on the west side of the Schuylkill River opposite Manayunk. At the bottom of the exit ramp, turn across the river and follow Green Lane 0.9 mile straight uphill through Manayunk to an intersection with Ridge Avenue. Turn left and follow Ridge Avenue 3 miles to an intersection at a traffic light where Spring Lane intersects from the left and Bells Mill Road intersects from the right. Turn right and follow Bells Mill Road 0.9 mile downhill to a parking lot on the right. If the lot is full, there is another lot in 0.2 mile on the other side of Wissahickon Creek.

From the west on the Pennsylvania Turnpike: Leave the Turnpike at Exit 25 for Norristown. After paying the toll, take the first ramp down to the right (it is unmarked); the ramp leads onto **Route 422 (Germantown Pike)** east toward Philadelphia. Follow Germantown Pike east 4.2 miles, then turn right at a traffic light onto West Bells Mill Road. Go 0.3 mile downhill to a parking lot on the right. If the lot is full, there is another lot in 0.2 mile on the other side of Wissahickon Creek.

From the east on the Pennsylvania Turnpike: Leave the Turnpike at Exit 26 for Fort Washington. After paying the toll,

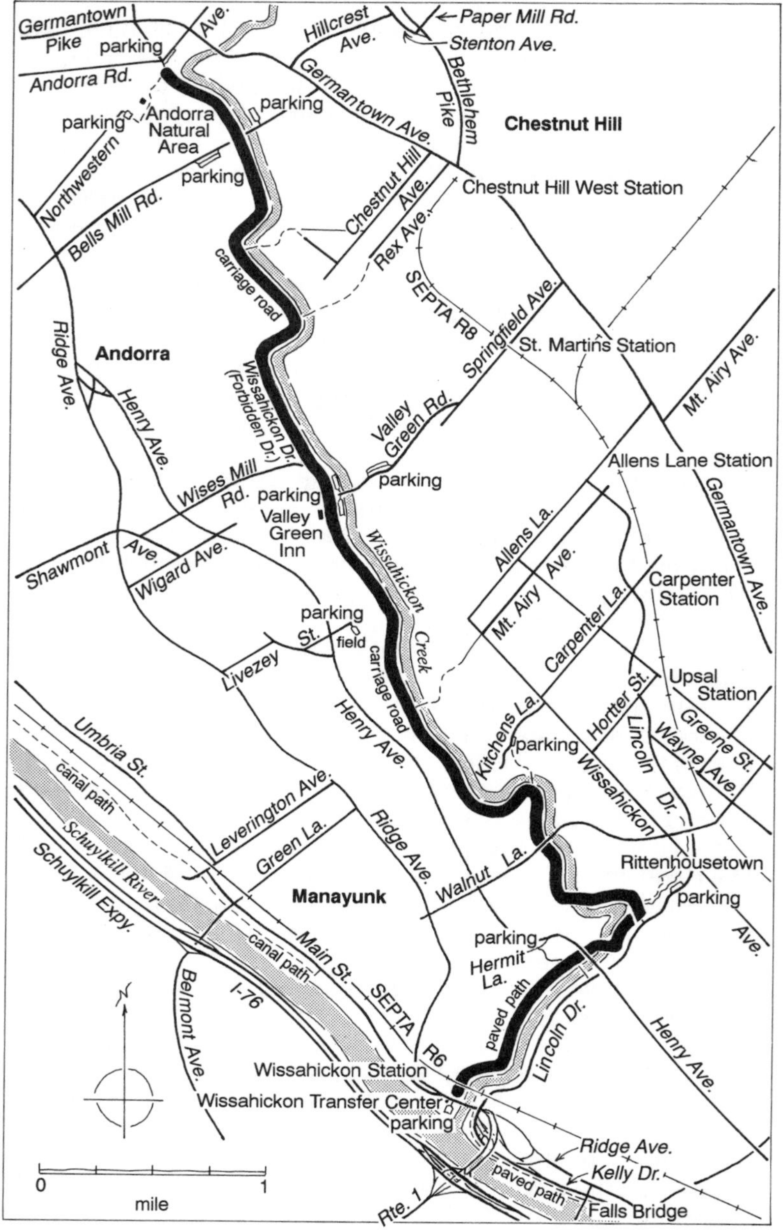

MAP 25—Wissahickon Valley: carriage road (closed to motor vehicles) and bikeway

take **Route 309 South (Fort Washington Expressway)** toward Philadelphia. Go 2.2 miles, then take the exit for Paper Mill Road. At the bottom of the exit ramp, turn right toward Chestnut Hill. Go 1.4 miles to a crossroads at a traffic light with Bethlehem Pike, and there continue straight through the intersection onto Stenton Avenue, which immediately curves right. Follow Stenton Avenue only 0.2 mile, then turn left onto Hillcrest Avenue toward West Bells Mill Road. Go 0.5 mile, then turn left onto Germantown Avenue toward West Bells Mill Road. Go uphill just 0.2 mile, then turn right onto West Bells Mill Road. Go 0.3 mile downhill to a parking lot on the right. If the lot is full, there is another lot in 0.2 mile on the other side of Wissahickon Creek.

From the north or south on Interstate 476 (the Blue Route): The southern end of I-476 starts at Exit 7 off Interstate 95 near Chester; the northern end of I-476 starts at Exits 25-25A off the Pennsylvania Turnpike. <u>If you are coming from the south</u>, leave I-476 at Exit 7A for Conshohocken and Ridge Pike toward Philadelphia. Follow Ridge Pike 3.7 miles to a crossroads at a traffic light where Bells Mill Road intersects from the left and Spring Lane intersects from the right. Turn left onto Bells Mill Road and go 0.9 mile downhill to a parking lot on the right. If the lot is full, there is another lot in 0.2 mile on the other side of Wissahickon Creek.

<u>If you are coming from the north on I-476</u>, take Exit 7 for Norristown, then—after going only 0.1 mile from the top of the exit ramp—bear right just beyond a traffic light onto Alan Wood Road. Go around the jug handle back to the light, and there turn left, which will put you onto Ridge Pike headed toward Philadelphia. Follow Ridge Pike 4 miles to a crossroads at a traffic light where Bells Mill Road intersects from the left and Spring Lane intersects from the right. Turn left onto Bells Mill Road and go 0.9 mile downhill to a parking lot on the right. If the lot is full, there is another lot in 0.2 mile on the other side of Wissahickon Creek.

From the intersection of Bethlehem Pike and Germantown Avenue in Chestnut Hill: Go north on Germantown Avenue 0.8 mile, then turn left onto West Bells Mill Road and follow it 0.3 mile downhill to a parking lot on the right. If the lot is full, there is another lot in 0.2 mile on the other side of Wissahickon Creek.

WALKING AND BICYCLING: **Map 25** opposite provides an overview of the Wissahickon Valley and Wissahickon Drive.

Broad, well-graded, and paved with finely-crushed rock, Wissahickon Drive is the main walkway and bikeway, passable even by thin-tired road bicycles.

Maps 26, 27, and 28 on page 159-161 are more detailed than Map 25 and show footpaths and horse trails along the sides and rim of the Wissahickon Valley. Less used and more rugged than Wissahickon Drive, the trails shown on Maps 27 and 28 are good not only for hiking but also for **mountain biking**—provided that you are prepared to dismount fairly frequently because of rocks, roots, erosion, and steep grades. As a gesture of courtesy, mountain bikers should also dismount as they pass hikers and equestrians on these narrow trails. Please note that bicycles are prohibited from the trails of the Andorra Natural Area shown on Map 26 opposite.

Finally, although I have provided maps, I should add that you really do not need them, except perhaps in the Andorra area. Because the valley is so narrow and steep-sided, its general "organization" is obvious. Wissahickon Drive runs down the bottom of the valley, mostly on the west side of the creek. Other paths follow the sides and rim of the valley, occasionally crossing trails that descend to Wissahickon Drive, to which you can always get by taking one or another path downhill. The yellow-blazed trail follows the western flank and rim of the valley. The orange-blazed trail and—farther up the slope—the white-blazed trail follow the eastern side of the valley. Frequent bridges provide the means to cross Wissahickon Creek from one side of the valley to the other.

An obvious approach to exploring the valley's various trails is to follow one set of blazes down the valley and then to follow another set of blazes, or Wissahickon Drive, back up again. Happy wandering.

MAP 26—Wissahickon Valley: Andorra Natural Area

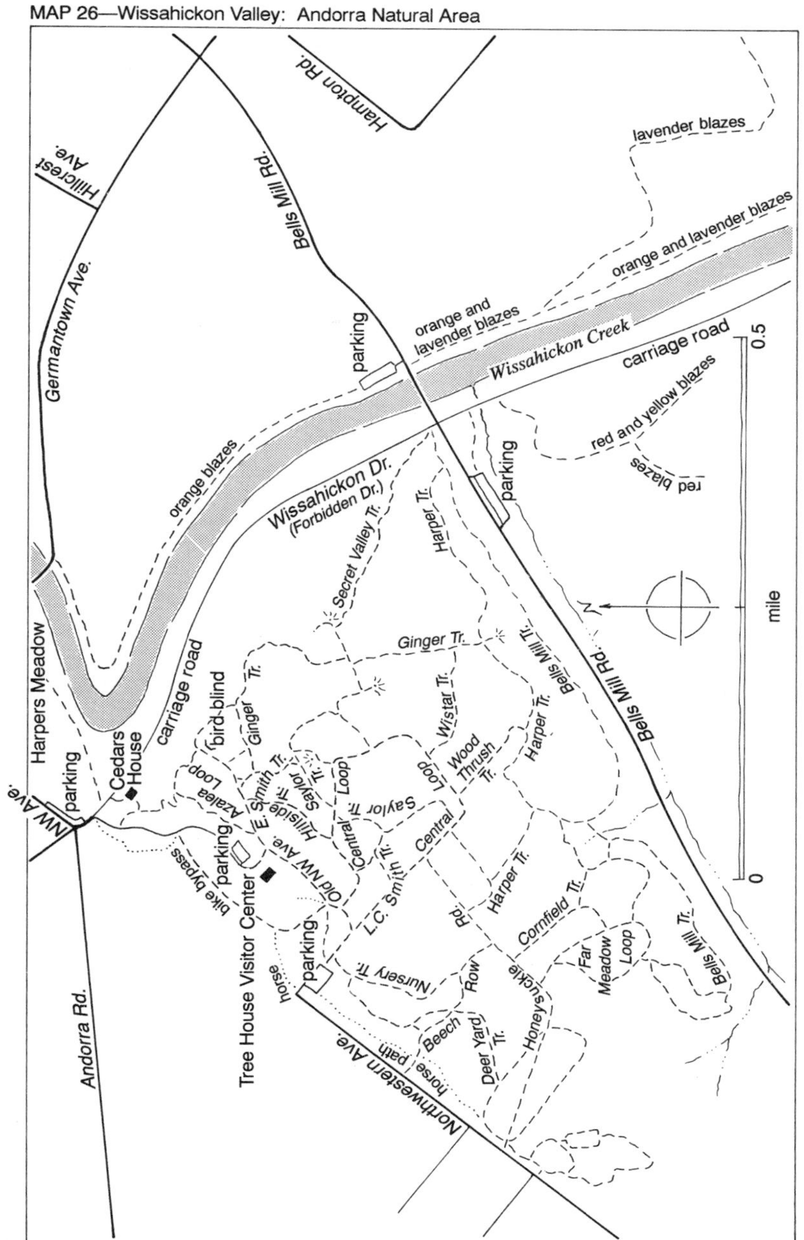

MAP 27—Wissahickon Valley: northern half

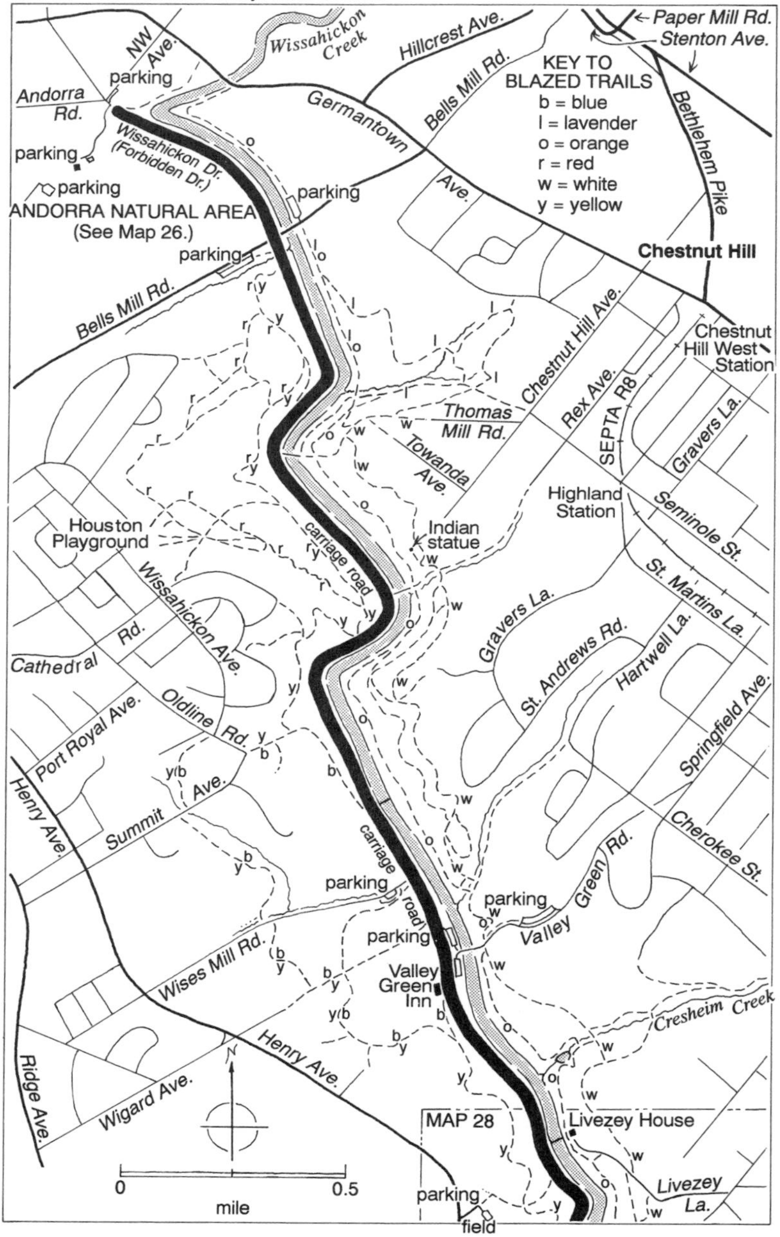

KEY TO BLAZED TRAILS
b = blue
l = lavender
o = orange
r = red
w = white
y = yellow

MAP 28—Wissahickon Valley: southern half

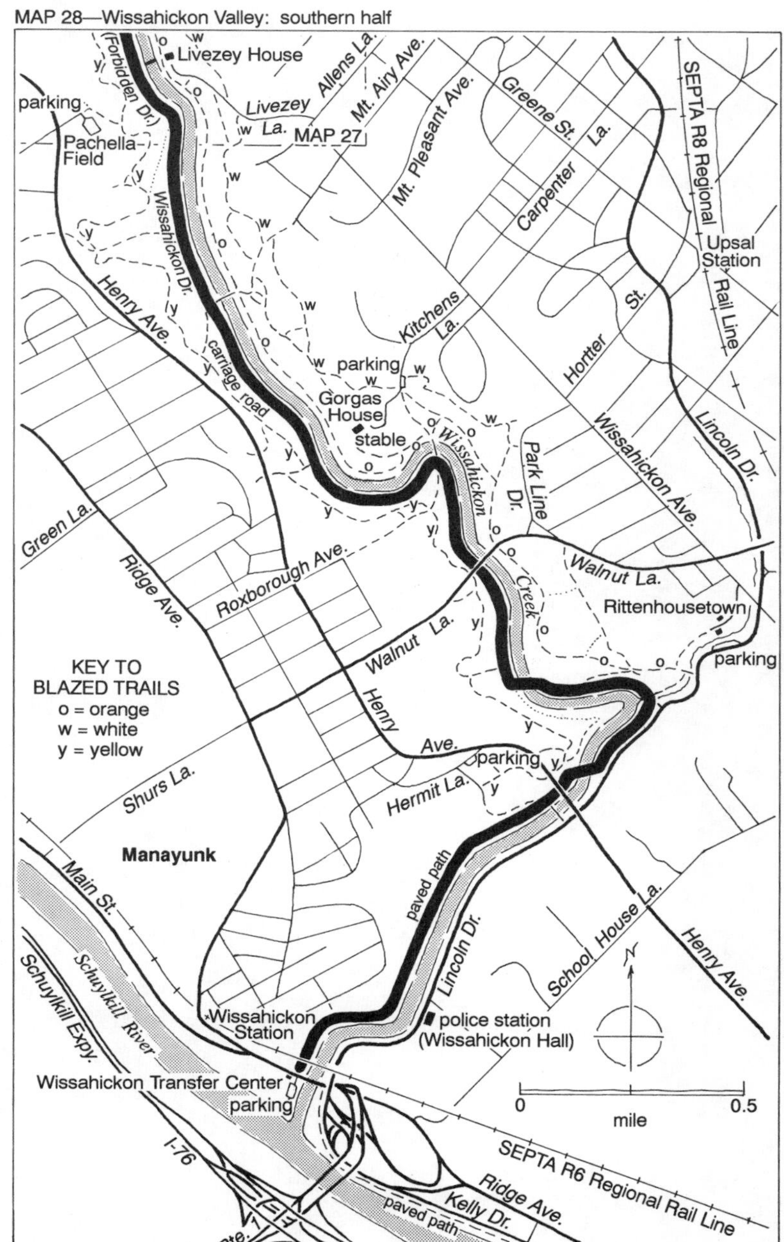

12

THE SCHUYLKILL CENTER FOR ENVIRONMENTAL EDUCATION

Walking and ski touring. As shown on Map 29 on page 167, about 5 miles of foot trails lead through meadows and wooded ravines where the Upper Roxborough highlands slope steeply toward the Schuylkill River at the northwest corner of Philadelphia. This private, 500-acre wildlife preserve also includes an interpretive building that houses exhibits, classrooms, a laboratory, auditorium, bookstore, and library. For information on the programs, courses, field trips, demonstration projects, and family events conducted by The Schuylkill Center for Environmental Education, telephone (215) 482-7300.

The Schuylkill Center is open Monday through Saturday from 8:30 to 5, and on Sunday from 1 to 5. It is closed Sundays in August and major holidays. An admission fee is charged. Dogs and off-road bicycling are prohibited.

THE LARGE TRACT of fields and woods at The Schuylkill Center for Environmental Education probably has changed less during the last three centuries than any other area of comparable size in Philadelphia. Even the Wissahickon and Pennypack valleys have seen the development and demise of numerous mills and quarries. Fairmount Park, crisscrossed with roads and dotted with eighteenth-century mansions, nineteenth-century monuments, and twentieth-century recreational and cultural amenities, tells its own story of change. But the land at the Schuylkill Center, from the time of William Penn to the establishment of the nature preserve in 1965, was simply farmland and pasture. Now much of the area has reverted to woods, presumably as it was before the first European settlers arrived.

Traces of the farms remain. Several farmhouses are occupied by staff members of the nature center. A ruined springhouse is set into the bluff. Old aerial photographs show that as late as 1936 most of the

Common Milkweed, *Asclepias syriaca*

property was still fields. The last farming done here was a dairy operation, which ceased in 1957. Now a few fields are kept clear only by periodic mowing and burning in order to provide varied wildlife habitat. Deer are a common sight at dusk.

In 1694 the land that is now The Schuylkill Center was included in a grant from William Penn to several of his creditors, including Isaac Norris, whose name was later given to Norristown. During the following two centuries the property was divided into many parcels that were reassembled in 1886, when Henry Howard Houston acquired the entire tract. A director of the Pennsylvania Railroad and an investor in Pennsylvania oil fields and western gold mines, Houston bought a large area on both sides of the Wissahickon Valley. For the next seventy years his family held the tract that later was to become the preserve, leasing it to farmers. In 1946 the United Nations almost purchased the property as the site of its headquarters, but at the last moment, while the Houston family representatives were on the train to New York to close the deal, John D. Rockefeller, Jr., scotched the transaction by offering the United Nations $8.5 million to buy land bordering the East River on Manhattan. Twenty years later the Houstons sold their property for a nominal price to the newly organized Schuylkill Valley Nature Center, a non-profit organization that later changed its name to The Schuylkill Center for Environmental Education.

≈ ≈ ≈ ≈

SEPTA: Buses 9, 27, and 32 pass Port Royal Avenue either on Henry Avenue or Ridge Avenue. (See the northeast corner of **Map 29** on page 167.) However, getting from one or the other of these two bus stops to The Schuylkill Center entails walking about half a mile along Port Royal Avenue and Hagys Mill Road, neither of which have sidewalks.

Telephone (215) 580-7800 for current information on schedules, routes, and connections from your starting point.

AUTOMOBILE DIRECTIONS: The Schuylkill Center in northwest Philadelphia occupies, in part, the wooded bluff that one sees across the Schuylkill River while driving in and out of the city on the Schuylkill Expressway. The center is located on the high ridge that separates the Schuylkill Valley from the Wissahickon Valley. Access is off Ridge Avenue (Ridge Pike) not far south of the boundary with Montgomery County. (See •12 on **Maps 1 and 2E** on pages 6 and 7.) Several avenues of approach are described below.

From the north or south on Interstate 95: Take Exit 17 for Interstate 676 West toward central Philadelphia. Stay on I-676 past the exits for Broad Street and the Benjamin Franklin Parkway, then merge with Interstate 76 West (Schuylkill Expressway). Once you are on I-76 westbound, follow the directions in the next paragraph.

From the east or west on Interstate 76 (Schuylkill Expressway): Leave the expressway at Exit 31 for Belmont Avenue and Green Lane on the west side of the Schuylkill River opposite Manayunk. At the bottom of the exit ramp, turn across the river and follow Green Lane 0.9 mile straight uphill through Manayunk to an intersection with Ridge Avenue. Turn left and follow Ridge Avenue 2.2 miles to an intersection at a traffic light with Port Royal Avenue. Turn left and follow Port Royal Avenue just 0.2 mile, then turn right and follow Hagys Mill Road 0.3 mile to the entrance to The Schuylkill Center on the left.

From the west on the Pennsylvania Turnpike: Leave the Turnpike at Exit 25 for Norristown. After paying the toll, take the first ramp down to the right (it is unmarked); the ramp leads onto **Route 422 (Germantown Pike)** east toward Philadelphia. Follow Germantown Pike east 4.2 miles, then turn right at a traffic light onto West Bells Mill Road. Go 1.4 miles down into the Wissahickon Valley and up the other side to an intersection at a traffic light with Ridge Avenue. Cross Ridge Avenue and continue straight on Spring Lane 0.6 mile, then turn left onto Hagys Mill Road and go 0.3 mile to the entrance to The Schuylkill Center on the right.

From the east on the Pennsylvania Turnpike: Leave the Turnpike at Exit 26 for Fort Washington. After paying the toll, take **Route 309 South (Fort Washington Expressway)** toward Philadelphia. Go 2.2 miles, then take the exit for Paper Mill Road. At the bottom of the exit ramp, turn right toward Chestnut Hill. Go 1.4 miles to a crossroads at a traffic light with Bethlehem Pike, and there continue straight through the intersection onto Stenton Avenue, which immediately curves right. Follow Stenton Avenue only 0.2 mile, then turn left onto Hillcrest Avenue toward West Bells Mill Road. Go 0.5 mile, then turn left onto Germantown Avenue toward West Bells Mill Road. Go uphill just 0.2 mile, then turn right onto West Bells Mill Road. Follow it 1.4 miles, descending into the Wissahickon Valley and up the other side to an intersection at a traffic light with Ridge Avenue. Cross Ridge Avenue and continue straight on Spring Lane 0.6 mile, then turn left onto Hagys Mill Road and go 0.3 mile to the entrance to The Schuylkill Center on the right.

From the north or south on Interstate 476 (the Blue Route): The southern end of I-476 starts at Exit 7 off Interstate 95 near Chester; the northern end of I-476 starts at Exits 25-25A off the Pennsylvania Turnpike. If you are coming from the south, leave I-476 at Exit 7A for Conshohocken and Ridge Pike toward Philadelphia. Follow Ridge Pike 3.7 miles to a crossroads at a traffic light where Bells Mill Road intersects from the left and Spring Lane intersects from the right. Turn right onto Spring Lane and follow it 0.6 mile, then turn left onto Hagys Mill Road and go 0.3 mile to the entrance to The Schuylkill Center on the right.

If you are coming from the north on I-476, take Exit 7 for Norristown, then—after going only 0.1 mile from the top of the exit ramp—bear right just beyond a traffic light onto Alan Wood Road. Go around the jug handle back to the light, and there turn left, which will put you onto Ridge Pike headed toward Philadelphia. Follow Ridge Pike 4 miles to a crossroads at a traffic light where Bells Mill Road intersects from the left and Spring Lane intersects from the right. Turn right onto Spring Lane and follow it 0.6 mile, then turn left onto Hagys Mill Road and go 0.3 mile to the entrance to The Schuylkill Center on the right.

From the intersection of Bethlehem Pike and Germantown Avenue in Chestnut Hill: Go north on Germantown Avenue 0.8 mile, then turn left onto West Bells Mill Road and follow it 1.4 miles, descending into the Wissahickon Valley and up the other side to an intersection at a traffic light with Ridge Avenue. Cross Ridge Avenue and continue straight on Spring Lane 0.6 mile, then turn left onto Hagys Mill Road and go 0.3 mile to the entrance to The Schuylkill Center on the right.

WALKING: After paying the admission fee at the education center, where there are interesting exhibits and an excellent bookstore, you can reach the trail system shown on **Map 29** opposite by exiting from the back of the building.

The paved Widener Trail is suitable for wheelchairs and can be reached from an exit at the northeast end of the education center, where there is a handicap parking area.

MAP 29—The Schuylkill Center for Environmental Education

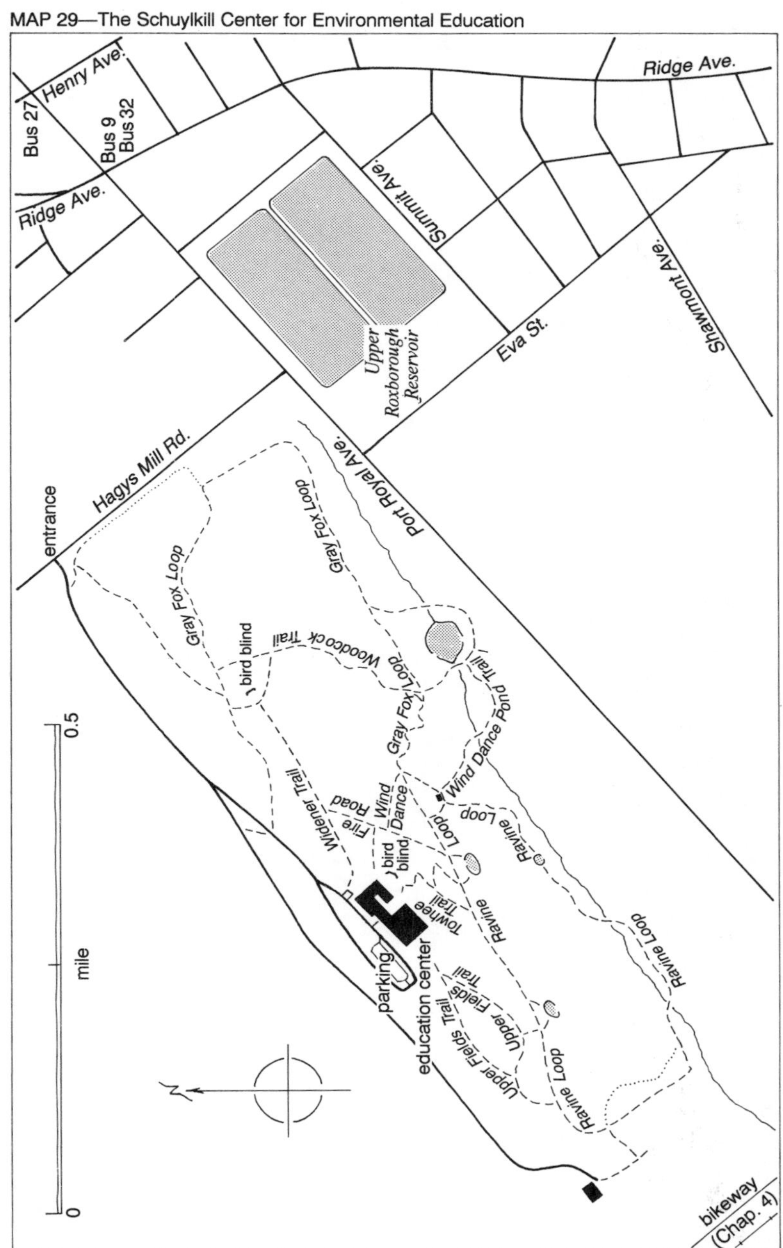

13

PENNYPACK PARK
LORIMER PARK

Walking, jogging, ski touring, and bicycling. Stretching from Pine Road near the boundary with Montgomery County to Torresdale Avenue near the Delaware River, Pennypack Park in northeast Philadelphia provides the opportunity to follow a winding and wooded stream valley for as much as 17 miles round-trip on a paved hike-bike path. If you have an infant or small child, the paved path next to Pennypack Creek is an excellent promenade for buggies and strollers, although occasionally the grade is fairly steep. The park also has many miles of foot trails and horse paths, nearly all of which are excellent for mountain biking. And just upstream from Pennypack Park is Montgomery County's Lorimer Park, with still more trails suitable for hiking and mountain biking.

The bold line on Map 30 on page 173 shows the 8.4-mile paved hike-bike path. Maps 31 and 32 on pages 176 and 177 show the Pennypack Valley in greater detail, including other trails. A glimpse at the maps shows that between Pine Road in the north and Frankford Avenue in the south, it is possible to walk or cycle up one side of Pennypack Creek and down the other. Along the way are four small bridges (in addition to the regular road bridges) that will enable you to cross safely from one side of the creek to the other in order to make a circuit of whatever length you want.

On Verree Road just east of Pennypack Creek is the Pennypack Environmental Center; telephone (215) 671-0440 or stop by for information on guided hikes, workshops, and events at Pennypack Park. Although the main path though the Environmental Center is open to hikers, equestrians, and cyclists alike, please note that the other trails in the area bounded by Verree Road, Bloomfield Avenue, Pine Road, and Pennypack Creek are for walkers only.

Pennypack Park is open from dawn until dusk and Lorimer Park is open from 8 A.M. until sunset. Dogs must be leashed. Bicyclists must yield to other trail users, keep their speed to a moderate, safe pace, and ride single file.

Pennypack Park is managed by the Fairmount Park Commission; telephone (215) 685-0000. Lorimer Park is managed by the Montgomery County Department of Parks and Recreation; telephone (610) 278-3555.

BEFORE AMERICAN INDUSTRY converted from water power to steam during the second half of the nineteenth century, Pennypack Creek (like Wissahickon Creek) was the site of a chain of water-driven mills and factories, some of which are still evidenced by occasional mill dams or recalled by the names of various roads. In the Holmesburg section of Philadelphia there is Mill Street, site of several old factories. Farther upstream are Axe Factory Road and Verree Road, named for Robert Verree and his descendants, owners of a small mill complex. In Montgomery County are Fetter's Mill Road, Paper Mill Road, Mill Road, and Saw Mill Lane. The first recorded mills were erected in the late seventeenth century, but there may have been earlier, unrecorded mills built by the Swedish settlers who preceded the establishment of Penn's colony. By one estimate about thirty-five mills—including gristmills, sawmills, fulling mills, linseed oil mills, powder mills, shovel works, and other factories—were powered by Pennypack Creek and its tributaries in the early 1800s.

Smedley's 1862 *Atlas of the City of Philadelphia* shows ten mills along the portion of Pennypack Creek within the municipal boundaries. At Holmesburg—at that time separated from the center of Philadelphia by open farmland—there were Pennock's Grist and Saw Mill, Jonathan Large & Brothers' Cotton Factory, and an "old saw mill," all on the west bank downstream from the bridge of the Bristol Turnpike (Frankford Avenue). Part of the Holmesburg dam still stands above the bridge. The remains of a mill race—now a shallow trough—are discernible stretching from the west end of the dam, under Frankford Avenue, and downstream toward Torresdale Avenue. Incidentally, the present-day Frankford Avenue bridge is said to incorporate within its structure the original stone spans built in 1697, making it one of the oldest bridges in the United States. It was part of the King's Highway linking Philadelphia and New York. In 1803 a tollgate was erected at the bridge when the road became part of the Frankford and Bristol Turnpike. The bridge was widened in 1895, so it is not likely that any of the original stonework is visible.

Rowland's Shovel Works, founded in 1826, is shown in Smedley's atlas at the confluence of Pennypack Creek and Wooden Bridge Run about three-quarters of a mile above Holmesburg. Nearby was a gristmill, and upstream above Welsh Road was the small factory community—including the mill and about eighteen houses—of Andrew Hartel & Company's Pennypack Print Works, where calico was bleached, dyed, and printed. Still intact, the Hartel dam is located upstream from the lower Rhawn Street Bridge near a park access road and parking lot to which the automobile directions at the end of the chapter will guide you. Rowland's and Hartel's were large operations. The former employed fifty hands and the latter one hundred fifty hands by the late 1800s, when both factories were powered by steam as well as by water.

A photograph of Hartel's factory in about 1910 shows not only a substantial mill building but also a valley covered with scrubby, immature forest. During the eighteenth and early nineteenth centuries, the valley probably was stripped of trees, with pastures sloping down to the creek.

Other Pennypack mills shown in Smedley's atlas are Lathrop's Cotton Factory in LaGrange, a small community of about two dozen houses clustered near the creek at the Bustleton Pike bridge. At Krewstown Road (shown as Krenstone Lane) there was the Walnut Mill, and about half a mile upstream, Prince's Mill. The community of Verreeville, where axes, hatchets, and shovels were made, was located where Verree Road crosses the creek. The dam still stands upstream from the road, along which there are a couple of old Verreeville houses.

By the beginning of the twentieth century, when the 8-mile stretch of Pennypack Valley within Philadelphia was acquired by the Fairmount Park Commission, most of the Pennypack mills had been abandoned. The advent of steam power freed manufacturers from the need to locate their factories in narrow stream valleys, where the works were subject to periodic flooding. Also, the shift in wheat cultivation from the eastern states to the northern Great Plains and beyond doomed the many small gristmills of the mid-Atlantic region. Minneapolis became the nation's chief grain milling center. Those factories which remained in the Pennypack Valley in the early 1900s, such as Rowland's Shovel Works and Hartel's Pennypack Print Works, were purchased by the city starting in 1905 and eventually torn down. Now the chief relics of the various Pennypack mills are an occasional dam in a valley that has otherwise reverted to deep woods. Developed with footpaths, horse trails, and a paved hike-bike path, the valley is now an outstanding linear park.

≈ ≈ ≈ ≈

SEPTA: As shown on **Map 30** opposite, the R7 Regional Rail Line passes near the southern end of Pennypack Park. Get off the train at Holmesburg Junction. Descend the stairs next to the bridge at the end of the platform, then turn left and follow Rhawn Street a few hundred yards to an intersection with Torresdale Avenue. Turn right onto Torresdale Avenue and go 0.3 mile. After crossing Pennypack Creek, turn left onto the paved bikeway opposite the old Philadelphia Prison.

Telephone (215) 580-7800 for current information on schedules, routes, and connections from your starting point. You may also want to inquire about the large number of bus routes that provide access to Pennypack Park at various points. And telephone (215) 580-7852 for information about taking your bicycle on the R7 train.

AUTOMOBILE DIRECTIONS: Pennypack Park in northeast Philadelphia extends from the Montgomery County line south to Torresdale Avenue near the Delaware River. (See •13 on **Map 1** on page 6; see also **Map 30** opposite.)The directions below guide you to a set of parking lots off Rhawn Street, which provides good access from Interstate 95 and Route 1 (Roosevelt Boulevard). Several avenues of approach are described below.

There are, of course, other access points and parking lots, notably at Frankford Avenue just west of the bridge across Pennypack Creek (the lot here is small and is located across the river from the paved path), at Krewstown Road east of the creek and under a high railroad bridge, at Verree Road just west of the creek, and on Pine Road just west of the bridge at the park's northern end. The lot at Pine Road is large and provides access not only to the Pennypack hike-bike path, but also to Lorimer Park, which can be reached by crossing Pine Road and following the creek upstream. (Be cautious; there is no traffic light at the Pine Road crossing.) The official entrance and parking lot for Lorimer Park are off Moredon Road, which intersects with Pine Road east of Pennypack Creek. These various parking lots are shown on the maps, but if you are coming from any distance and are unfamiliar with the area, I suggest that you start by going to the large lot off Rhawn Street, as described below.

From the north or south on Interstate 95: Take Exit 22 for Academy Road toward the Northeast Philadelphia Airport. Follow Academy Road only as far as the first traffic light, and

MAP 30—Pennypack Park: 8.4-mile hike-bike path

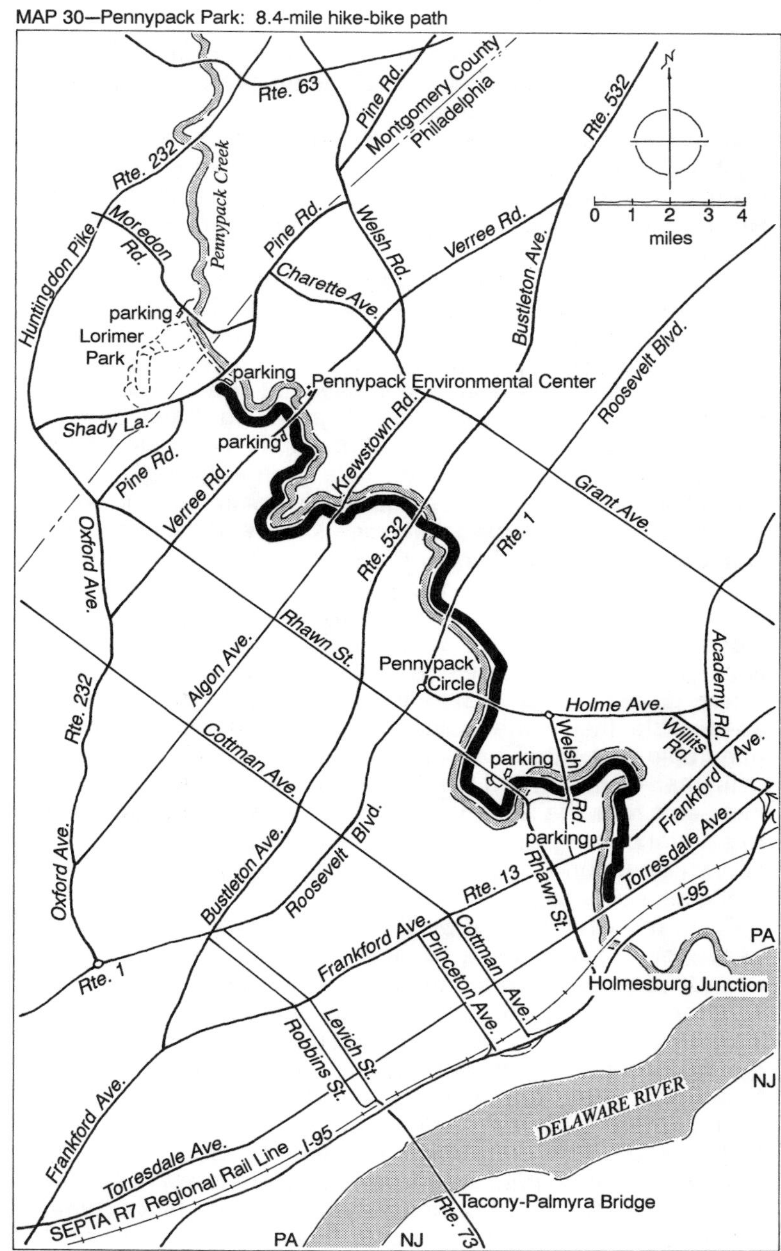

there turn left onto Frankford Avenue. Go 1.2 miles (in the process crossing Pennypack Creek) to an intersection at a traffic light with Rhawn Street. Turn right onto Rhawn Street and follow it 0.8 mile—taking care (after 0.4 mile) not to fork right onto Cresco Avenue—then turn left onto a park road that leads to several parking lots. Curve left downhill and under the Rhawn Street bridge to the lowermost parking lot, located next to the hike-bike path.

From Interstate 76 (the Schuylkill Expressway): Leave the expressway at Exit 34 for Route 1 North (Roosevelt Boulevard). Follow **Route 1 North** about 9 miles; toward the end of this distance you will want to be on the frontage road as far to the right as possible. If you have not already gotten onto the frontage road, do so at a large sign saying "Pennypack Circle, local traffic," then turn right at a traffic light onto Rhawn Street. Follow Rhawn Street 0.7 mile, then—just beyond a traffic light where Holmehurst Street intersects from the left—turn right onto a park road that leads to several parking lots. Curve left downhill and under the Rhawn Street bridge to the lowermost parking lot, located next to the hike-bike path.

From the north—or that is, from Bucks County—on Route 1: Follow Route 1 South into Philadelphia and past Northeast Philadelphia Airport. As you approach Pennypack Circle, do *not* exit for local traffic. Instead, get as far to the left as possible, then—after going through the underpass—turn left at a traffic light onto Rhawn Street. Follow Rhawn Street 0.7 mile, then—just beyond a traffic light where Holmehurst Street intersects from the left—turn right onto a park road that leads to several parking lots. Curve left downhill and under the Rhawn Street bridge to the lowermost parking lot, located next to the hike-bike path.

From the east or west on the Pennsylvania Turnpike: Leave the turnpike at Exit 28 for Route 1 South toward Central Philadelphia. Stay toward the right to pay your toll, then fork right for Route 1 South. From the top of the ramp, follow Route 1 South 6.6 miles. As you approach Pennypack Circle, do *not* exit for local traffic. Instead, get as far to the left as possible, then—after going through the underpass—turn left at a traffic light onto Rhawn Street. Follow Rhawn Street 0.7 mile, then—just beyond a traffic light where Holmehurst Street intersects from the left—turn right onto a park road that leads to several parking lots. Curve left downhill and under the Rhawn Street bridge to the lowermost parking lot, located next to the hike-bike path.

WALKING AND BICYCLING: Map 30 on page 173 provides an overview of Pennypack Park and the 8.4-mile hike-bike path. Paved with asphalt, the hike-bike path is suitable even for thin-tired road bicycles.

Maps 31 and 32 on pages 176 and 177 are more detailed than Map 30 and show footpaths and horse trails at Pennypack Park and Lorimer Park. Less used and more rugged than the paved path, these trails are good not only for hiking but also for **mountain biking**—provided that you are prepared to dismount occasionally because of rocks, roots, erosion, and steep grades. As a gesture of courtesy, mountain bikers should also dismount as they pass hikers and equestrians on these narrow trails.

MAP 31—Pennypack Park (northern section) and Lorimer Park

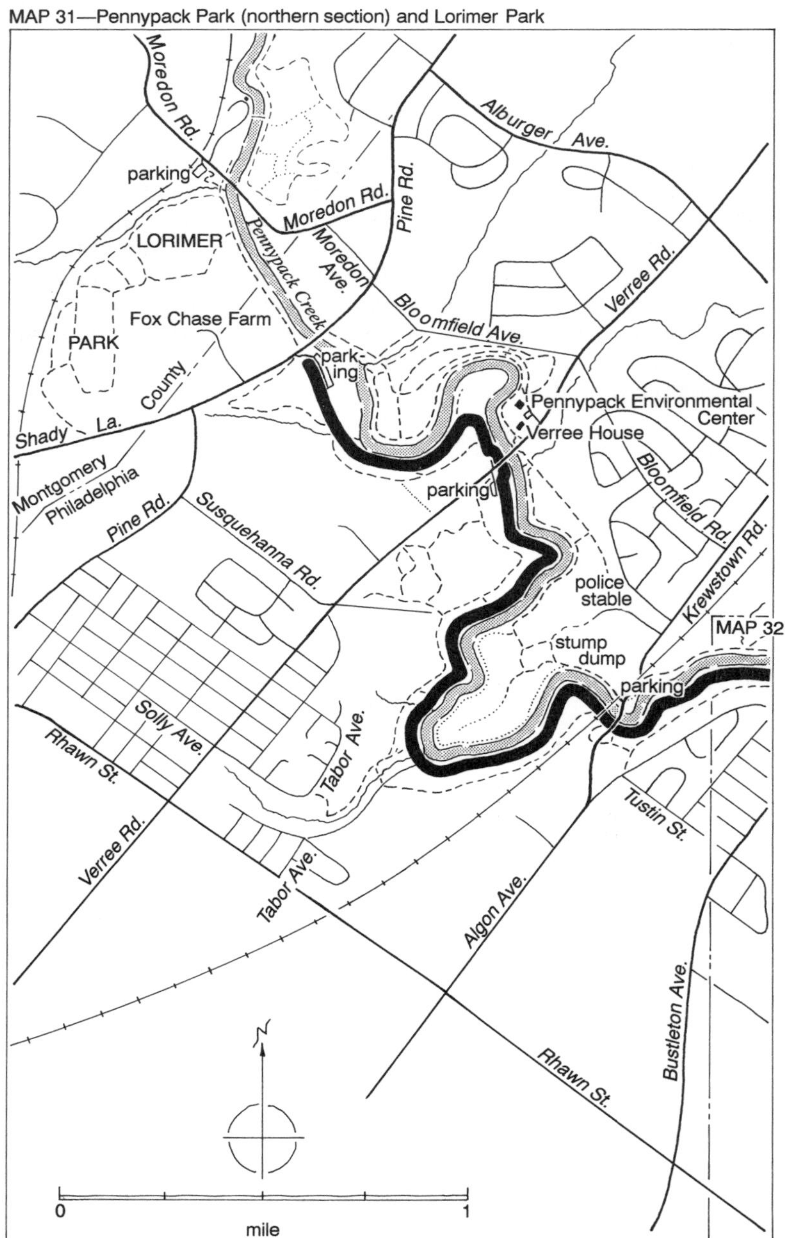

MAP 32—Pennypack Park (southern section)

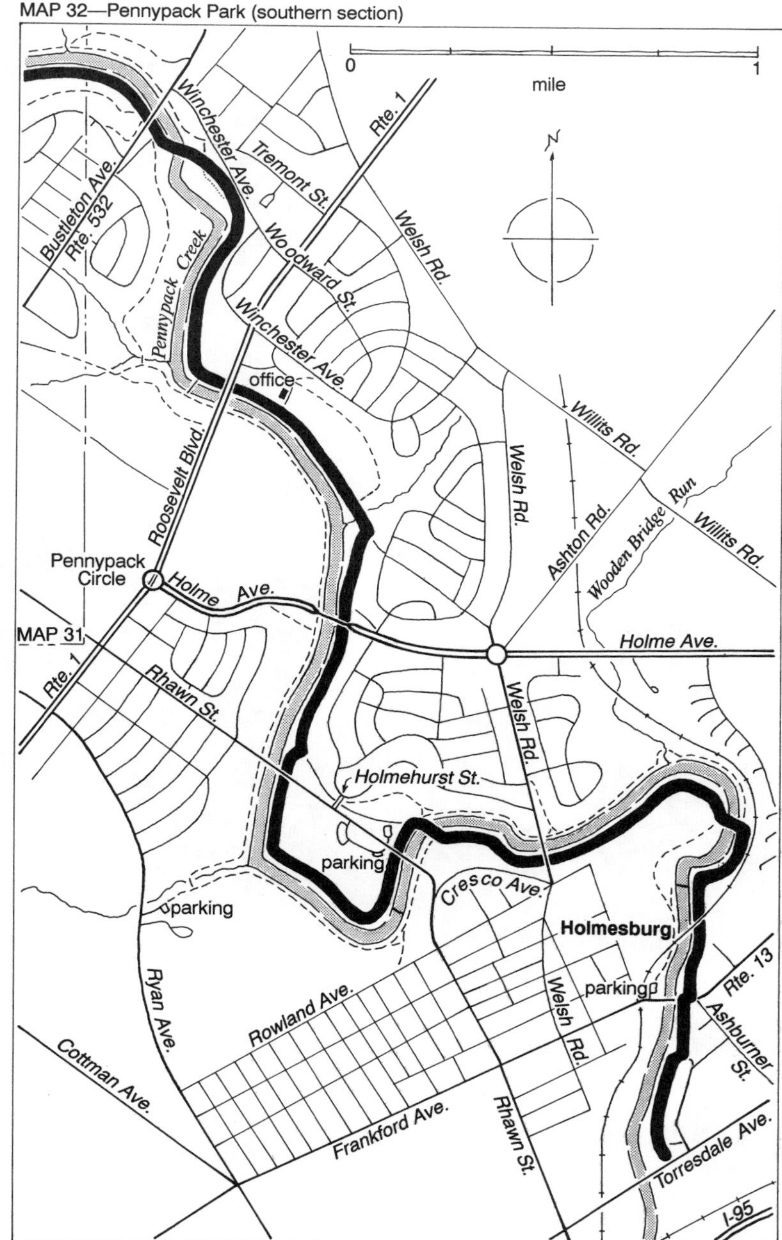

14

FAIRMOUNT PARK

Riverside paths, Belmont circuit, and Tour de Fairmount

Walking, jogging, and bicycling. This chapter outlines three excursions through different parts of Fairmount Park.

The 8-mile loop shown by the bold line on Map 33 on page 184 is probably the most popular exercise circuit in Philadelphia. The loop follows paved paths along both banks of the Schuylkill River between Falls Bridge and the art museum. Although the paths are never far from roads and often are merely glorified sidewalks, the river and its bordering bluffs, greenery, and gardens provide outstanding scenery. For this circuit, the pertinent automobile directions start on page 183, and the corresponding walking or cycling directions start on page 185. The best time to go is on Saturday and Sunday, April through October, between 7 A.M. and noon, when West River Drive is closed to cars. (On the same days between noon and 5 P.M., automobile access to the parking lots on West River Drive is permitted via Montgomery Drive, but through-traffic is still prohibited.) To avoid crowds, go early. Cyclists using the riverside paths must ride single file, keep their speed to a moderate, safe pace, and yield to pedestrians.

Very different from the riverside paths is the 3-mile hiking and mountain-biking circuit shown by the bold line on Map 34 on page 188. The loop starts at the Belmont Plateau and follows a dirt road and wide paths through the woods that occupy the west side of the Schuylkill Valley, then returns via the mile-long allée next to Chamounix Drive. (**Note:** The dirt road and wide paths are often used on autumn Saturdays for cross-country running meets that preclude other activities.) For this circuit, the pertinent automobile directions start on page 186, and the corresponding walking or cycling directions start on page 189. For short distances, cyclists must follow park roads open to automobile traffic. Near the end of the circuit, the route passes the historic and handsomely-furnished Belmont Mansion, which is open Tuesday through Friday from 10 to 4 and for which there is a modest admission fee. The Belmont Mansion is managed by the American Women's Heritage Society; telephone (215) 878-8844.

Finally, the bold line on Map 35 on page 195 outlines the Tour de Fairmount, an 18-mile bicycle circuit that—except for the stretches along the riverside paths—follows park roads used also by cars. For this circuit, the pertinent automobile directions start on page 192, and the corresponding cycling directions appear on page 194 opposite Map 35. The map also shows the locations of a dozen historic houses located within the park. Like Belmont Mansion mentioned earlier, most of the houses are open to the public under the management of different civic organizations. For elegance and magnificence, there is no greater collection of eighteenth- and early nineteenth-century show houses anywhere. Although schedules vary from one house to the next, most are open Tuesday through Sunday from 10 to 4; simply knock or ring and wait for a guide to open the door. For most, an admission fee is charged. Early in December and again in mid-April, the Philadelphia Museum of Art sponsors guided tours of the Fairmount Park houses: telephone (215) 684-7926.

Fairmount Park is managed by the Fairmount Park Commission; telephone (215) 685-0000 for information, including fees and hours of the park houses and whether the time when West River Drive is closed to cars has changed.

DURING THE LATTER HALF of the eighteenth century, the land on both sides of the Schuylkill River north of "Faire Mount" (the rocky hill that is now the site of the Philadelphia Museum of Art) comprised the private estates of some of Philadelphia's leading families. Prosperous merchants, bankers, shipowners, judges, and other members of the city's aristocracy of wealth and accomplishment established summer homes and farms along the highlands overlooking the river.

A few of these houses were at first simple summer homes or farmhouses that later were improved and expanded; most, however, were opulent mansions from the start. Mount Pleasant, built atop the east bluff by sea captain and privateersman John Macpherson, was called by John Adams in 1775 "the most elegant seat in Pennsylvania."

Between 1770 and 1799, financier Robert Morris had a farm and elaborate complex of gardens and greenhouses at The Hills just north of Faire Mount. After Morris's bankruptcy the property was acquired by Henry Pratt, who erected the Lemon Hill mansion, now regarded as one of the most elegant Federal-style houses in the country. In 1797 Samuel Breck, later a state senator and congressman, built Sweetbriar on the west bank of the Schuylkill to escape the yellow-fever epidemic that killed ten thousand Philadelphians in the older, crowded part of the city between 1793 and 1800. These and nearly a dozen other eighteenth- and nineteenth-century houses still stand within the park. As noted in the introduction to this chapter, many of the houses have been restored, handsomely furnished with period items, and opened to the public.

Between 1812 and 1822 Philadelphia excavated a reservoir atop Faire Mount and constructed the Fairmount waterworks and dam to supply the city with drinking water. In the following years pressure slowly mounted for public acquisition of the land bordering the river, in order both to protect the purity of the water and to provide a park for the growing city. A small public garden at the waterworks was expanded in 1844 by the purchase of Pratt's Garden at Lemon Hill, a privately-owned tract of 45 acres that previously had been open to the public on an admission-fee basis. In 1855 this land was dedicated as Fairmount Park. Sedgeley, an estate of 34 acres to the north of Lemon Hill, was acquired by the city in 1857.

Galvanized into action by the realization that Philadelphia's "cup of water was in danger of becoming a poisoned chalice," the state legislature established the Fairmount Park Commission in 1867 and authorized the city to expand Fairmount "as open public ground and Park for the preservation of Schuylkill water and of the health and enjoyment of the people forever." Still larger appropriations of land, including the Wissahickon Valley, were approved in 1868. During the next few years the city purchased the estates of Mount Pleasant, Woodford, Sweetbriar, Belmont, Ridgeland, Chamounix, and hundreds of other properties large and small. Jesse George and his sister Rebecca donated the land at Georges Hill, now the site of the Mann Music Center. Chemical works, breweries, paper and cotton mills, carpet and dye works, and other factories along the Schuylkill River and Wissahickon Creek were acquired and demolished.

By 1868 the park's land along the Schuylkill and Wissahickon valleys totaled 4,077 acres. By comparison, New York's Central Park, established in 1854, totals 840 acres. Maps published in conjunction with the Centennial Exhibition, a world's fair held in western Fairmount in 1876 to celebrate the nation's first hundred years of independence, show a configuration of park boundaries and roads little different from what exists today.

≈ ≈ ≈ ≈

THE FAIRMOUNT TROLLEY: Consisting actually of buses fixed up to look like old trolleys, the Fairmount Trolley runs from Independence Hall and other downtown historic sites to Fairmount Park, alternating daily between the west park and east park, where it stops at each of the historic houses.

≈ ≈ ≈ ≈

SEPTA DIRECTIONS TO THE RIVERSIDE CIRCUIT SHOWN ON MAP 33 : Bus 76 provides access to the circuit at the Philadelphia Museum of Art.

The Wissahickon Transfer Center, which is served by several bus routes, is located adjacent to a bikeway that leads downriver 0.6 mile to Falls Bridge and the riverside circuit. (As of 1994, the path at the transfer center consists merely of a sidewalk next to Ridge Avenue and Kelly Drive.) Just uphill from the transfer center is Wissahickon Station on the R6 Regional Rail Line.

Telephone (215) 580-7800 for current information on schedules, routes, and connections from your starting point. And telephone (215) 580-7852 for information about taking your bicycle on the R6 train.

AUTOMOBILE DIRECTIONS TO THE RIVERSIDE CIRCUIT SHOWN ON MAP 33: The main part of Fairmount Park straddles the Schuylkill River north of the Philadelphia Museum of Art. Several avenues of approach are described below.

From downtown Philadelphia: Follow the Benjamin Franklin Parkway northwest toward the art museum. Just before reaching the art museum, fork right for Kelly Drive and follow it north along the river 2.3 miles to a large parking lot on the left. If the lot is full, there is another lot 0.4 mile farther along the river.

From the north or south on Interstate 95: Take Exit 17 for Interstate 676 West toward central Philadelphia. After passing the exit for Broad Street, leave I-676 at the exit for the museum area and Benjamin Franklin Parkway. At the top of the exit ramp, turn right. Go 100 yards, then turn left onto the

MAP 33—Fairmount Park: 8-mile riverside circuit of paved paths

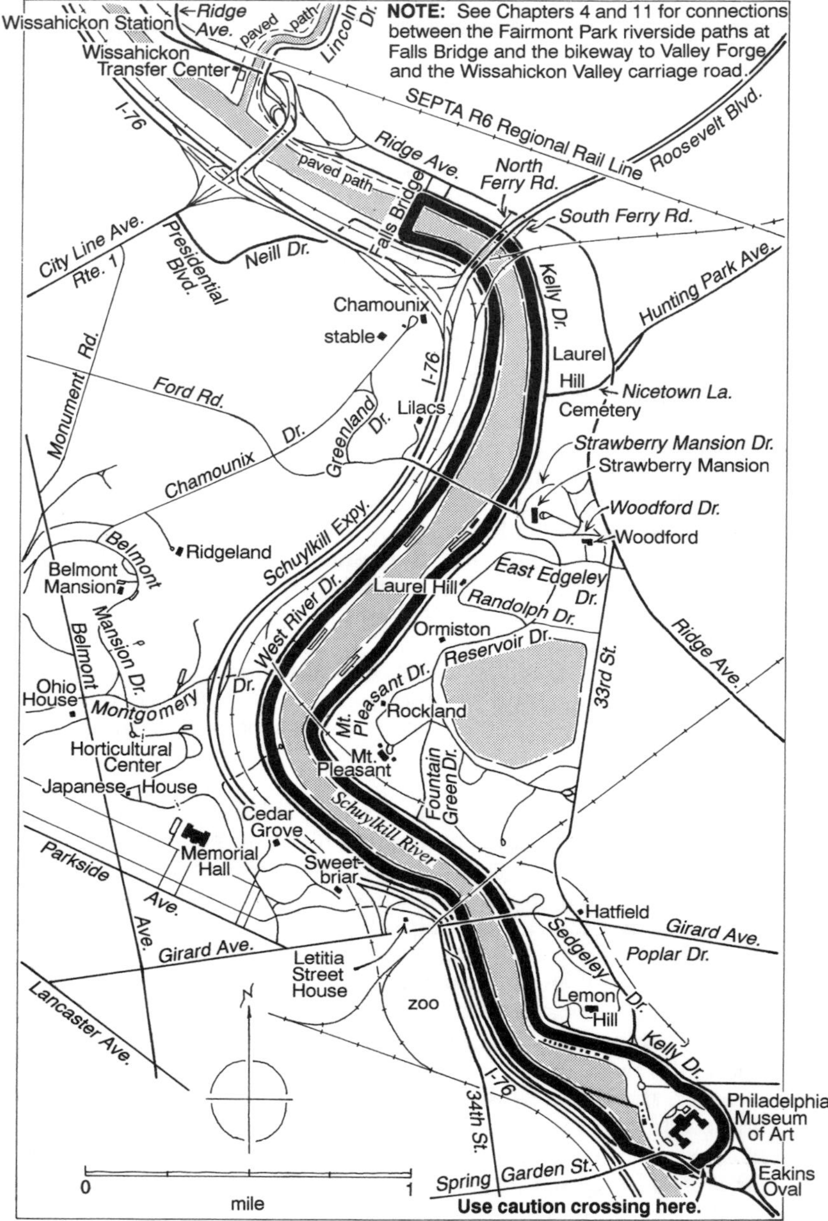

Benjamin Franklin Parkway and move to the right-hand lanes. Just before reaching the art museum, fork right for Kelly Drive and follow it north along the river 2.3 miles to a large parking lot on the left. If the lot is full, there is another lot 0.4 mile farther along the river.

From the east or west on Interstate 76 (Schuylkill Expressway): Exit 35 for Montgomery Drive provides quick access to West River Drive. At the bottom of the exit ramp, turn downhill into the park. At a T-intersection with West River Drive, turn left and continue to the parking lots next to the river. **Remember, however,** that there is no automobile access to West River Drive on Saturday and Sunday, April through October, between 7 A.M. and noon, so on those weekend mornings, you should follow the directions in the next paragraph in order to reach a parking lot on the east side of the river.

Get off I-76 at Exit 32 for Lincoln Drive and Kelly Drive. (If you are coming from the west, the exit is on the left.) After crossing the Schuylkill River, curve tightly left for Kelly Drive. At the bottom of the exit ramp, follow Kelly Drive 1.9 miles to the large parking lot on the right for the East Park Canoe House. If the lot is full, there is another lot 0.4 mile farther along the river.

From the south on City Avenue: Follow City Avenue (Route 1) north. After passing the exits for Interstate 76 (Schuylkill Expressway) and after crossing the Schuylkill River, curve tightly left for Kelly Drive. At the bottom of the exit ramp, follow Kelly Drive 1.9 miles to the large parking lot on the right for the East Park Canoe House. If the lot is full, there is another lot 0.4 mile farther along the river.

WALKING OR BICYCLING ALONG THE RIVER: As shown by the bold line on **Map 33** opposite, paths extend along both banks of the Schuylkill River between the Falls Bridge in the north and the Philadelphia Museum of Art in the south, making possible a circuit of 8 miles. Be cautious wherever cars are near, such as on bridge sidewalks and at parking lots.

Because of protracted construction at the old Fairmount Waterworks, you should circle around the art museum on the landward side. To get to or from the West River Drive bridge south of the museum (not far from the museum's front steps), you must cross an approach-road for the Spring Garden Bridge. There is no traffic light or crosswalk, so be cautious.

Alternatively, by following the sidewalk north from the Falls Bridge along the Schuylkill's east bank for 0.6 mile, you can reach the Wissahickon Valley, where there are many more miles of paths (see Chapter 11). The round-trip distance between the art museum and the northern end of Wissahickon Drive (also called Forbidden Drive) at the boundary with Montgomery County is about 24 miles. Another option is to follow the Schuylkill Valley upriver via the Philadelphia-Valley Forge Bikeway (see Chapter 4). Finally, the Schuylkill River Development Council intends to build a path from the art museum south along the river to Spruce Street. Plans call for the path eventually to extend to the vicinity of Philadelphia International Airport.

≈ ≈ ≈ ≈

SEPTA DIRECTIONS TO THE BELMONT PLATEAU CIRCUIT SHOWN ON MAP 34: Bus 38 follows Belmont Avenue through western Fairmount Park. Get off at the intersection with Montgomery Drive opposite South Georges Hill Drive. Follow Montgomery Drive downhill to the Belmont Plateau.

Telephone (215) 580-7800 for current information on schedules, routes, and connections from your starting point.

AUTOMOBILE DIRECTIONS TO THE BELMONT PLATEAU CIRCUIT SHOWN ON MAP 34: Several avenues of approach are described below, all leading to a parking lot off Montgomery Drive in western Fairmount Park.

From downtown Philadelphia: Take Interstate 76 West (Schuylkill Expressway), then follow the directions two paragraphs below.

From the north or south on Interstate 95: Take Exit 17 for Interstate 676 West toward central Philadelphia. Stay on I-676 West past the exits for Broad Street and the Benjamin Franklin Parkway, then merge with Interstate 76 West (Schuylkill Expressway). Once you are on I-76 westbound, follow the directions in the next paragraph.

From the east or west on Interstate 76 (Schuylkill Expressway): Exit 35 for Montgomery Drive and West River Drive provides quick access to western Fairmount Park. At the bottom of the exit ramp, turn uphill and follow Montgomery Drive only 0.1 mile to the entrance to the Belmont Plateau parking lot on the right.

MAP 34—Fairmount Park: 3-mile circuit from the Belmont Plateau

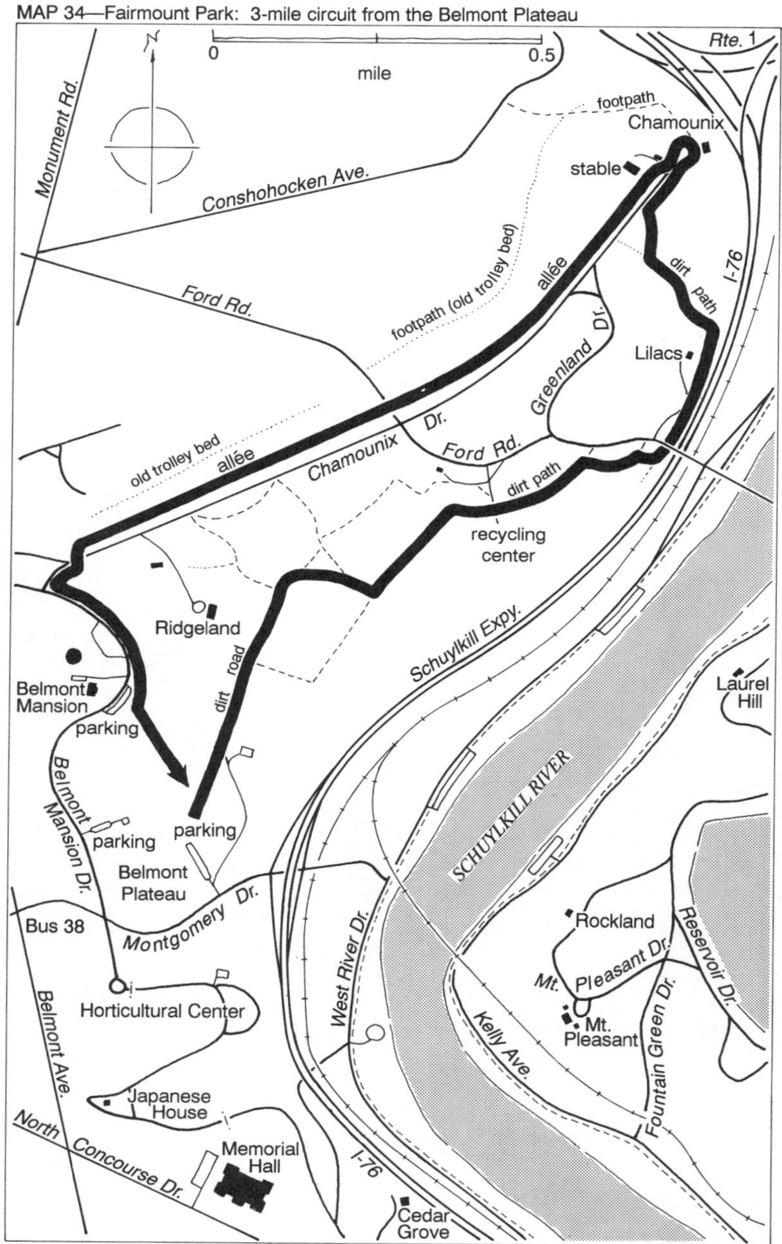

WALKING OR MOUNTAIN BIKING FROM THE BELMONT PLATEAU: The circuit shown by the bold line on **Map 34** opposite starts at the far end of the parking lot. Head out across the grass toward woods in the distance, keeping more or less parallel with a narrow paved road about 100 yards away on your right. From the point where the paved road ends at the entrance to a maintenance area, continue straight into the woods on a gravel road.

The gravel road passes through a forest that was once part of Ridgeland Farm, which during the first half of the nineteenth century was the summer home of Jacob S. Waln, a member of the City Council and Pennsylvania legislature. The simple stone Ridgeland house, of which the oldest part was built in 1719, is uphill to the left out of sight of the path. Entered from Chamounix Drive, the house now serves as a park office.

Continue through the woods on the main track, which is fairly level and passes lesser trails intersecting from left and right. After nearly a mile, cross the entrance drive to a recycling center and continue half-left downhill. Cross a small bridge, then turn right to continue through the woods. Just before the trail reaches Greenland Drive, fork right downhill, then follow the old roadbed of the Fairmount trolley under Greenland Drive.

The original Fairmount trolley system was built during 1896-97 and operated until 1946, providing an easy way to get from one part of the park to another. The western terminus was at the intersection of Belmont Avenue and Elm (now Parkside). The eastern terminus was at 33rd and Dauphin streets. The trolley crossed the Schuylkill River on the Strawberry Mansion bridge. From the Greenland Drive underpass, one arm of the system followed the flank of the valley north around Chamounix and south along the western edge of the park.

With the Schuylkill Expressway on the right, continue straight past a driveway on the left serving Lilacs, a plastered stone farmhouse later enlarged by Philadelphia gentry and now occupied by a drug rehabilitation organization. Continue straight on the trolley roadbed next to the expressway, then curve left uphill away from the din of the traffic. Cross a field diagonally toward a former police stables in the distance, then follow the edge of Chamounix Drive right to its end at the Chamounix carriage house and mansion.

Chamounix Mansion was built in 1802 by George Plumstead, a Quaker merchant whose father and grandfather had been mayors of Philadelphia. In 1806 the property was purchased by Benjamin Johnson, who moved here with his family from Ridgeland Farm, which he sold to Jacob Waln. After Philadelphia purchased the Chamounix estate from the Johnsons for Fairmount Park in 1876, the house became a restaurant.

Chamounix is now operated by the American Youth Hostels Association. It has dormitory accommodations and cooking facilities for forty-eight visitors, with still more capacity during the summer when the carriage house is open. The house is closed from 11 A.M. to 4:30 P.M. People who want to look at the house's first floor are welcome but should check first with one of the hostel's staff. Telephone (215) 878-3676 for information.

With Chamounix Drive on your left, follow a broad paved path away from the Chamounix carriage house, past tennis courts, and over Ford Road. Continue to the end of the path, then—with caution—bear left across Chamounix Drive in order to cross a bridge with stone parapets. Turn left again and continue along the grass next to Belmont Mansion Drive—or, if you are cycling, follow Belmont Mansion Drive itself. Go 300 yards to the entrance to Belmont Mansion on the right.

The oldest part of Belmont Mansion may have been built before 1717 and certainly predates 1742, when the property was purchased by Judge William Peters, who during his career filled various offices for the Penn family. His estate of more than 200 acres extended from the Schuylkill River to a point approximately 2,000 feet west of present-day Belmont Avenue. An amateur architect of considerable distinction, Peters greatly expanded the house in about 1746 by adding the first two floors of the section that now overlooks the city to the southeast. He also developed an elaborate formal garden in the vicinity of the house, and beyond that a "wilderness" cut through with vistas. With a symmetrical facade, quoins at the corners, and a slightly projecting frontispiece topped (originally) by an ornate pediment, Peter's elegant villa is one of the earliest examples of Palladian classicism in the colonies. Somewhat more exuberant is the plaster ceiling in the main hall or drawing room, featuring musical instruments in nearly full relief.

William Peters was a loyalist who returned to England during the Revolution, but his son Richard was a patriot who served as secretary of the Continental Board of War (which procured provisions for the army) and later as a member of Congress, speaker of the Pennsylvania

Senate, and a judge of the U.S. District Court of Pennsylvania for thirty-seven years. Described by his neighbor Samuel Breck of Sweetbriar as "unceremonious, communicative, friendly," Richard Peters continued the development of Belmont into a model farm and country seat where George Washington, James Madison, Benjamin Franklin, and other national leaders and also dignitaries from abroad often dined during the period from 1790 to 1800, when Philadelphia was the capital of the new republic. Breck wrote of Peters:

> The playfulness of his conversation always enlivened by flashes of the gayest pleasantry was forever quick and unrestrained and varied by casts of true humour, sometimes as broad and well enacted as the most exaggerated farce, and at others convolved in double meaning, fit only for the ready perception of the most practiced ear and polished taste . . . .
>
> When a morning of leisure permitted that great man [Washington] to drive to Belmont . . . . it was his constant habit to do so. There, sequestered from the world, and the torments and cares of his business, Washington would enjoy . . . a wholly unceremonious intercourse with the judge, walking for hours side by side, in the beautiful gardens of Belmont, beneath the dark shade of lofty hemlocks placed there by his ancestors a century ago.

Richard Peters died at Belmont in 1828. In 1854 state legislation that greatly increased the size of Philadelphia brought the area west of the Schuylkill River into the city, and in 1868 Philadelphia purchased the Belmont estate for inclusion in Fairmount Park. During the Centennial Exhibition of 1876, Belmont Mansion and its garden were a European-style cafe. In the 1970s the mansion sometimes functioned as a restaurant open in the summer during the season of the adjacent Playhouse in the Park (now largely defunct). Neglected and deteriorating, the Belmont Mansion in 1986 came under the stewardship of the American Women's Heritage Society, a volunteer organization formed to restore and operate the house as an historic site and museum, focusing in particular on African-American history. The Society raises funds not only through admission fees but also by making the mansion available for meetings, luncheons, lectures, weddings, and receptions, often involving the preparation of food in the large kitchen left over from the mansion's restaurant days. To accommodate these special events, the mansion is closed to the public on weekends (and also on Mondays). Among the Society's plans is acquisition of the site of Playhouse in the Park for development of a multipurpose cultural center.

From the front of the Belmont Mansion overlooking central Philadelphia, head downhill across the grass to the parking area where you started. Toward the right is the greenish dome of Memorial Hall, which served as the art gallery for the Centennial Exhibition and is now the headquarters for the Fairmount Park Commission and park police.

≈ ≈ ≈ ≈

SEPTA DIRECTIONS TO THE TOUR de FAIRMOUNT SHOWN ON MAP 35: The Tour de Fairmount is for bicycles. Telephone (215) 580-7852 for information about taking your bicycle on SEPTA Regional Rail trains.

One option is to go to Wissahickon Station on the R6 Regional Rail Line. From the station, follow Ridge Avenue downhill to the Wissahickon Transfer Center, and there join the bikeway that leads downstream along the river. (As of 1994, the bikeway at the transfer center consists merely of a sidewalk next to Ridge Avenue and Kelly Drive.) You can join the circuit at the Falls Bridge. (See **Map 35** on page 195.)

Another option is to go to Wynnefield Avenue Station on the R6 Regional Rail Line. Follow Wynnefield Avenue east past the intersection with Parkside Avenue, then turn right at the next intersection in order to join the circuit at the Mann Music Center. (Wynnefield Avenue is shown entering Map 35 at the middle of the left edge.)

Telephone (215) 580-7800 for current information on schedules, routes, and connections from your starting point.

AUTOMOBILE DIRECTIONS TO THE TOUR de FAIRMOUNT SHOWN ON MAP 35: The circuit starts at the large parking lot for the Canoe House off Kelly Drive in eastern Fairmount Park. Several avenues of approach are described below.

From downtown Philadelphia: Follow the Benjamin Franklin Parkway northwest toward the Philadelphia Museum of Art. Just before reaching the art museum, fork right for Kelly Drive and follow it north along the river 2.7 miles to a large parking lot on the left.

From the north or south on Interstate 95: Take Exit 17 for Interstate 676 West toward central Philadelphia. After passing the exit for Broad Street, leave I-676 at the exit for the museum area and Benjamin Franklin Parkway. At the top of the exit ramp, turn right. Go 100 yards, then turn left onto the Benjamin Franklin Parkway and move to the right-hand lanes. Just before reaching the art museum, fork right for Kelly Drive and follow it north along the river 2.7 miles to a large parking lot on the left.

From the east or west on Interstate 76 (Schuylkill Expressway): Get off I-76 at Exit 32 for Lincoln Drive and Kelly Drive. (If you are coming from the west, the exit is on the left.) After crossing the Schuylkill River, curve tightly left for Kelly Drive. At the bottom of the exit ramp, follow Kelly Drive 1.9 miles to the large parking lot on the right.

From the south on Route 1: Follow Route 1 (City Avenue) north. After passing the exits for Interstate 76 (Schuylkill Expressway) and after crossing the Schuylkill River, curve tightly left for Kelly Drive. At the bottom of the exit ramp, follow Kelly Drive 1.9 miles to the large parking lot on the right.

BICYCLING ON THE TOUR de FAIRMOUNT: The directions for the circuit shown by the bold line on **Map 35** are on page 194 opposite the map. As noted there, the numbered paragraphs refer to the corresponding numbers on the map. Capital letters on the map refer to the buildings listed at the bottom of the map.

The numbered directions below refer to the corresponding numbers on Map 35 on the facing page.

CAUTION: Most of the route shown by the bold line on Map 35 follows roads open to motor vehicles. For information on hours when West River Drive is closed to cars so that bicyclists can ride more safely in the roadway, see the introduction to this chapter. During periods when West River Drive is open to motor vehicles, cyclists should use the paved path next to the road.

1. With the Schuylkill River on your right, follow the paved path south. Continue past Boat House Row.
2. With caution, cross Kelly Drive at the seated statue of Abraham Lincoln. Follow Sedgeley Drive uphill.
3. Turn sharply left to circle past Lemon Hill, a very handsome federal-style mansion. After passing Lemon Hill, descend steeply, then turn right uphill.
4. Turn right onto Sedgeley Drive and return downhill to the statue of Lincoln. With caution, cross back over Kelly Drive. With the river on your left, follow the paved path north.
5. With caution, cross Kelly Drive at Fountain Green Drive, where an equestrian statue of Ulysses S. Grant is located. Follow Fountain Green Drive uphill.
6. Turn left toward Mt. Pleasant, a spectacular Georgian mansion.
7. After passing Rockland, turn left onto Reservoir Drive past Ormiston Mansion.
8. Turn left toward Laurel Hill Mansion.
9. Pass straight through a crossroads where there is a statue of an Indian on horseback.
10. Turn left past Woodford Mansion. Pass Woodford Drive (which intersects from the left), then continue more or less straight through a four-way intersection so as to follow a long, straight drive to Strawberry Mansion.
11. Turn left out the Strawberry Mansion driveway. Curve left downhill past Robin Hood Dell, then bear right across the Strawberry Mansion Bridge. Stay in the bicycle lane far to the right.
12. Climb steeply, forking right twice.
13. At the top of the slope, bear right and follow Chamounix Drive to Chamounix Mansion, now a hostel.
14. From the Chamounix carriage house, follow a paved path between rows of trees with Chamounix Drive on your left.
15. At the end of the paved path, fork left across a bridge with stone parapets.
16. Turn left and descend past Belmont Mansion. Cross Montgomery Drive and continue to the Horticultural Center.
17. If the Horticultural Center is open, follow the road to the Japanese House and back.
18. Follow Montgomery Drive uphill to Belmont Avenue.
19. Cross Belmont Avenue and follow South Georges Drive past the Ohio House and steeply uphill to the Mann Music Center.
20. Circle left around the Mann Music Center and continue downhill.
21. At the bottom of the hill, bear left toward a distant group of statues.
22. Continue straight on North Concourse Drive across Belmont Avenue and past Memorial Hall.
23. After passing tall columns topped by statues, cross a four-way intersection, then fork left to Sweetbriar Mansion at the end of the road.
24. Continue with the Schuylkill Expressway on your right, then fork right to Cedar Grove. After returning out the Cedar Grove road, turn right then turn right again so as to leave the tall columns behind on your left.
25. Fork right past a pair of gates and descend to West River Drive. Even if the gates are closed, bicycles ususally are permitted. In fact, the main reason the gates are closed is to improve bicycling on West River Drive.
26. With caution, cross West River Drive. With the river on your right, continue to Falls Bridge.
27. Turn right across Falls Bridge, then turn right again to continue on the paved path with the river on your right.

MAP 35—18-mile bicycle Tour de Fairmount

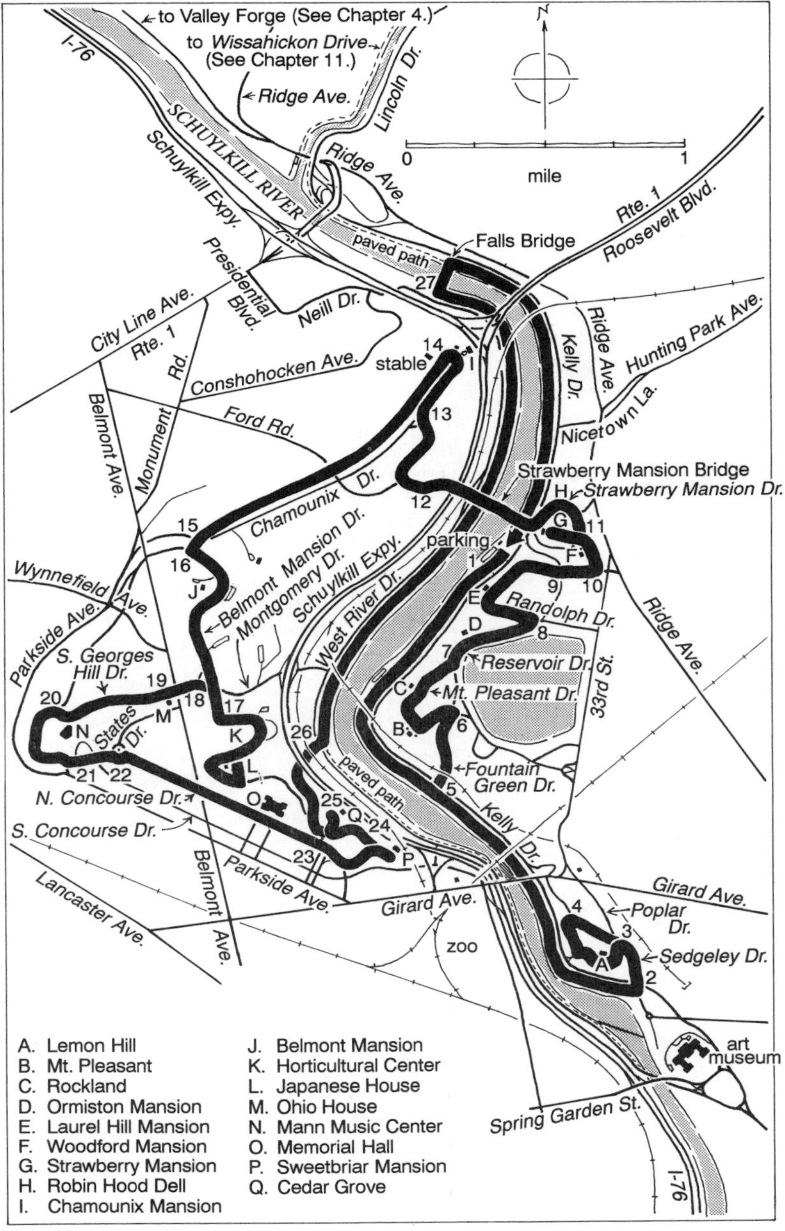

15

RIDLEY CREEK STATE PARK

Walking, jogging, ski touring, and bicycling.

The dashed lines on Map 36 on page 205 show an extensive network of hiking trails, none of which is open to off-road bicyclists. Most of the trails are marked with paint blazes, and of these the white trail forms a circuit of about 4.5 miles, almost all of it through deep woods. For a still longer outing, hikers can follow paths that connect with the trails at Tyler Arboretum to the south (see Chapter 16).

The bold line on Map 37 on page 207 shows a 5-mile circuit for walking, jogging, and bicycling. This loop follows paved country roads that are now closed to automobiles—except for the cars of a few park residents who are accustomed to driving very slowly and sharing the road with pedestrians and cyclists. Part of the loop borders Ridley Creek, and a short spur leads downstream to Sycamore Mills, now a quiet backwater but once an industrial hamlet, as discussed starting on page 202. Bicyclists should ride single file, yield to other trail users, and keep their speed to a moderate, safe pace. If you have an infant or small child, the roads are an excellent promenade for buggies and strollers.

The 3-mile loop shown by the bold line on Map 38 on page 209 follows Ridley Creek upstream, then circles back through the woods. The trail is also used by horseback riders, but is closed to bicyclists. Most of the loop—the part north of Gradyville Road—is on a well-graded carriage road paved with rock grit. As shown on the map, there is an opportunity for a longer circuit that passes close to Delchester Road.

Also shown on Map 38 is the Colonial Pennsylvania Plantation, a restored eighteenth-century farm where visitors can observe and even join authentically dressed guides as they perform household and farm tasks using tools appropriate to the period from 1760 to 1790. The plantation is open mid-April through mid-November on Saturday and Sunday from 10 to 4—or until 5 when Daylight Saving Time is in effect. There is a small admission fee. Dogs are prohibited; the farm animals roam freely. Group tours are given on weekdays and Saturday by previous arrangement. This is also a popular place for children's birthday parties. The plantation is operated by the Bishop Mills Historical Institute; telephone (610) 566-1725 for information, including the schedule of special weekend events, such as the May Crafts Fair, Children's Day, and the Harvest Feast.

Also well worth seeing at Ridley Creek State Park are the walled and terraced gardens next to the park office, which occupies the former Jeffords Mansion. The mansion is in the style of an English Tudor Manorhouse. The grounds were laid out by the Olmsted Brothers of Boston, who in the early part of the twentieth century served as park-planning consultants to many eastern cities. Paved footpaths loop out from the gardens and through the woods.

Ridley Creek State Park is open daily year-round from 8 A.M. until sunset. Dogs must be leashed. The office is open weekdays from 8 to 4. The Park is managed by the Pennsylvania Bureau of State Parks; telephone (610) 566-4800.

THE SMALL FAMILY FARM—each isolated farmhouse surrounded by its own outbuildings, fields, and woodlot—flourished from the start in colonial Pennsylvania. It defined the norm aspired to by poor or modestly-capitalized settlers coming to Pennsylvania from abroad and from the other colonies—from Maryland and Virginia, for example, where slumping tobacco prices and the increasing use of slaves had by the 1680s already curtailed economic opportunity for freed indentured servants in the tidewater region. Yet despite the popularity and success of the small family farm, the fact is that this form of rural development and agricultural organization is not at all what William Penn had in mind for his colony, which was granted to him in 1681 by King Charles II in repayment of a loan made to the Crown by Penn's father. Pennsylvania, incidentally, was named by the king. Penn suggested "Sylvania," (meaning woods) and Charles II added the "Penn." Penn himself was so mortified by the appearance of vanity that he tried to bribe the royal secretaries to quash the name.

Penn's idealism, proprietary power, and control over land policy combined to produce Utopian visions for the organization of rural Pennsylvania. A convert to Quakerism, Penn was a strong believer in community institutions and mutual aid. He thought that settlers should live in agricultural hamlets located at the center of small, tidy townships. "For the more convenient bringing up of youth . . . so that neighbors may help one another . . . and that they may accustom their children also to do the same," Penn advocated the establishment of hundreds of villages where farmers, craftsmen, tradesmen, teachers, ministers—in fact, all rural residents—would live near a meetinghouse or church. He published two township plans showing suggested farm shapes and sizes. According to both proposals, townships were to consist of 5,000 acres. The boundaries and road pattern would be rectilinear. One plan suggested up to twenty farms of 100 acres each, bordering a road that divided the township in half, and with a village at the center. The remaining land would be reserved for children of the original settlers. According to the other plan, ten houses would occupy lots of 50 acres each at the township center, from which ten wedge-shaped farms of 450 acres each would radiate outward to the edge of the township.

To some extent Penn's township plans reflected the typical European village of the feudal era, with its tradition of communal decision-making and cooperation. Indeed, as proprietor of Pennsylvania, Penn possessed many feudal powers. Under his charter he could and did demand perpetual quitrent from the settlers in lieu of feudal services. And his land grants provided for escheat—reversion of the land to him—if an area remained unoccupied three years after being granted to a settler.

At first the process of surveying and occupying the Pennsylvania countryside proceeded in an orderly fashion, but few of the many townships that were established conformed even remotely to the village pattern Penn advocated. Established in 1681, Newtown near Ridley Creek State Park was one of the few townships that actually developed into a village. Usually community institutions, such as meetinghouses, schools, mills, inns, and stores, were scattered without regard for the township centers or any particular plan. Dwellings were dispersed throughout the countryside, since the overwhelming majority of farmers preferred to build homes in the middle of their fields. Even as late at the 1790s a traveler observed that between Philadelphia and Lancaster he found "not any two dwellings standing together," except at Downingtown.

Several explanations have been offered to account for the rejection of agricultural villages similar to what many settlers in Pennsylvania had known in England and Germany, and the development instead of dispersed, individual farms. With notable exceptions (such as the Moravians), the settlers did not like communalism. Economic individualism was the prevailing philosophy, reinforced by the religious individualism of the Quakers and other dissenters. Farmers wanted to make their own decisions and to reap the full and exclusive benefit of their own efforts. As a matter of simple convenience, travel time to and from the fields was reduced by living at the center of the farm. Because

Penn had established peaceful relations with the Indians, settlers in his colony did not have to live in villages for mutual defense, as had at first been thought necessary in New England. There the early villages were surrounded by open fields and each farmer was granted several small, scattered parcels in order to guarantee an equitable distribution of different qualities of land, as had been done in Europe. But even in New England, settlers began to move to scattered family farms after 1680, and in the tobacco colonies too the rush to acquire and to cultivate one's own land thoroughly dispersed the population onto a myriad of small farms and plantations. In Maryland and Virginia numerous acts were passed for the establishment of towns, most of which never came into being. Even in Europe the agricultural village was on the wane as communally cultivated fields were enclosed to create large privately owned tracts.

The family farm system was well established in Pennsylvania by 1700, but during the following century family holdings tended to shrink with each generation as lands were divided among sons, for the English system of primogeniture frequently was rejected in Pennsylvania. By 1760 the average farm in Chester County (which at that time included Delaware County) was about 125 acres. More than two dozen of these old farmsteads still stand in Ridley Creek State Park, plus the ruins of still more, now surrounded by woods in a region that once was mostly cultivated farm fields. A similar pattern of small, closely spaced farms is evident at Tyler State Park (see Chapter 8).

≈ ≈ ≈ ≈

The Colonial Pennsylvania Plantation in northern Ridley Creek State Park provides a look at a typical eighteenth-century farm on which a wide variety of crops and livestock was raised for home use and for sale. Between a half and two-thirds of production was consumed on the farm. Still, most Pennsylvania farmers aimed for more than bare self-sufficiency, so that an international market economy developed, with particular emphasis on wheat.

James T. Lemon in *The Best Poor Man's Country*, a geographical study of early southeastern Pennsylvania, estimates that the typical farmer in 1760 planted yearly about 8 acres in wheat at a yield (very low by modern standards) of about 10 bushels per acre. "Wheat is the grand article of the province. They sow immense quantities," proclaimed the anonymous author of *American Husbandry*, commenting in 1775 on agriculture in Pennsylvania. Both wheat and rye were sown in autumn and harvested in late spring or early summer. Other grains were planted in spring: about 4 aces of oats, 2 acres of barley, 2 acres of buckwheat, and 8 acres of Indian corn—all yielding 15 bushels per acre. Wheat brought the highest price, and substantial quantities of flour were sent to Philadelphia and later to Baltimore for export to New England, the West Indies, South America, and southern Europe. Wheat also was distilled for whiskey, as was rye. Oats were used primarily for horsefeed and barley for beer. Buckwheat was eaten by the poor or was plowed under to improve the soil. Corn primarily was fed to hogs and other livestock. Other crops grown in small quantities were potatoes, turnips, and flax for linen, linseed oil, and fodder. About 20 acres on a typical farm were planted in hay, which was mown twice yearly. Perhaps 25 acres were forest, a valuable crop in an era when wood was the only fuel. The remaining acreage was fallow.

Virtually every farm had an orchard. One writer in 1748 stated, "Every countryman, even the poorest peasant, had an orchard with apples, peaches, chestnuts, walnuts, cherries, quinces, and such fruits, and sometimes we saw vines climbing in them." (Grape vines are a common sight throughout the woods at Ridley Creek.) Apples were grown for cider, and an orchard of fifty trees was considered small. The average farm had about 2 acres devoted to orchard, at sixty to seventy trees per acre.

Just as eighteenth-century farmers did not specialize in the production of a single crop, so a variety of livestock was raised in modest numbers. The average farmer might have a half-dozen cattle, including three cows. In fact, Chester County gradually became know for its production of cheese. Three to four horses were common, since they were all-purpose draft animals. Eight to ten swine and as many sheep were also usual, the former for meat and the latter for wool. The amount of pork consumed was approximately twice that of beef. Chickens, ducks, geese, turkeys, and other fowl were raised for meat and eggs. Finally, one or two hives of bees were kept for honey and to pollinate the fruit trees and clover.

Field rotation was standard practice, but fertilizing was not. Because of the emphasis on wheat as the main cash crop, livestock herds were small and so, in consequence, was the quantity of manure that was available. After 1750 lime and gypsum were introduced as fertilizers, but they were not popular, perhaps because those who experimented with these products often applied too much and hurt their soil. More usual was a simple reliance on a three-field or four-field rotation pattern, with one field being left fallow each year or perhaps planted in clover. Sometimes exhausted fields were left fallow for many years and allowed to grow into scrubby woods.

By modern standards the typical eighteenth-century Pennsylvania farm was deficient in other ways also. Before 1750 barns were the exception rather than the rule. Hay was left in stacks and livestock were wintered in the open, often simply in woodlots or fallow fields.

The great barns of the Pennsylvania Dutch were not built until after the Revolution. Tools also were primitive. Light wooden plows with strips of iron on the moldboards could not penetrate deeply into the soil, so fields had to be plowed three times. Cast-iron plows were not introduced until the end of the eighteenth century. Harvesting also was laborious: grain was cut with hand sickles, and threshing was done with flails or by treading on the sheaves.

In general, then, the typical farm in southeastern Pennsylvania during the eighteenth century was a family operation producing a variety of food for home consumption, a small surplus of vegetables and livestock for market, and a large surplus of wheat. Agricultural reformers of the day lamented poor animal husbandry and the lack of fertilizing, but they failed to recognize that most farmers were comfortable and saw little reason to change.

≈ ≈ ≈ ≈

The emphasis on the cultivation of wheat in Pennsylvania during the eighteenth and early nineteenth centuries led in turn to the development of numerous water-powered gristmills along the region's many rivers and streams. Some of these operations were very small, grinding grain of all varieties for home consumption by local farmers in exchange for a share of the product. More than half the grain grown was used on the farm. Nonetheless, there was a substantial surplus of wheat, and much of this went to large merchant mills whose owners bought grain outright and sent their flour to distant markets. A map of southeastern Pennsylvania published in 1792 shows mills of one sort or another—including sawmills, fulling mills, linseed oil mills, paper mills, and other such works—located about every 2 miles on permanent streams. In 1782 Chester County (including present-day Delaware County) had 123 gristmills, of which Sycamore Mills, now in Ridley Creek State Park, was one.

When first built in 1718 by John and Jacob Edge, this gristmill was called Providence Mill because it was located in Upper Providence Township. The mill stood on the northeast side of Ridley Creek about 125 yards upstream from the present-day bridge where Bishop Hollow Road, Chapel Hill Road, Ridley Creek Road, Barren Road, and Sycamore Mills Road all converge. (See Map 37 on page 207.) Here grain from nearby farms was ground, using different sets of millstones for wheat, rye, barley, buckwheat, and corn.

In 1748 a sawmill was erected next to the Providence gristmill. The sawmill—powered by water from the same race and perhaps even by the same waterwheel that served the gristmill—was operated only when the gristmill was idle. Both structures were demolished by fire in 1901, but the milldam survives.

Although the gristmill and sawmill are gone, the former office, a slender, two-story structure, still stands a few dozen yards up the road from the site of the mills. This building was fireproof. It had cement floors and (originally) a metal roof. In 1818 the second story was converted to the Union Library, a proprietary or subscription library that by 1834 had more than eight hundred volumes. The arrangement did not last, however, for in 1862 the library was liquidated and its books were sold at a sheriff's sale. Now the building is a residence.

Behind the former mill office and library is another residence, at one time a blacksmith and wheelwright shop built in the middle of the eighteenth century. Like gristmills, blacksmith shops were numerous; they might be compared to present-day service stations. Blacksmiths served a local clientele, shoeing horses, repairing wagons and tools, and making custom iron fittings of all kinds. For a period the shop was owned by Amor Bishop, grandson of Thomas Bishop, Sr., who had acquired Providence Mill in 1781. The mill complex then came to be called Bishop's Mill. In 1868 ownership of the property changed again, and the mill was renamed Sycamore Mills.

Across the road from the site of the gristmill and sawmill is a large stucco-covered house, which was the mill owner's residence. The oldest part of the house was built of logs early in the eighteenth century.

Next to the gristmill and sawmill but closer to the bridge over Ridley Creek there was a large, one-story rolling and slitting mill that operated between 1810 and 1830 (hence Forge Road approaching from the southwest). Iron hardware was fashioned from pig iron transported here from rural iron furnaces similar to Hopewell Furnace, discussed in Chapter 2. The rolling mill eventually failed, however, probably because transportation costs were high compared to those of similar plants located near the new canals, improved turnpikes, and growing cities of the nineteenth century.

The wall standing at the corner of Bishop Hollow Road and Chapel Hill Road is part of an old wagon shed thought to have been used in connection with the sawmill to shelter log-hauling equipment and to store lumber. The high stone walls of a barn built in 1848 and used to store grain are visible 40 yards up Chapel Hill Road on the left.

On the southwest side of Ridley Creek a small nail factory was located by the dam upstream from the bridge. Three houses (and the remains of a fourth) stand at intervals along Sycamore Mills Road. Built between 1785 and 1830, the cottages were workers' homes during the hamlet's most prosperous period. But the failure of the rolling mill precipitated the community's gradual descent into the obscurity shared by the hundreds of other gristmills and small industrial operations that once were spaced at intervals along small streams and rivers throughout southeastern Pennsylvania before steam engines came into widespread use during the last third of the nineteenth century.

≈ ≈ ≈ ≈

SEPTA: Buses 110 and 117 run to Penn State University's Delaware County Campus. However, from there you still have to walk about a mile on local roads that lack sidewalks to reach Ridley Creek State Park.

From the bus stop at the university, follow Yearsley Mill Road back to Middletown Road (Route 352). With caution, cross Middletown Road toward the left in order to follow Old Middletown Road. At an intersection with Blacksmith Lane, turn right. At a T-intersection with Horseshoe Drive, turn left. Follow Horseshoe Drive as it bends right to a T-intersection with Carriage Drive. Turn left onto Carriage Drive, then left again at a T-intersection with Painter Road. Pass the entrance to Tyler Arboretum and continue 0.2 mile to an intersection with Forge Road. Turn right past a gate at Forge Road in order to join (at its southernmost point) the circuit of paved roads shown on **Map 37** on page 207.

Telephone (215) 580-7800 for current information on schedules, routes, and connections from your starting point.

AUTOMOBILE DIRECTIONS: Ridley Creek State Park is located about 15 miles west of downtown Philadelphia near Newtown Square and Media. (See •15 on **Maps 1 and 2F** on pages 6 and 7.) Several avenues of approach are described below.

From the Pennsylvania Turnpike 's Exit 25 or 25A for Interstate 476 South (the Blue Route): Follow I-476 South past Norristown and Conshohocken to Exit 4 for Route 3. Take Route 3 West about 3 miles to Newtown Square, then follow the directions two paragraphs below.

From the east on Interstate 76 (the Schuylkill Expressway): Take Exit 28A for Interstate 476 South toward Chester. Leave I-476 at Exit 4 for Route 3. Take Route 3 West about 3 miles to Newtown Square, then follow the directions in the next paragraph.

From Newtown Square at the intersection of Route 3 and Route 252: Follow Route 252 South 1 mile, then turn right

MAP 36—Ridley Creek State Park: southern section

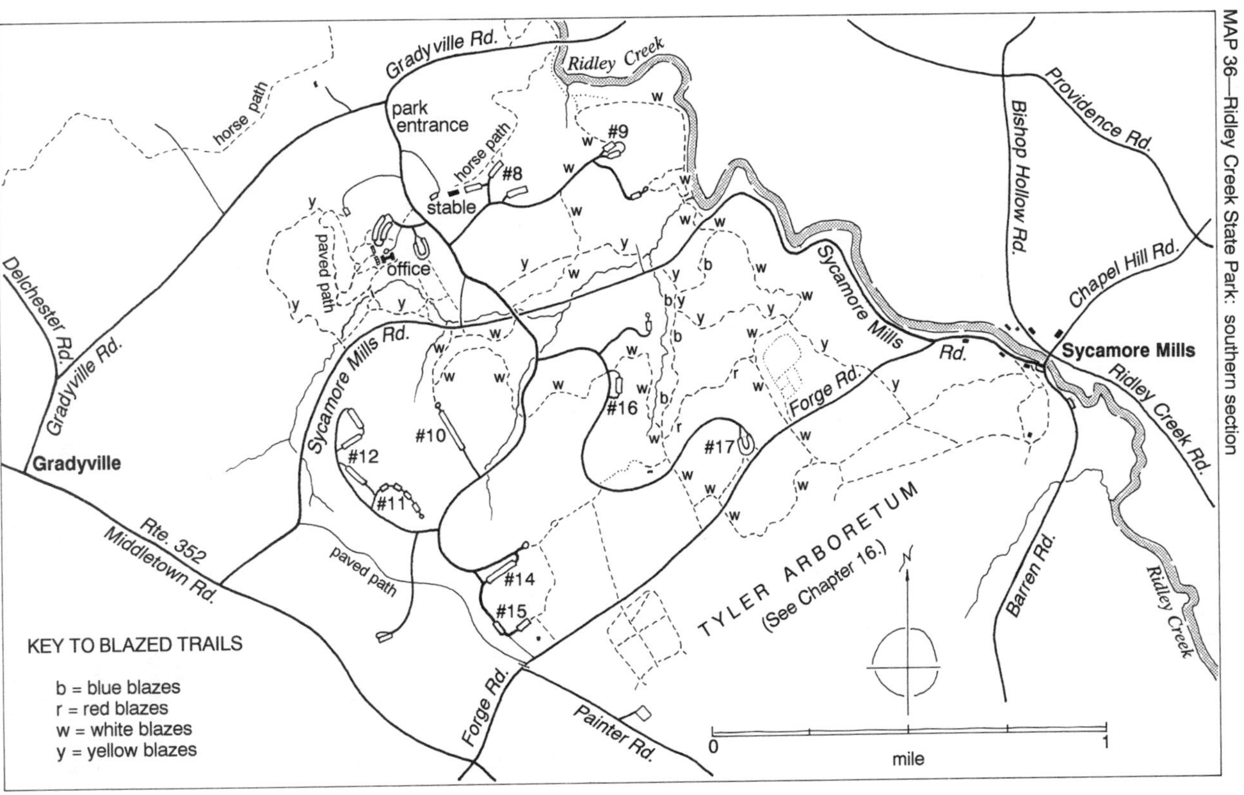

onto Gradyville Road. Go 3 miles on Gradyville Road, then turn left into the entrance for Ridley Creek State Park.

From Interstate 95 's Exit 7 for Interstate 476 North (the Blue Route): Follow I-476 North to Exit 3 for Route 1. Take Route 1 South toward Lima about 1 mile to the exit for Route 252, then follow the directions in the next paragraph.

From the point where Route 252 crosses Route 1: Follow Route 252 North toward Newtown Square for 2.6 miles, then turn left onto Gradyville Road at a traffic light. Go 3 miles on Gradyville Road, then turn left into the entrance for Ridley Creek State Park.

WHERE TO PARK? That depends:

If you plan to walk on the blazed trails shown on Map 36, follow the park road only 0.3 mile. Turn right toward the park office, then immediately turn left downhill into a large parking lot.

If you plan to walk or bicycle on the circuit of paved roads shown on Map 37, follow the park road as straight as possible at each intersection. After passing roads for Picnic Areas 10 and 11-12-13, turn right and then right again for Picnic Area 15, which has two parking lots, one after the other.

If you plan to walk on the circuit shown on Map 38, follow the park road only 0.4 mile, then turn left for Picnic Areas 8-9. At the next intersection turn left again, then fork right to a large parking lot for Area 8, opposite the stable parking lot.

THE BLAZED HIKING TRAILS: If you want to get off by yourself, the trails shown by dashed lines on **Map 36** on page 205 are far less used than the circuit of paved roads shown on Map 37 opposite. Of course, the trails are also more strenuous, going up hill and down dale through the woods.

A good place to start is the large parking lot below the park office. From the bottom end of the parking lot, follow a wide path more or less straight downhill to the old Jeffords driveway. Cross a bridge at an intersection with Sycamore Mills Road. You can pick up the white trail on the far (i.e., south) side of Sycamore Mills Road.

WALKING AND BICYCLING ON THE CIRCUIT OF PAVED ROADS: This loop is shown by the bold line on **Map 37** opposite. Begin at the short segment of road that connects the two parking lots at Picnic Area 15. Follow a paved path 150

MAP 37—Ridley Creek State Park: 5-mile circuit of paved roads for walkers and bicyclists

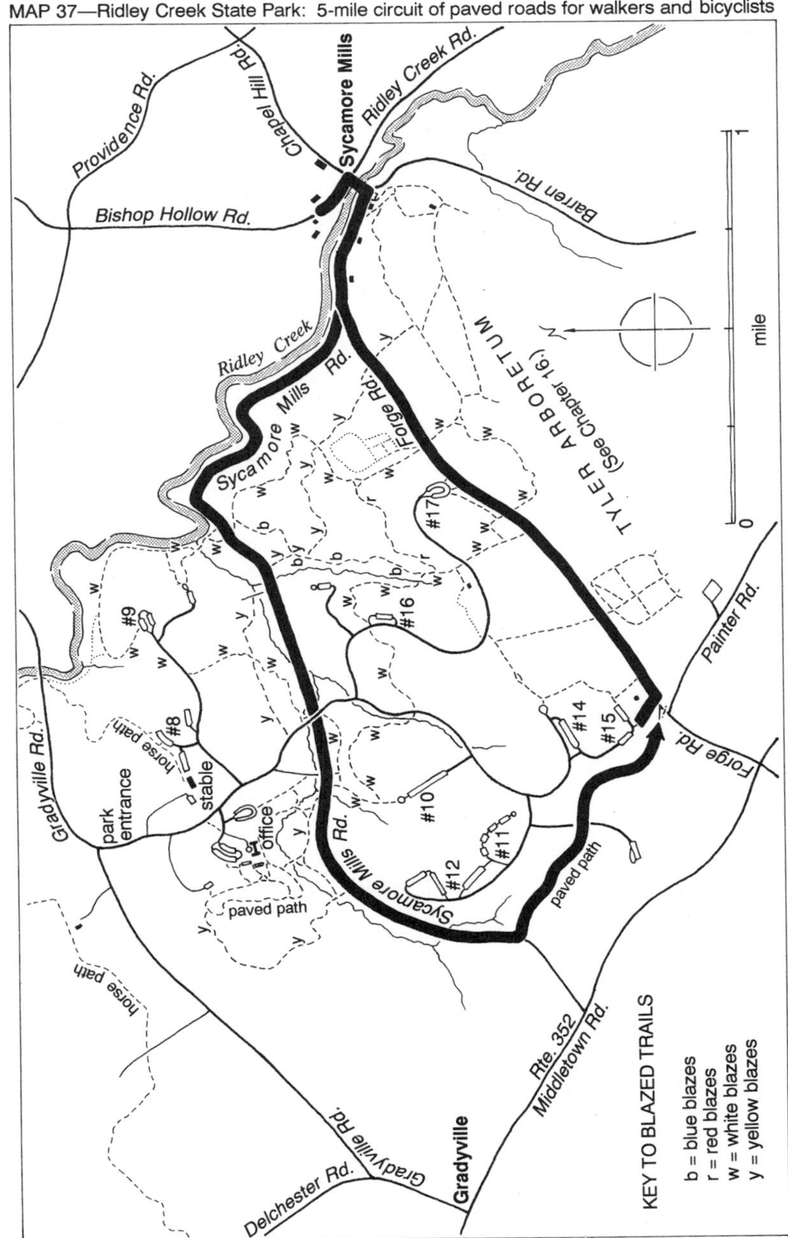

yards to join Forge Road near a barrier at the intersection with Painter Road. On the right is the paved path by which you will return at the end of the circuit.

Because this circuit is used by walkers, bicyclists, and even an occasional car going to and from residences within the park, walkers should stay to the left, facing the oncoming traffic. Cyclists should stay to the right and sound a warning well before they pass.

From the barricade at the intersection of Forge Road and Painter Road, follow Forge Road east more than 1 mile to Sycamore Mills Road and Ridley Creek. To see the remains of Sycamore Mills, follow Sycamore Mills Road to the right (with the creek on your left), then return by the way you came.

From the intersection of Sycamore Mills Road and Forge Road, continue around the loop by following Sycamore Mills Road with Ridley Creek on your right. Continue for more than 2 miles as the road curves left away from the river, goes through a short tunnel, and passes a road and bridge on the right. (This road and bridge are the old entrance to the Jeffords Mansion, which is now the park office. In 1966 Pennsylvania bought the 2,000-acre Jeffords estate for $5.6 million. An additional 500 acres was purchased from adjoining owners.)

Eventually, Sycamore Mills Road reaches an intersection with an asphalt path on the left. (The path is bordered on one side by a large field.) Turn left onto the path and follow it uphill and across an asphalt road. Continue to your starting point on Forge Road near the intersection with Painter Road.

WALKING IN THE AREA NORTH OF GRADYVILLE ROAD: The trails in this part of the park are shown on **Map 38** opposite.

From the middle of the uphill side of the parking lot for Picnic Area 8, follow a narrow track that leads a few yards to a bridle path. Turn right onto the bridle path and follow it as it winds downhill. Pass under the Gradyville Road bridge next to Ridley Creek. Follow a wide gravel track, occasionally passing trails that intersect from the left; you will return by one of these later.

Continue with Ridley Creek on your right. Eventually, you will reach a fork in the path. As shown by the bold line on Map 38, I recommend that you bear left, for a total walking distance of 3 miles. However, you can add 2 miles by forking right and following a somewhat rougher loop that passes near Delchester Road.

MAP 38—Ridley Creek State Park: northern section

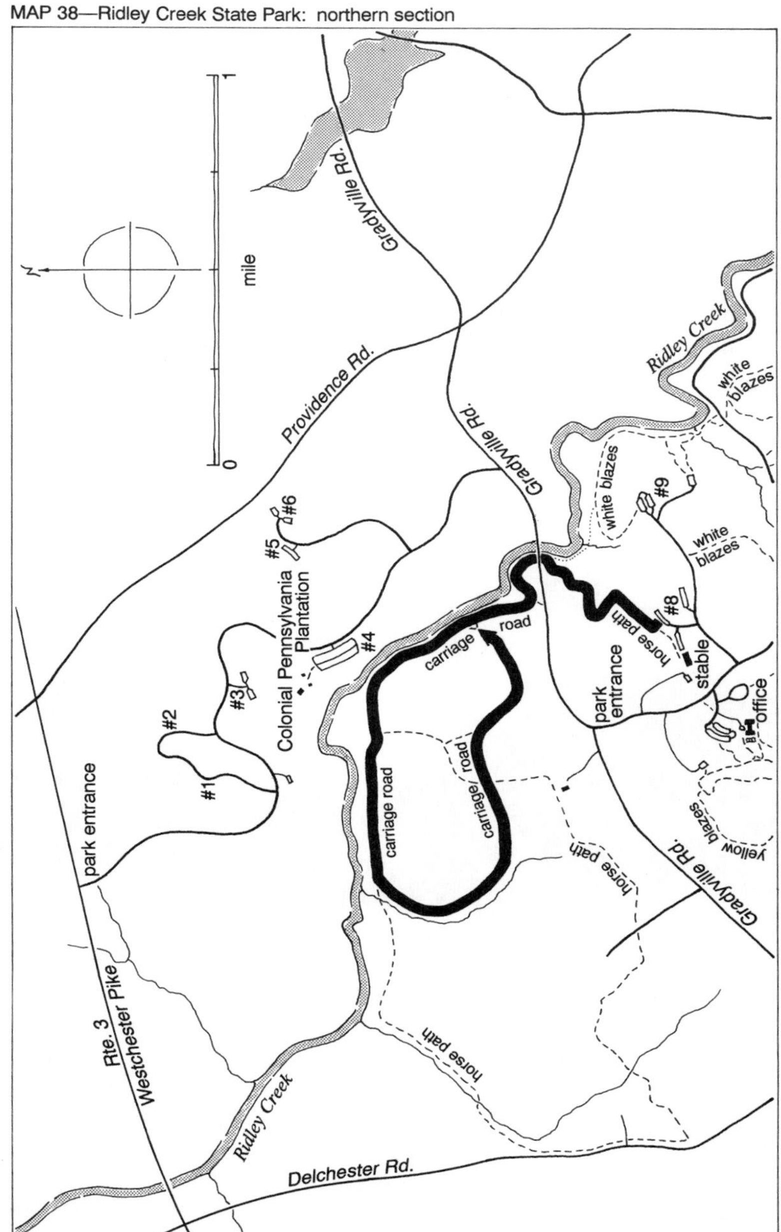

Assuming that you forked left, simply follow the wide path gradually uphill. Continue as straight as possible past trails intersecting from either side. Eventually, after descending a long hill, fork right to return along Ridley Creek (with the stream on your left), under Gradyville Road, and uphill to the parking lot at Picnic Area 8.

16

TYLER ARBORETUM

Walking and ski touring. Off-road bicycling is not permitted on the trails at Tyler Arboretum.

This outstanding arboretum features exotic and native trees, flowering shrubs, several specialty gardens, meadows, and woods—all interconnected by a network of trails marked with paint blazes. The arboretum is rich also in field and forest wildflowers.

A walk of almost any length is possible here. I recommend the 3.8-mile loop shown by the bold line on Map 39 on page 217. Marked with red blazes and called the Painter Brothers Trail, it offers variety and provides a good introduction to the main part of the arboretum. Shorter walks are outlined on Maps 40 and 41 on pages 219 and 221. Far longer walks are possible by following trails to the northwest into Ridley Creek State Park (Chapter 15).

The arboretum is open daily from 8 A.M. to dusk. An admission fee is charged. Dogs must be leashed. Picnicking is prohibited. For information—including upcoming events and educational programs—telephone (610) 566-5431.

THE LAND AT TYLER ARBORETUM first became a showcase for exotic trees during the middle of the nineteenth century. At that time the property was owned by the brothers Minshall and Jacob Painter, prosperous descendants of Thomas Minshall, an English Quaker to whom William Penn in 1681 conveyed a tract that included the site now occupied by the arboretum. The Painter brothers inherited about 500 acres and added another 150 acres during their lives. In addition to managing and improving their farm, the brothers read widely in the field of natural science and even erected a building for their library. Between 1825 and 1875 they planted more than a thousand trees and shrubs in the vicinity of their house and barn and along Painter Road. More than 20 of these specimens survive, including a Giant Sequoia and some other unusual species.

The Tyler Arboretum was established in 1944 by the bequest of Laura Tyler in honor of her deceased husband (and cousin), John J. Tyler. Laura Tyler was a great-great-great-great-great-granddaughter of Thomas Minshall. Her husband was a nephew of the Painter brothers.

≈ ≈ ≈ ≈

Although Tyler Arboretum has comprehensive plantings of pines, hollies, magnolias, cherries, crabapples, rhododendrons, and other ornamental trees and shrubs, most of the land is meadow and forest. In contrast to the collections of trees and shrubs—most of which are provided with their own space—the woods demonstrate that in a natural setting relatively few species predominate.

The eventual dominance of a few varieties of trees in any given tract of woods is the end result of the gradual process by which distinct plant communities succeed one another. An obvious example is the process by which an abandoned farm field grows up in weeds, followed in turn by woody brush—including crabapples, cherries, plums, hawthorns, persimmons, red cedars, gray birch, sumac, aspens, and pines—most of which eventually give way to large, long-lived, deciduous trees that shade and kill their competitors. Plants themselves can contribute to changes in soil, moisture, sunlight, wildlife, and other conditions, and these changes may favor the rise to dominance of yet entirely different plant species than were formerly present. This displacement of one biotic community by another is called *ecological succession*, and it can continue through several stages until change eventually becomes so slow—depending, perhaps, on shifts in the climate itself—that a virtual equilibrium is achieved between the physical environment and the climax community of plants and animals. At any time, however, hurricanes, ice storms, fires, infestations, floods, and other such events can abruptly undo decades of gradual change and rejuvenate the mix of trees, shrubs, and other plants.

The climax plant community of southeastern Pennsylvania has traditionally been called the "oak-chestnut" forest—a glaring misnomer ever since the early twentieth century, when chestnut blight killed all mature American chestnut trees. The disease continues to kill chestnut saplings as they sprout from old root systems. From Maryland northward, tulip trees (also called yellow-poplar) have filled the gap left by the chestnuts and now occupy a position of co-dominance with the oaks. Other species of hardwoods are also common, including beech, black cherry, and varieties of ash, hickory, and maple. Dogwood is widespread in the understory.

Although many trees are tolerant of a broad range of soil and moisture conditions, some are usually found in a particular type of terrain. For example, as its name suggests, swamp white oak generally grows in moist or even soggy soils inimical to other species. Willow oak and pin oak often are found in heavy bottomland soils. Most oaks, however, including white, scarlet, black, and chinquapin oak, prefer drier soils. Southern red oak usually grows in upland regions. Black-jack oak, post oak, and to a lesser extent chestnut oak have a high tolerance for dry, gravelly hilltops or poor, sandy soils. So do the evergreen Eastern red cedar, pitch pine, and Virginia pine, which are among the first trees to grow in abandoned fields. White pine is another sun-loving tree found in former farmland, often forming pure stands in sandy loam soils.

Each type of terrain is associated with certain groups of trees. Stream banks and bottomland support river birch, boxelder, hornbeam, red and silver maple, sycamore, black locust, American elm, sourgum, witch-hazel, varieties of willow, and black, green, and pumpkin ash. The slopes of hills and valleys sustain white ash, beech, Hercules'-club, mountain maple, striped maple, sweetgum, tulip tree, flowering dogwood, and mountain laurel. Cool, shady ravines and moist, north-facing slopes provide a suitable environment for Eastern hemlock. On upper slopes and ridgetops the balance shifts toward the dry oaks and shagbark and pignut hickory. As you follow the trails up and down the hills and stream valleys described in this book, and as the slopes face sometimes north and sometimes south, notice how the vegetation changes.

≈ ≈ ≈ ≈

SEPTA: Buses 110 and 117 run to Penn State University's Delaware County Campus. However, from there you still have to walk 0.8 mile on local roads that lack sidewalks to reach Tyler Arboretum.

From the bus stop at the university, follow Yearsley Mill Road back to Middletown Road (Route 352). With caution, cross Middletown Road toward the left in order to follow Old Middletown Road. At an intersection with Blacksmith Lane, turn right. At a T-intersection with Horseshoe Drive, turn left. Follow Horseshoe Drive as it bends right to a T-intersection with Carriage Drive. Turn left onto Carriage Drive, then left again at a T-intersection with Painter Road. Continue to the entrance to Tyler Arboretum on the right.

Telephone (215) 580-7800 for current information on schedules, routes, and connections from your starting point.

AUTOMOBILE DIRECTIONS: Tyler Arboretum is located about 15 miles west of downtown Philadelphia near Media and Lima. (See •16 on **Maps 1 and 2F** on pages 6 and 7.) Several avenues of approach are described below.

From the Pennsylvania Turnpike 's Exit 25 or 25A for Interstate 476 South (the Blue Route): Follow I-476 South past Norristown and Conshohocken to Exit 3 for Route 1. Take Route 1 South toward Lima about 2.5 miles to the exit for Route 352. Follow Route 352 North 2 miles to an intersection with Forge Road. Turn right onto Forge Road and go 0.2 mile to Painter Road. Turn right again and follow Painter Road 0.2 mile to the entrance for Tyler Arboretum on the left.

From the east on Interstate 76 (the Schuylkill Expressway): Take Exit 28A for Interstate 476 South toward Chester. Leave I-476 at Exit 3 for Route 1. Take Route 1 South toward Lima about 2.5 miles to the exit for Route 352. Follow Route 352 North 2 miles to an intersection with Forge Road. Turn right onto Forge Road and go 0.2 mile to Painter Road. Turn right again and follow Painter Road 0.2 mile to the entrance for Tyler Arboretum on the left.

From Interstate 95 's Exit 7 for Interstate 476 North (the Blue Route): Follow I-476 North to Exit 3 for Route 1. Take Route 1 South toward Lima about 2.5 miles to the exit for Route 352. Follow Route 352 North 2 miles to an intersection with Forge Road. Turn right onto Forge Road and go 0.2 mile to Painter Road. Turn right again and follow Painter Road 0.2 mile to the entrance for Tyler Arboretum on the left.

From the point where Route 352 crosses Route 1: Follow Route 352 North 2 miles to an intersection with Forge Road. Turn right onto Forge Road and go 0.2 mile to Painter Road. Turn right again and follow Painter Road 0.2 mile to the entrance for Tyler Arboretum on the left.

WALKING: From the arboretum parking lot, go first to the large stone barn, where the visitor center/bookstore is located, and where you can obtain pamphlets about the arboretum's programs. From the visitor center/bookstore, circle clockwise down around the barn to the education center.

From the education center at the barn's lower level, descend across the grass to a bridge over a brook. This is the trailhead for a complex network of paths marked with paint blazes.

The best route is the 3.8-mile **Painter Brothers Trail** (red blazes). This is the trail shown by the bold line on **Map 39** opposite and described starting in the next paragraph. Also

MAP 39—Tyler Arboretum: Painter Brothers Trail (red blazes)

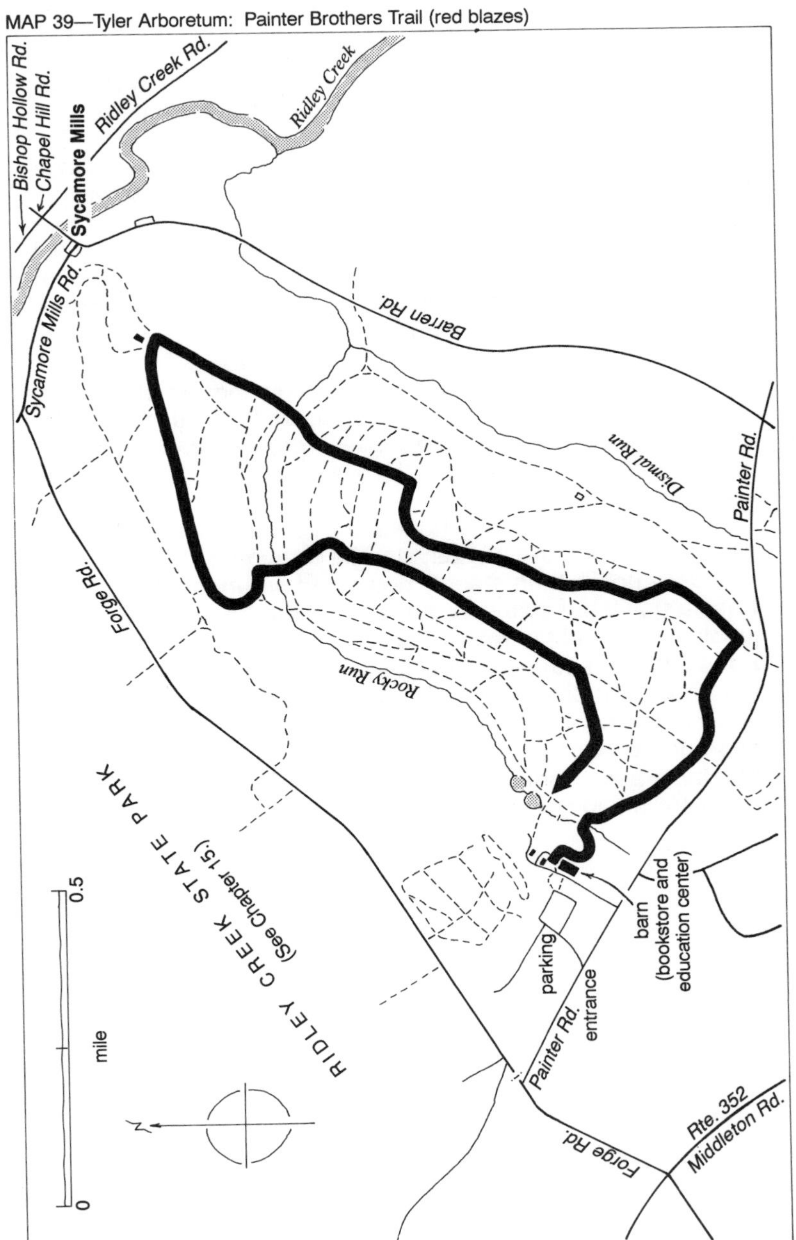

pleasant are the orange-blazed **Dismal Run Trail** shown on **Map 40** opposite and the blue-blazed **Rocky Run Trail** shown on **Map 41** on page 221, both of which are mostly in the woods.

Red-blazed Painter Brothers Trail: Follow the red-blazed track, keeping Painter Road toward your right. Eventually, enter the woods, then turn left. After 220 yards, veer left to emerge from the woods and continue along the edge of a field. Pass through a short stretch of woods, then continue along the edge of the meadow. Eventually, at a corner of the meadow, follow the red-blazed path downhill into the woods.

Continue straight where several trails intersect. Gradually curve right, then turn abruptly left to follow the red-blazed path. Pass through a series of trail junctions as the path descends steeply. At the bottom of the slope, cross a stream and continue straight through the woods with the slope falling off to your right.

At an abandoned stone house, turn abruptly left. Follow a dirt road through the woods, straight through a clearing, gradually uphill, then steeply down and around to the left. Pass a trail intersecting from the right. At the next trail junction, turn right to follow the red blazes across a stream. Pass through a four-way trail intersection and climb half-left. Continue past diverging trails as the red-blazed path curves uphill to the right. At the top of the slope, continue along the edge of the woods, then straight across an open area of brush and tall grass. Fork right to follow the red blazes back to the small stream in the vicinity of the trailhead and barn.

MAP 40—Tyler Arboretum: Dismal Run Trail (orange blazes)

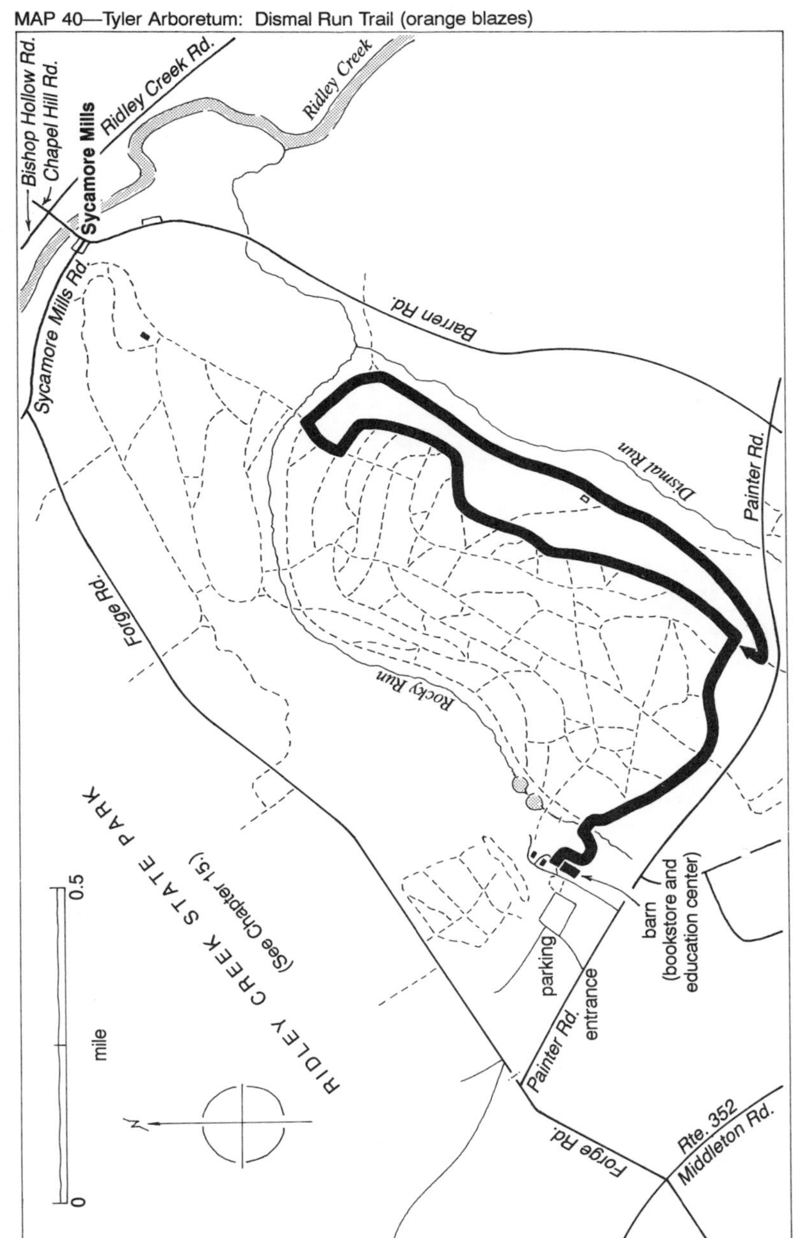

MAP 41—Tyler Arboretum: Rocky Run Trail (blue blazes)

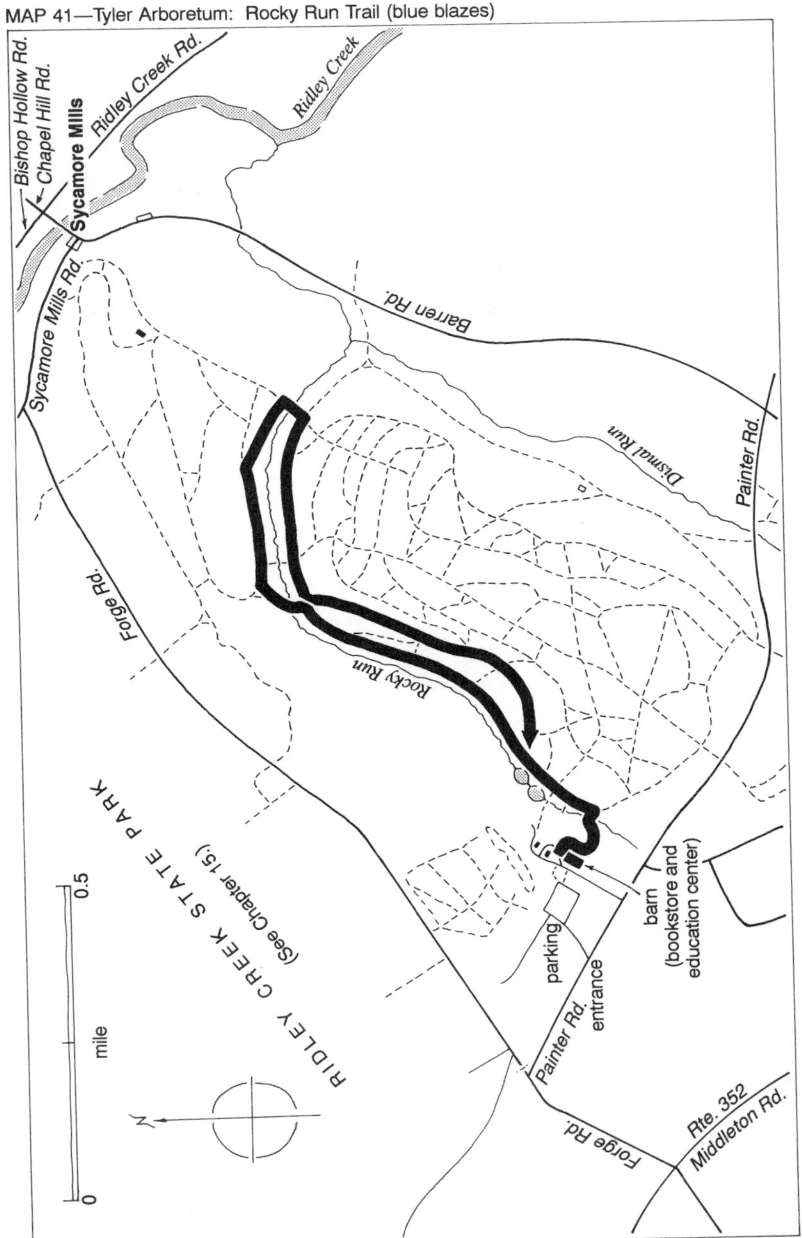

17

JOHN HEINZ NATIONAL WILDLIFE REFUGE AT TINICUM

Walking, ski touring, bicycling, and canoeing. The 3-mile circuit shown by the bold line on Map 42 on page 229 starts by following a dike that borders Darby Creek, a tributary of the Delaware River west of Philadelphia International Airport. The wide, well-graded dike trail provides easy walking, outstanding views over a freshwater impoundment and a freshwater (yet tidal) marsh, and excellent opportunities for bird watching. The route returns on a wide trail through the woods east of the impoundment.

As shown by Map 43 on page 231, other trails at the Tinicum refuge extend downstream along Darby Creek almost to its mouth. The round-trip distance from the visitor contact station to the farthest point west of Route 420 is nearly 9 miles, but I recommend going no farther than the tidal marsh at point A on the map—about 7 miles round-trip. Part of the trail along Darby Creek is rough and sometimes becomes choked by encroaching reeds and brush.

Walking is not the only way to see the refuge. If you have a fat-tired or hybrid bicycle that can handle the sometimes loose, gravelly surface, the refuge's main path around the impoundment provides good bicycling. Cyclists must ride single file, yield to other trail users, and keep their speed to a moderate, safe pace.

Alternatively, if you have a canoe, a canoe trail extends downstream along Darby Creek from a dock near the visitor contact station, where a canoe trail brochure is available. There is a strong tidal current. Moreover, canoeing is only possible during the 6-hour interval when the level of the water is above mid-tide. For information on the tide, call the visitor contact station.

The refuge is open daily from 8:00 A.M. until sunset; the visitor contact station is open daily from 9 to 4. Dogs must be leashed. There are no picnic facilities and fires and barbecues are prohibited. The refuge is managed by the U.S. Fish and Wildlife Service. The visitor contact station telephone is (215) 365-3118;

the headquarters telephone is (610) 521-0662. Call for information about unusual bird sightings or the refuge's calendar of guided nature walks on weekends.

ABOUT 325 SPECIES OF BIRDS are seen regularly in the Delaware Valley and southern New Jersey. Looking for them can take you as far afield as the Pocono Mountains, Hawk Mountain, the New Jersey coast, and Bombay Hook bordering Delaware Bay. Or you can drive (or ride the bus) 6 miles from downtown Philadelphia to the national wildlife refuge at Tinicum in Philadelphia's southwestern corner. More than 290 species—nearly 90 percent of the Delaware Valley and New Jersey bird lists—have been recorded at Tinicum's shallow impoundment, fields, thickets, woods, mud flats, and freshwater tidal marsh.

In late winter and early spring geese, ducks, grebes, and coots pass through the refuge on their way north. They are followed by herons, egrets, ibises, a myriad of shorebirds, and the usual land birds of eastern Pennsylvania and New Jersey. About 85 species nest at Tinicum, including harriers, kestrels, herons, bitterns, rails, owls, and many songbirds and waterfowl. In late summer the shorebirds return to feed on the mud flats. Migrating hawks and owls also pause at the refuge. By fall waterfowl crowd the impoundment and creek. Some stay for the winter if the freshwater impoundment and creek do not freeze.

The concentration of birds at Tinicum is all the more remarkable for occurring within sight of downtown Philadelphia, in a sector of the city and Delaware County that for the most part has been given over to tank farms, warehouses, and residential development. About 90 percent of the tidal marshland that formerly bordered the Delaware River between Darby Creek and the Schuylkill River has been filled in during the last half-century, yet Tinicum continues to be a major stopover on the Atlantic flyway. Delaware Bay funnels northbound waterfowl and shorebirds through the Philadelphia region. Land birds are deflected along the bay's western shore and up the Delaware Valley. Heading south, many birds again follow the Delaware River.

In geologic terms, Tinicum's low marsh landscape is of extremely recent origin. When the continental glacier that covered eastern Canada, the Great Lakes region, New England, New York, and northeastern Pennsylvania began its final retreat about ten thousand or twelve thousand years ago, an immense quantity of meltwater was released. The Delaware was one of the principal meltwater rivers, fed by a continuous torrent pouring off the receding glacial front in southern New York. Gradually the sea rose from a level that—because so much water had been locked up in the form of glacial ice—was as much as 300 feet lower than at present. (Even today, the Ice Age continues at higher latitudes, where enough ice remains in the polar ice caps and the Greenland ice sheet to raise the ocean another 130 feet if the ice were to melt, as no doubt some of it will.) The rising sea flooded the lower Delaware Valley to create Delaware Bay. Then as now, rivers carrying mud in suspension dumped their load of sediment as their currents dissipated in the estuary at tidewater. In this manner the Tinicum region became an extensive settling basin. Test borings at Tinicum show deposits of sand, silt, and clay as thick as 28 feet.

Although Darby Creek is tidal to the 84th Street bridge and the Delaware River is tidal as far north as Trenton, the downstream current usually prevents salt water from reaching Tinicum Marsh. However, brackish water, which is heavier than fresh water, occasionally creeps upstream in the bottom of the channels during periods of low rainfall.

Because of the constant influx of nutrient-laden mud and the unfailing flow of water (whether salt or fresh), tidal marshes achieve extraordinary natural productivity. Their warm, sunlit waters enable photosynthesis to take place at a rapid rate. Great quantities of algae and animal microorganisms are produced; algae are even able to grow during the winter. Insects, worms, snails, mollusks, crustaceans, and bait fish thrive on the algae and rotting vegetation. Although stream pollution has left Tinicum with only a meager variety of invertebrates and fish compared to less-contaminated wetlands, its marsh still yields more vegetable matter than the most fertile farmland.

Unfortunately, however, large areas of the refuge are dominated by spatterdock (a variety of water lily), purple loosestrife, and tall, plumed phragmites (or giant reed), none of which have much food value for wildlife. As of 1994, a variety of programs were underway to reduce the abundance of these plants. Measures include draining the impoundment during summer in order to discourage the spatterdock and introducing a variety of weevil that feeds on the roots of purple loosestrife. The rotting vegetation in the impoundment during summer, in combination with the hot temperature and low level of dissolved oxygen in the water, have on occasion fostered bacteria that cause avian botulism in waterfowl. (This disease does not affect people.) Although the refuge staff monitor the impoundment closely for avian botulism, they also encourage you to report any dead birds that you see.

The fertility of the alluvial soil at Tinicum, and the ease of enclosing large treeless tracts of marsh with dikes and converting the meadows to conventional agriculture, were not lost on the early European settlers.

Tinicum Island—located at the mouth of Darby Creek, and the site of one of the first European communities in the Delaware Valley—was settled by Swedes under Johann Printz in 1643, five years after an earlier Swedish settlement at Fort Christina (now Wilmington) and forty years before William Penn founded Philadelphia. At the time of the Swedish settlement, Tinicum Island, which now is merged physically with the surrounding land, was an isolated hill overlooking a broad marshy plain that was flooded at high tide. Printz established his colony here because it was easily defended and near Dutch Fort Nassau at present-day Gloucester, New Jersey. Printz thought that the new base of Swedish activity at Tinicum would enjoy an advantage in trade with the Indians to the west and would thwart the expansion of the New Netherlands colony at Gloucester. In 1655, however, the Swedish colony was annexed by New Netherlands, which was centered at New Amsterdam on Manhattan Island. The Dutch in turn gave way to the English. During one of a series of three Anglo-Dutch wars fought between 1652 and 1678 for mercantile and maritime dominance, Great Britain in 1664 seized New Amsterdam and all the Dutch outposts south to Delaware.

A system of dikes enclosing the vast stretches of tidal marsh along the Delaware River between Darby Creek and the Schuylkill River was well established by the time of the Revolutionary War. Planted in hay, the diked flats were used to graze cattle and sheep. By 1788 the Pennsylvania legislature had passed four acts governing the maintenance and extension of the dikes. A map dating from the middle of the nineteenth century bears a note superimposed over the area now occupied by Philadelphia International Airport: "Flats formerly covered by reeds and bushes and partially submerged at high water, now reclaimed from the tides by banks."

Management of the system of dikes and drainage courses was the responsibility of two companies comprising owners of the enclosed land. According to a 1936 report of the U.S. Army Corps of Engineers, the companies eventually were dissolved during the first decade of the twentieth century. Earlier, the dikes had deteriorated, and for a period the enclosed land reverted to marshy meadows.

However, development of efficient hydraulic dredges during the late nineteenth century portended the obliteration of most of the wetlands. These machines suck mud from the bottom of a river or harbor and pump the material through a floating line to areas to be filled on shore. It was only a matter of time before the technique was applied to the Delaware River and its bordering wetlands. At the outset of World War I, 400 acres of marsh at Hog Island east of Tinicum were filled for a shipyard. During the 1930s much of the site of Philadelphia International Airport was filled hydraulically with an estimated hundred million cubic feet of sand and silt pumped from the Delaware ship channel. Other large sections of marsh, including tracts now within the boundaries of the wildlife refuge, were buried at intervals. The last such operation occurred in the early 1970s. The high Interstate 95 bridge over the Schuylkill River provides a panoramic view over a vast area of riverside marsh that has been filled. In 1991, in partial mitigation for the destruction of wetlands along the newly built Interstate 476, the Pennsylvania Department of Transportation restored 18 acres of marshland that previously had been filled along Interstate 95 at the Tinicum refuge.

Efforts to preserve at least some of Tinicum Marsh began in 1952, when a committee of the Delaware Valley Ornithological Club proposed to Mayor Joseph A. Clark, Jr., that Philadelphia establish a municipal wildlife refuge. The mayor's response was encouraging, but as the committee explored the matter it learned that Gulf Oil Corporation, owner of the land, had already contracted with the Corps of Engineers and state and local agencies to let the area be used as a basin for spoil dredged from the Schuylkill River. Eventually another site was found for disposal of the silt. In 1953 Philadelphia Conservationists, Inc., was organized to continue working for the creation of a wildlife preserve. After assurance that its pipeline rights-of-way would be protected, Gulf Oil agreed to *donate* the land to Philadelphia, and in 1955 the city established the Tinicum Wildlife Preserve. Comprising at first only 145 acres, the refuge included the dike, impoundment, and woods at the eastern end of the present-day refuge.

The remaining wetlands at Tinicum were threatened in the late 1960s by highway plans to route Interstate 95 through the area. Part of the expressway was in fact built through the western stretches of Tinicum Marsh before national and local conservation groups and area congressmen (including John Heinz) convinced the federal Department of the Interior that the area should be added to the National Wildlife Refuge System. In 1971 the unfinished portion of the highway was realigned along the southern edge of the marsh, and the following year Congress created the Tinicum National Environmental Center administered by the U.S. Fish and Wildlife Service, to which Philadelphia then gave the original Tinicum refuge. In 1991 the refuge was renamed to honor John Heinz following his death in a helicopter crash while serving as U.S. senator.

The refuge at Tinicum now totals slightly more than 900 acres. Acquisition of an additional 300 acres has been approved by Congress but not yet funded or successfully negotiated. A master plan proposes a long-range program to restore former tidal wetlands and to dig several freshwater ponds immediately southwest of the present impoundment. Other filled areas are managed as forests or fields to create a wide diversity of wildlife habitats.

≈ ≈ ≈ ≈

SEPTA: Bus 37 passes the corner of 84th Street and Lindbergh Boulevard just north of the wildlife refuge. (See **Map 42** opposite.) From the corner of 84th and Lindbergh, walk south on Lindbergh Boulevard 0.2 mile to the entrance to the John Heinz National Wildlife Refuge at Tinicum. Turn right into the refuge, then bear left and follow the entrance road several hundred yards to the visitor contact station.

Telephone (215) 580-7800 for current information on schedules, routes, and connections from your starting point.

AUTOMOBILE DIRECTIONS: The John Heinz National Wildlife Refuge at Tinicum straddles the boundary between Philadelphia and Delaware County just west of Philadelphia International Airport and just north of Interstate 95. (See •17 on **Map 1** on page 6; see also **Map 43** on page 231.) Three avenues of approach are described below.

From the north on Interstate 95: After crossing the high bridge over the Schuylkill River, take Exit 10 for Route 291 and Philadelphia International Airport. The process of exiting here is rather protracted, but eventually fork right for Route 291 toward Lester.

At a traffic light at the bottom of the exit ramp, turn right onto Bartram Avenue East and go 0.7 mile to the intersection with 84th Street. Turn left onto 84th Street and continue 0.7 mile to an intersection with Lindbergh Boulevard. Turn left onto Lindbergh Boulevard and go 0.2 mile to the entrance to the John Heinz National Wildlife Refuge at Tinicum. Turn right into the refuge, then immediately bear left and follow the entrance drive several hundred yards to the parking lots and visitor contact station.

From the south on Interstate 95 : After passing Chester, take Exit 10 for Route 291 East and Philadelphia International Airport. At the first traffic light, turn left onto Bartram Avenue. Follow Bartram Avenue 1.5 miles to the intersection with 84th Street. Turn left onto 84th Street and continue 0.7 mile to an intersection with Lindbergh Boulevard. Turn left onto Lindbergh Boulevard and go 0.2 mile to the entrance to the

MAP 42—John Heinz National Wildlife Refuge at Tinicum: 3-mile dike trail

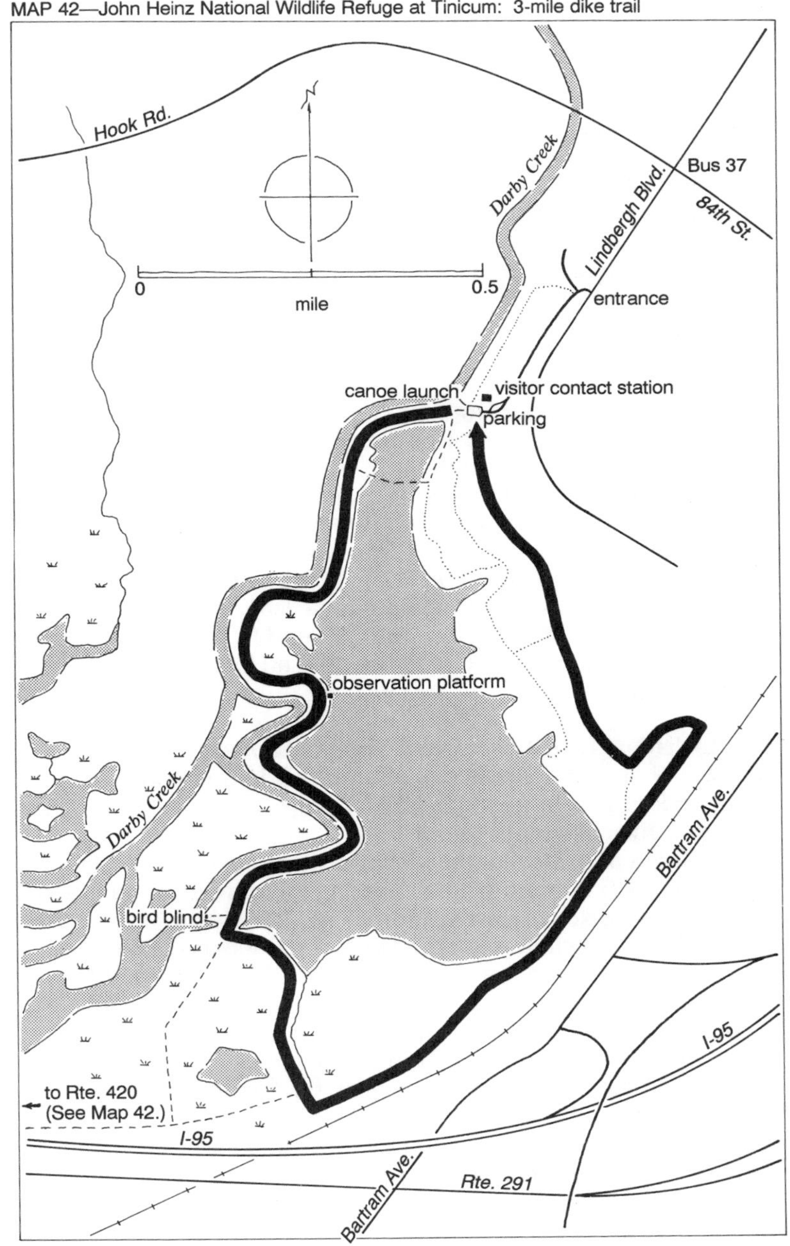

John Heinz National Wildlife Refuge at Tinicum. Turn right into the refuge, then immediately bear left and follow the entrance drive several hundred yards to the parking lots and visitor contact station.

From the west on Interstate 76 (Schuylkill Expressway): Stay on I-76 East through the city. Eventually, after passing the downtown exits, follow the signs indicating that you should stay in the left lanes for Exit 43A toward Route 291, I-95 South, and International Airport.

After exiting, go 1.3 miles, then turn right at a traffic light onto Route 291 West toward International Airport. Immediately after crossing the Schuylkill River on the George C. Platt Bridge, fork right for I-95 South and International Airport. After 1.3 miles, take Exit 10 for Route 291 and Philadelphia International Airport, then fork right for Route 291 toward Lester.

At a traffic light at the bottom of the exit ramp, turn right onto Bartram Avenue East and go 0.7 mile to the intersection with 84th Street. Turn left onto 84th Street and continue 0.7 mile to an intersection with Lindbergh Boulevard. Turn left onto Lindbergh Boulevard and go 0.2 mile to the entrance to the John Heinz National Wildlife Refuge at Tinicum. Turn right into the refuge, then immediately bear left and follow the entrance drive several hundred yards to the parking lots and visitor contact station.

WALKING AND BICYCLING: The bold line on **Map 42** on page 229 shows a 3-mile circuit around a large freshwater impoundment. For a longer walk or bicycle ride to the refuge's western end, use **Map 43** opposite.

In either case, start at the visitor contact station and follow the main path through a small parking lot and out along the top of the broad dike, which the federal Work Projects Administration (WPA) and state and county governments reconstructed during the 1930s on the site of an earlier dike. On the left is a freshwater impoundment; on the right is tidal Darby Creek.

After 1.4 miles, fork left if you want to continue around the freshwater impoundment on the 3-mile circuit. Or, to reach the western trails, continue straight, then bear right at a T-intersection near Interstate 95. On Map 43, the trail segments shown by dotted lines bordering Interstate 95 are not actually part of the refuge and are, of course, marred by the sight and sound of the highway.

MAP 43—John Heinz National Wildlife Refuge at Tinicum

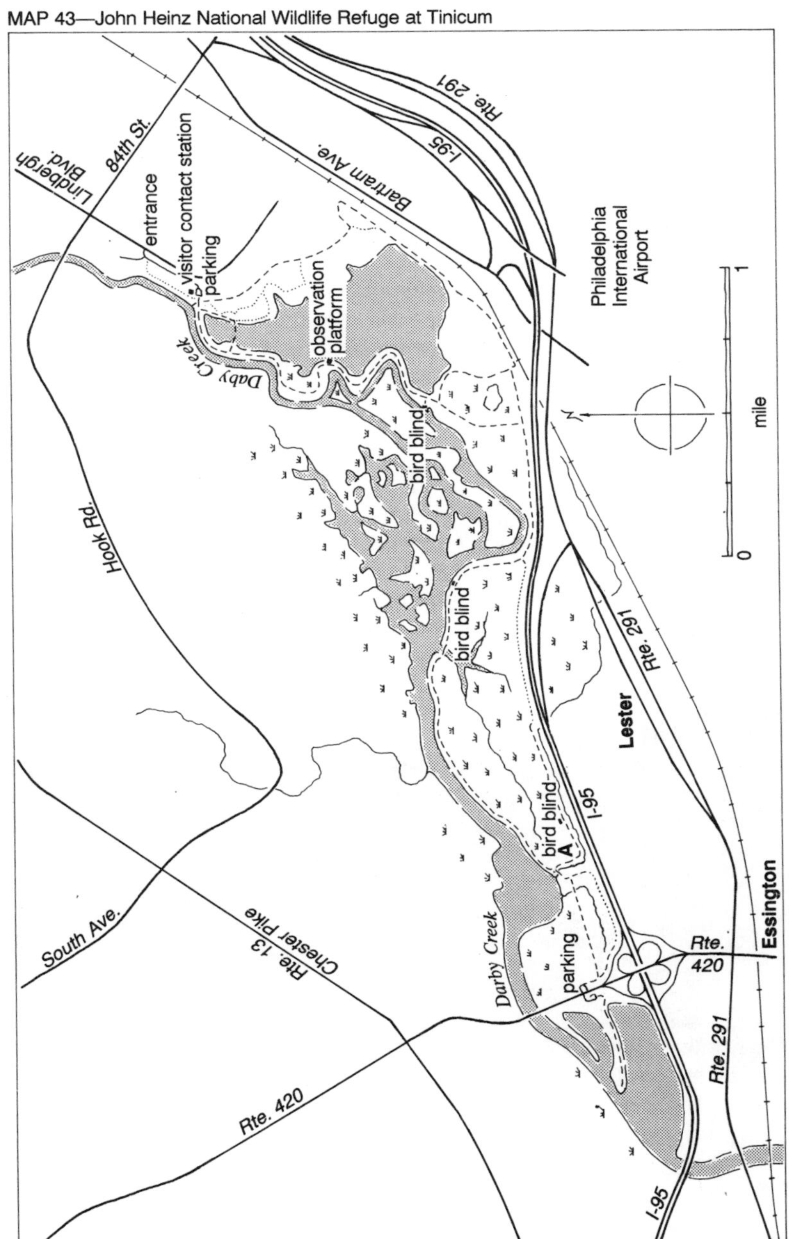

18

BRANDYWINE CREEK STATE PARK

Walking and mountain biking. Bicycles, however, are restricted to the multi-use trail on the river's east bank. From the park the multi-use trail extends upstream into a large tract owned by Woodlawn Trustees, Inc., where trails that are open to public use provide many miles of off-road bicycling. But please see first the discussion starting on page 237. The Woodlawn Property is used also by horseback riders and, of course, hikers. Cyclists should yield to people on foot and on horseback, pass with care, and keep their speed to a moderate, safe pace.

Located in northern Delaware's Piedmont region, Brandywine Creek State Park consists of rolling meadows and woods that slope down to the river. Map 44 on page 236 shows the park's extensive network of footpaths, where you could easily walk for an hour or an afternoon. Some of the trails are marked with colored blazes, as discussed on page 235.

Brandywine Creek State Park is open daily year-round from 8 A.M. to sunset. An admission fee is charged from Memorial Day through Labor Day and on weekends in May, September, and October. The park is managed by the Delaware Department of Natural Resources and Environmental Control, Division of Parks and Recreation. For information, including the schedule of nature walks and other events, telephone the park office at (302) 577-3534; for the Brandywine Creek Nature Center, telephone (302) 655-5740.

RESIDENTS OF THE FIRST STATE may object to the suggestion that Brandywine Creek State Park north of Wilmington is part of the Philadelphia region—as inclusion of the park in this book would seem to imply. Yet even apart from proximity (the park is only 40 minutes' drive from downtown Philadelphia, and far less from the western suburbs), the fact remains that for most of its colonial history, all of

Delaware was part of Pennsylvania. True, Delaware secured a separate legislature in 1704 and a separate executive council in 1710, but the governor of Pennsylvania, with his capital at Philadelphia, was the chief executive until 1776, when Delaware's Revolutionary War government terminated subservience to London and Philadelphia alike.

Still, a glance at a map shows that Brandywine Creek State Park clearly belongs in Pennsylvania, lying as it does well up into that peculiar bulge that protrudes above the eastward extension of the Mason-Dixon Line separating Maryland and Pennsylvania. Defined as the arc of a circle with a radius 12 miles long and with its center at New Castle, the northern boundary of Delaware was established in 1683 in a grant from Charles II to his brother the duke of York (later James II). This boundary was intended to prevent other settlements from encroaching on Delaware's colonial administrative center at New Castle, but even before the formal grant was made, the duke of York leased his Delaware territory in 1680 to William Penn for ten thousand years. Today Delaware's circular northern boundary is unique among the states and may even be unique in the world (although I am told that the ill-defined and disputed northern border of Kuwait has a circular component). Any reader who knows of other circular boundaries is urged to let me know via a letter to the publisher.

If Delaware is not to be made to rejoin Pennsylvania or at least to cede its northern Piedmont area, there is the claim of Maryland to consider. When King Charles I gave Maryland to Cecilius Calvert in 1632, the grant delineated boundaries that included the Delaware territory. However, the grant covered only "land hitherto uncultivated and occupied by savages." This clause, coupled with the fact that there was a failed Dutch settlement at Lewes near Cape Henlopen in 1631 (where all the colonists were killed by Indians), eventually resulted in Delaware being carved out of Maryland after the Netherlands relinquished claim to the region by treaty with England in 1674.

≈ ≈ ≈ ≈

Before Brandywine Creek State Park was established in 1965, most of the property on the west bank was a dairy farm owned by the Du Pont family, for whom in the late 1800s Italian masons constructed the massive stone walls that cross or border the former pastures. Particularly attractive is the fact that large areas have been preserved as meadows, although necessarily some fields have been allowed to revert to forest. The Tulip Tree Woods Nature Preserve behind the Brandywine Creek Nature Center has remained more or less undisturbed for two hundred years. The park's mixture of meadow, scrubby new woods, old growth forest, freshwater marsh, and placid river provides a wide range of habitats where about 170 species of birds have been recorded. A bird checklist is available at the nature center.

≈ ≈ ≈ ≈

AUTOMOBILE DIRECTIONS: Brandywine Creek State Park is located in northern Delaware a few miles above Wilmington. (See • 18 on **Map 1** on page 6; see also the insert in the upper-right corner of **Map 44** on page 236.)

From the north or south on Interstate 95: Leave I-95 at Delaware's Exit 8 for Route 202 North toward West Chester (Exit 8B if you are approaching from Philadelphia). From the top of the exit ramp, follow Route 202 North only 0.9 mile, then turn left onto Route 141. Follow Route 141 for 0.7 mile, then turn right onto Rockland Road . Follow Rockland Road 1.4 miles past Rockland Mills and across Brandywine Creek, then fork right onto Adams Dam Road and continue 0.5 mile to the entrance to the state park on the right. From the fee booth at the park entrance, follow the winding road uphill 0.5 mile to the parking lot by the park office and nature center.

From the intersection of Route 1 and Route 202: Follow Route 202 South 3.7 miles, then turn right onto Route 92 West. After only 0.3 mile, turn left to continue on Route 92 West for 2.8 miles, in the process crossing Brandywine Creek and passing the entrance to the park's Thompsons Bridge Area. At a crossroads where Route 92 ends and where Route 100 intersects from the right, turn left and go 0.3 mile to the park's main entrance on the left. From the fee booth at the park entrance, follow the winding road uphill 0.5 mile to the parking lot by the park office and nature center.

WALKING: Some of the trails shown on **Map 44** on page 236 are blazed with colored swatches. When using these blazes, it is important to realize that they designate different specific routes or itineraries. Thus it sometimes occurs that a particular stretch of trail is blazed one color if you are following it in one direction and shows another color if you are following it in the opposite direction. Map 44 attempts to reflect this fact by showing little arrows next to the letters that stand for the different colored blazes.

Although all of Brandywine Creek State Park is attractive, the chief scenic features are the meadows in the southwestern

MAP 44—Brandywine Creek State Park

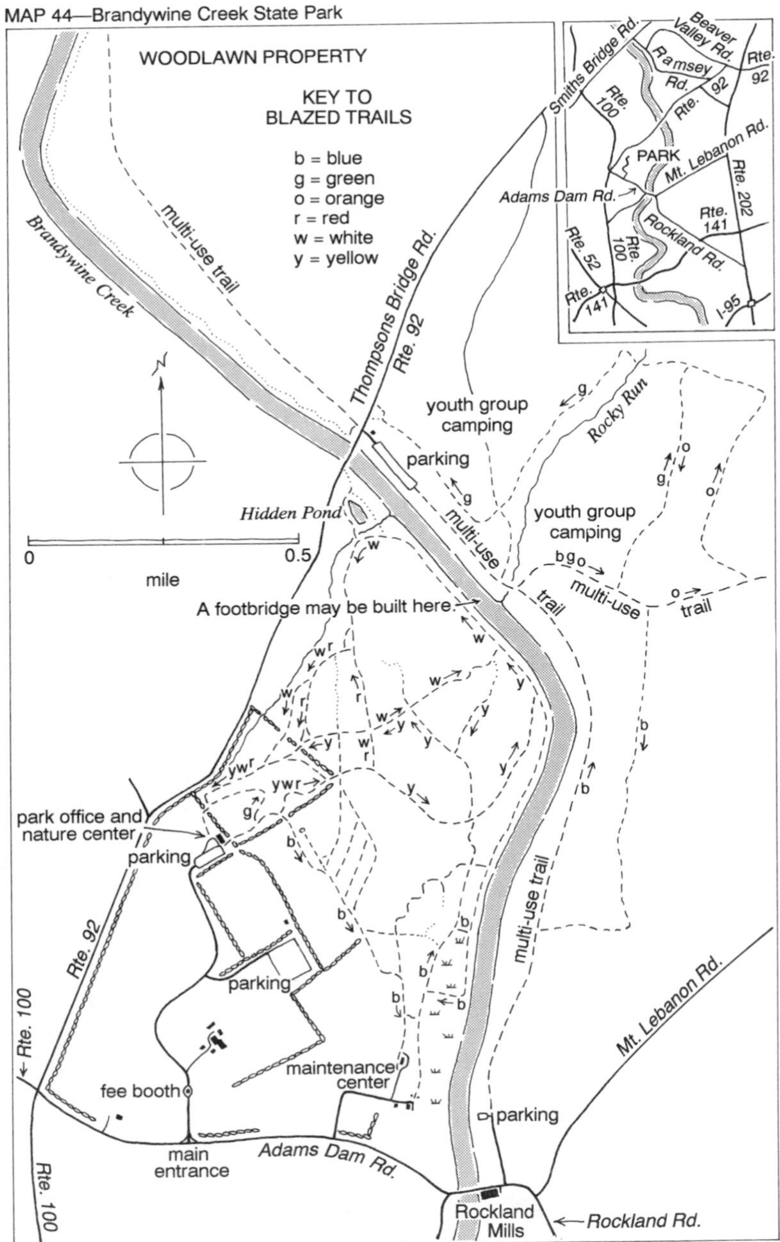

sector of the park, the tulip tree woods behind the park office and nature center, the freshwater marsh next to the river at the park's southern end, and the riverside path along the creek's west bank. An easy way to take in these different areas is to start at the trailhead to the right of the park office and nature center. Follow the **blue blazes** through the tulip tree woods, then downhill along the edge of the woods and meadow to the freshwater marsh and river. From there, with Brandywine Creek on your right, follow the riverside path upstream. Eventually, as you approach Thompsons Bridge Road, you will pick up the **white blazes**, which you can follow back to the park office and nature center. When you reach a gap in a stone wall within sight of the office and nature center, simply continue uphill across the grass. Altogether, this route is about 2.6 miles long.

HIKING AND MOUNTAIN BIKING ON THE MULTI-USE TRAIL and at the WOODLAWN PROPERTY: At Brandywine Creek State Park, off-road bicycling is permitted only on the multi-use trail on the river's east bank. However, as of 1994, hikers, horseback riders, and cyclists are welcome to use—at their own risk and during daylight hours only—the many trails on the Woodlawn Property, a huge tract of woods, meadows, and farm fields located north of the park on the river's east bank. This property belongs to Woodlawn Trustees, Inc. a non-profit corporation founded in 1918 by William Bancroft, who as early as 1906 had started buying land in the Brandywine Valley in order to preserve it from development. Most of the section of Brandywine Creek State Park that lies on the east side of the river was formerly the property of Woodlawn Trustees, Inc., which in 1981 transferred 350 acres worth $2.9 million to the state, half as a gift and half in a sale for which the money was supplied by the federal government's Land and Water Conservation Fund. The Trustees then donated the proceeds of the sale to the state as an endowment to help maintain the eastern section of the park.

Referring to the insert at the upper-right corner of **Map 44** opposite, Woodlawn Trustees, Inc. owns most of the land encompassed by Beaver Valley Road on the northwest and northeast, Route 92 on the southeast, and Brandywine Creek on the west. It also owns land beyond these bounds. Posted signs help to delineate the actual property lines.

Taken together, the multi-use trail at the park plus the many

trails at the Woodlawn Property provide an outstanding opportunity for extended walking and for off-road bicycling. However, because the Woodlawn Property is privately-owned, the activities permitted there are entirely at the discretion of the trustees, so you really have to take your cue from the posted signs and from the security guards who patrol the area.

I suggest that you start at the small parking lot located at the park's southern end on the east side of the river. This lot is reached via a narrow gravel road off Rockland Road, just uphill and opposite from the entrance to Rockland Mills condominiums. (See **Map 44**.) If you are at the park on a fee day, you must first pay for admission at the main park entrance across the river, then display your receipt in your window when you park your car in the small lot at the southern end of the multi-use trail.

From the parking lot, follow the multi-use trail north. With caution, cross Thompsons Bridge Road and continue upstream on the main track to Ramsey Road, where a narrow dirt track parallels the road on the side away from the river. This track soon climbs into the Woodlawn Property, where you can explore the many trails. Be careful—some of these trails are steep and very rough. And be considerate. Avoid eroded areas, skirt cultivated fields, stay away from houses, farm buildings, and active farm operations, and dismount from your bike when passing hikers and horseback riders.

Another way for cyclists to get to know the trails of the Woodlawn Property is first to ride around the area on Ramsey Road, Beaver Valley Road, and Route 92 (Thompsons Bridge Road), noting the posted signs, the parking areas, and the places where trails meet the roads. Even once you enter the property, getting lost is virtually impossible, since by heading downhill you will eventually reach Brandywine Creek, where you can return to the state park via the multi-use trail.

Finally, you may notice white paint blazes along the multi-use trail. The blazes designate the Brandywine Trail, a footpath that follows Brandywine Creek for 30-some miles. Although blazed, the trail for the most part crosses private property and is not open to the public except where the trail crosses the state park and the Woodlawn Property. For information, contact the Wilmington Trail Club, for which you can obtain a current telephone number from the park office.

IF YOU HAVE ENJOYED this book, you or your friends may also like some of the other guidebooks listed below. These guides are widely available at bookstores, nature stores, and outfitters, or you can write to Rambler Books, 1430 Park Avenue, Baltimore, MD 21217, for current prices and ordering information.

DAY TRIPS IN DELMARVA

This book explores the Delmarva Peninsula, consisting of southern Delaware and the Eastern Shore of Maryland and Virginia. Emphasis is on the region's scenic back roads, historic towns, wildlife refuges, parks, undeveloped beaches, and trails for hiking and bicycling. *Day Trips in Delmarva* includes detailed directions, 44 maps showing car tours, walks, and bicycle trips, and extensive commentary on local history and natural history.

"Few realize the wealth of sights the Delmarva Peninsula holds, which is why *Day Trips in Delmarva* is such an infinitely enjoyable book."—*Baltimore Magazine.* • "The best organized, best written, most comprehensive and practical guide to daytrips on the Delmarva Peninsula."—*The Easton Star Democrat*

COUNTRY WALKS NEAR BALTIMORE

"Fisher's books, with his own photos illustrating them, are models of pith and practicality. . . . The maps for '*Country Walks*' excel."—*Baltimore Sun*

COUNTRY WALKS NEAR WASHINGTON
MORE COUNTRY WALKS NEAR WASHINGTON

"Cream of the local outdoors-guide crop. . . . You could probably fit both of these precise and passionately unstuffy works by Alan Fisher into one pocket, but you'll want to have them in your hand for most of the trips. . . . He starts each trip/chapter with history, perspective and a map, and ends it with meticulous step-by-step directions."—*Washington Post.* • "The happy union between a utilitarian and historically informative guide."—*The Washington Times Magazine*

COUNTRY WALKS NEAR BOSTON

"An invaluable paperback."—*Boston Sunday Globe.* • "This is my favorite trail guide. . . . Unlike the others, it features a lot of social, cultural, and natural history."—*Boston Phoenix*

COUNTRY WALKS NEAR CHICAGO

"A handy guide. . . . The general information sections—which, if combined, constitute three-fourths of the book—are excellent."—*Chicago Tribune*